People and Employment

A. K. Whitehead MPhil, BA, PGCE
L. Baruch, BSc(Econ)
School of Management and Business Studies,
Leeds Polytechnic

with contributions from

E. M. Wilson, BSc(Econ)
O. D. Jones, BA
D. Golding, MSc, PhD

BUTTERWORTHS
London Boston Sydney Wellington Durban Toronto

First published 1981

©Butterworth & Co (Publishers) Ltd, 1981

British Library Cataloguing in Publication Data

Whitehead, A. K.
  People and employment.
  1. Industrial sociology
  I. Title   II. Baruch, L.
  '306'.3   HD6955

  ISBN 0–408–10691–3
  ISBN 0–408–10692–1 Pbk

Photoset by Butterworths Litho Preparation Department
Printed and bound by Cambridge University Press, Cambridge

Contents

Introduction

1   People, organizations and employment   1
1.1 Introduction   1
1.2 A simple pricing and allocation model   3
1.3 Characteristics of the market for labour services   6
1.4 Factors underlying supply and demand schedules   15
1.5 Wage differentials between occupations   22
Appendix 1.1: Elasticity   27
Appendix 1.2: Marginalism   28

**2   Demography and education: structure and quality of the
        workforce**   33
2.1 Introduction   33
2.2 Population and the economy   33
2.3 The population of Great Britain and the Demographic Transition
      Model   36
2.4 Education and the quality of the workforce   42
2.5 Education, productivity and earnings   47
2.6 Rate of return on investments in human capital   52
Appendix 2.1: Weekly earnings of male workers, employed full-time
(1978)   58

3   Organizations and employment   59
3.1 Introduction   59
3.2 Utilization of externally provided manpower   59
3.3 Effects of other markets   64
3.4 Demand elasticity and wage bargaining   66
3.5 Training and manpower development   68
3.6 Manpower demand and fixed labour costs   72
3.7 Some empirical evidence   74
Appendix 3.1: Market structures   78

4 Manpower, hiring allocation and planning by organizations 82
4.1 Introduction 82
4.2 Manpower recruitment and selection 83
4.3 Manpower allocation within organizations 90
4.4 Manpower planning 95

5 The individual in the organization 102
5.1 Introduction 102
5.2 Approaches to organization design 103
5.3 Some key aspects of interplanning 107
5.4 Organization structure 110
5.5 Role 112
5.6 Power and control 113
5.7 Approaches to the design of organizations 114

6 Pressure groups and work organizations 122
6.1 Introduction 122
6.2 The nature of political behaviour 122
6.3 Influence, power and authority 123
6.4 The importance of understanding power and pressure groups 128
6.5 Types of pressure group 132

7 Communication, change and conflict 141
7.1 Introduction 141
7.2 The nature of communication 141
7.3 One-way and two-way communication 142
7.4 Barriers to communication 144
7.5 Written communications 148
7.6 Oral communication 149
7.7 Change and conflict: introduction 149
7.8 Change 150
7.9 Conflict 160
Appendix 7.1: Case study 171

8 Discrimination in employment 174
8.1 Introduction 174
8.2 Women 174
8.3 Equal opportunities and race relations 188
8.4 Concluding observations 191

People and Employment

Other BEC Higher National Level core texts from Butterworths:

Business in Society: Consensus and Conflict
Organizations: Structure and Policy
Data Studies

9   Legal relationships between people and organizations   194
9.1 Introduction   194
9.2 Development of legislation   194
9.3 The Trade Union and Labour Relations Act 1974 (TULRA)   195
9.4 The closed shop   199
9.5 A code of practice to promote good industrial relations   200
9.6 Health and safety   201
9.7 Employment protection legislation   208
9.8 The Wages Councils   214

10   Organizations and collective bargaining   217
10.1   What is a bargain?   217
10.2   Organizations with which bargains are made   218
10.3   Who is included in the bargaining structure?   218
10.4   The law of contract and bargaining   220
10.5   The place of bargaining in law   221
10.6   The procedure for handling redundancies   222
10.7   Time off work   222
10.8   The Health and Safety at Work Act 1974   222
10.9   Steps followed in the collective bargaining process   222
10.10 The procedure agreement   224
10.11 The Advisory, Conciliation and Arbitration Service (ACAS)   225
10.12 Trade union objectives   227
Appendix 10.1: Structure of the TUC in the English regions   231
Appendix 10.2: Structure of a typical employers' organization — the
Engineering Employers' Federation   232

11   The outcome of collective bargaining   233
11.1 Introduction   233
11.2 The Truck Acts — payments in the coin of the realm   233
11.3 Wages payment systems   234
11.4 The social wage   235
11.5 The constraints on collective bargaining   235
11.6 Management techniques to establish wage rates   236
11.7 Local and national bargaining   237
11.8 The outcome of collective bargaining in public and private
      industry   237
11.9 Influence of trade unions on relative wages   244

12   People, organizations and the government   249
12.1 Introduction   249
12.2 Market failure and the government   249
12.3 Government manpower policy   252
12.4 Taxation policies   256
12.5 The economic and political background   260
Appendix 12.1: Facts and figures 1960–1980   267
Appendix 12.2: Postwar incomes policies   268

Index   269

Introduction

In writing this book the authors have attempted to use the various perspectives provided by social sciences to examine the relationships which develop between people in employment and the organizations which hire them. This area is both extensive and complex, and the intention is to furnish the reader with sufficient depth and breadth to appreciate both without claiming, as the chapter references will indicate, to be in any way exhaustive. Indeed, it is doubtful whether any single volume could claim to be comprehensive in any meaningful way.

One of the major problems presented by a book of this nature is that, while all scientists may claim to use the same basic methodological approach of developing theories and marshalling data with which to confront them, societal investigators are frequently interested in different aspects, view the same phenomena from different angles and develop different tools and concepts for accomplishing their respective tasks. Consequently, the study of man in his social environment encompasses several disciplines, so that there is no single science of human society. While this division of labour has been partly responsible over the years for considerable advances in our understanding, there is some difficulty in bringing the separate contributions together. To resolve these problems, we have written and ordered the material in what seems to us a logical and understandable way which will enable the student to appreciate contributions which these disciplines have to offer and the complementaries between them.

People in employment find themselves operating within organizations which vary in size and complexity, and, while some may enjoy relatively protected positions, all have external constraints imposed upon them. To accomplish the foregoing aims, therefore, it was clearly necessary to include both internal and external environmental influences. This is evident if one considers, for example, the effects of economic and legal factors. Variations in the state of the general economy and associated government policies, in addition to changes in factor and product markets, are highly significant in determining the external climate within which employing organizations operate and have strong implications for employment conditions within them. Similarly, the increasing volume of legislation which reaches the statute book, the new regulations and changes to existing obligations which it introduces, continuously modifies the legal areas of employment relationships within organizations.

An inspection of chapter headings will indicate something of the balance reached in the consideration of internal and external matters. Within the first two general chapters a discussion is included of the 'quality' of people, in so far as it is influenced by the educational system and in the sense that it is important in determining the state of human resources with which employing organizations must initially operate. The focus then shifts towards various internal aspects over the following five chapters, moving into the organization, from a consideration of its demand for human resources, to the various processes and influences which exist within it. Apart from the final chapter, which is wholly concerned with the external environment and its recent development, there is then an emphasis on constraints imposed from the outside but which are of such crucial importance for relationships at a local level that they cannot be divorced from their impact on employment relationships within individual organizations. Consequently, these chapters tend, in varying degrees, to be a mixture of the two.

We have thought it proper to include a chapter on discrimination in employment, since this is a significant feature in our society and has been the subject of important legislation. The chapter is mainly concerned with women, because their importance in employment has been increasing for many years and, indeed, continues to assume greater significance; but minority groups also receive attention. It is, of course, highly desirable for the reader, both as a student and as a participator in the employment complex, to appreciate the relevance of legislation in this and other contexts. We have not thought it necessary to include a description of legal principles but have concentrated rather on what the law actually says on relevant matters. Our experience (in teaching and in non-educational employment) is that there is a demand for this from both students and their employers. We have also noted that ambiguity can arise in publications which paraphrase the law, and direct quotations have therefore been used where possible so that misconceptions should not be created about what conditions have actually been expressed in legislation.

Chapter 1 presents an overview of the relationship between people as employees and organizations both as employers and as institutions which directly affect employment conditions, and draws attention to many aspects to be considered later in greater detail. It begins with a highly simplified view of the market for labour services and decision-making by people and organizations but, by introducing various characteristics of the market, proceeds to a more complicated picture of the situation which provides a basis for later development.

Following the outline presented in Chapter 1, the purpose of the second chapter is to explain the types, quality and distribution of human resources as provided by the external environment of employing organizations. The first part of the chapter considers the relationship between the economy and population. Then, together with appropriate data, the question of population size and its determinants is discussed, with consideration of the importance of these factors in a business context. An outline of the education system is presented with special reference to the further and higher education sectors. The importance of education and training is then analysed in the second part of the chapter in relation to earnings, productivity and occupational flexibility.

While Chapter 2 discussed the provisions of manpower resources by the external environment, the focus of Chapter 3 is upon the organization as an employer utilizing and altering manpower resources. The first part of the chapter relates the importance of wage costs to the value of the employee's contribution to output and discusses the effects of different market structures. After a consideration of the determinants of the elasticity of labour demand (which reappears in Chapter 11), the second part of the chapter examines the employing organization in relation to its development of human resources through training. The earlier discussion of wages is developed to include other employment costs and their effect on manpower demand and utilization.

Chapter 4 then considers in more detail some broadly related topics. It begins with a consideration of the recruitment and selection process which accompanies the hiring of labour, and follows this through to investigate internal allocation policies to which people become subject once they attain the status of an employee. The chapter concludes with a discussion of manpower planning at organization level, which is related to the corporate plan and the need to reconcile supply and demand imbalances.

The purpose of Chapter 5 is to enable students to attain some understanding of the forces that shape the behaviour of individuals within organizations. Following a brief consideration of the different perspectives that social scientists have typically adopted in studying organizational life, Chapter 5 focuses on a number of key aspects of behaviour in organizations (e.g. motivation, organization structure). This discussion provides the platform for a critical consideration of a number of different approaches to the design of organizations.

Chapter 6 commences by exploring the concepts of manpower and authority, and illustrates their relevance to the behaviour of people in employment. The behaviour of different types of pressure groups is described. The chapter then enumerates the various pressure groups, consisting of professional organizations, employers' organizations and trade unions. It deals in some detail with the actual function and organization of pressure groups, especially with shop-stewards, and a mention is made of the functions of the Economic League.

The first part of Chapter 7 is concerned with the general area of communication. It discusses the nature and types of communication in organizations and considers problems associated with communication systems which may lead to conflict. The second part of the chapter then examines conflict and change. The study of change in organizations is located in a framework of more general theories of social change and discussed in relation to the importance of underlying assumptions about the nature of people in society. This provides a foundation for an approach to the planning of change in organizations and for an introduction to organization development. The study of conflict is then approached by examining various arguments put forward for the origins of conflict together with relative and alternative theories of conflict. The discussion concludes with an analysis of forms of conflict and the arenas in which such conceived forms are said to occur.

Chapter 8 is then devoted to a consideration of discrimination in employment and to some of the recent legislation in this area. The main focus of the chapter is on women but minority groups are also discussed.

Chapter 9 is devoted to a consideration of the very large amount of legislation which has come into force in the post-war period and which affects people in an employment context. The chapter begins with a brief survey of legislation as it developed before this time and then concentrates on trade union, health and safety and minimum wage legislation. Such important developments as the Trade Union and Labour Relations Act (TULRA) of 1974 and the Employment Protection (Consolidation) Act of 1978 are considered in some detail.

Chapter 10 deals with the organization of collective bargaining and bargaining structures. It deals with the law of contract and the many items that are included in a bargaining procedure. It then deals with the role of ACAS and the structure of various bargaining agencies — i.e. employers' organizations and the TUC. The chapter concludes with a short general discussion of the objectives of trade unions and the possible sources of conflict which may arise in this respect.

Chapter 11 deals with the outcome of collective bargaining and how wage rates are established by the use of various management techniques. It then deals with the outcome in the form of enumerating various agreements concluded in the recent past as a result of collective bargaining procedures.

People and organizations have operated in the post-war period against a background of increasing government activity and legislation. While specific aspects of legislation are given earlier consideration, the purpose of Chapter 12 is to present the general economic justification for government involvement and to provide a broad picture of government policy which includes reference to industrial relations, taxation and manpower aspects, so that the reader may obtain an impression of the general environment in which people have found themselves as employees and within which organizations have operated.

At the end of each chapter the reader will find lists of references and questions. Individual students might have sufficient interest to pursue some of the references themselves, but they are also provided so that teachers who wish to develop particular aspects in greater depth can make use of them in directing their students towards appropriate material. Teachers may also wish to utilize some of the questions when setting course work; students may find them valuable enough to incorporate in their progress and revision programmes.

The primary aim of the book is to cover part of the Business Education Council (BEC) Higher Level material for core studies. It is therefore complementary to the three companion volumes in this series. However, it has also been written and structured in such a way as to make it 'free-standing' in the sense that it provides a comprehensive (though not exhaustive) treatment of its subject matter, and, where appropriate, this is facilitated by the provision of appendices. It should, therefore, appeal to a readership which extends beyond that of BEC students. For example, it is hoped that those intending to sit examinations for the Institute of Personnel Management will find it of value, in addition to may students following courses in management, business, administration and social studies.

Chapter 1

People, organizations and employment

1.1 Introduction

People and the organizations which employ them can be viewed from many different standpoints, and even the most cursory reflection is sufficient to indicate the many varied and complex relationships which arise between them. It is these which, in the context of a business environment, form the subject matter of this book. The primary focus is the employment relationship between people and organizations, of which this chapter presents an overview. Its purpose is to indicate briefly the nature of the employment market and its mechanisms and to draw attention to some of its more important characteristics.

In the following section a number of assumptions are made which allow of the construction of a simple theoretical model which is capable of subsequent elaboration, but which also serves to indicate several basic features which characterize the market for labour services in which people and organizations participate. It will provide some initial answers to such questions as why some people earn more than others, how human resources are allocated between alternative jobs and organizations, why people enter one occupation rather than another, and what determines relative and absolute employment levels in organizations. We shall find, however, that many other questions arise which cannot be fully answered by the basic model without the introduction of other factors. Such matters concern the importance of communications between people and within and between organizations; the transmission of information in the market for human resources; the emergence and effects of conflict, discrimination, legislation, differences in individual perceptions, and so forth.

One set of factors from which the simple model abstracts relates to the varying nature of organizations. It can be argued that organizations are a major locus of work in our society. Indeed, organizations impinge on almost every aspect of the individual's life cycle. Our society has been characterized by one sociologist (R. Presthus) as an 'organisational society'. Thus, if we wish to understand the nature of employment in our society, we need to consider how membership of an organization affects this relationship.

The concept of organization refers to a particular pattern of social relationships, such as the family or friendship groups, and has fundamental consequences for the employment relationship. Organizations have the feature of being deliberately set up to achieve particular goals with rules and prescriptions governing the allocation, performance, reward and co-ordination of activities and responsibilities. When an individual enters an organization, he is subject to a number of controls on his behaviour[1]. The scope of these controls varies from one organization to another and also within organizations. Thus, typically managers have more discretion in the performance of their work than machine operators. Similarly, individuals vary in their commitment to the official goals and mechanisms of control, for when individuals enter an organization, they come with a set of *prior* orientations and expectations and these have implications for the experience of, and commitment to, the organization.

Organizations are essentially social entities. They are comprised of people who organize their behaviour in pursuit of shared goals or objectives. For example, students may share the view that part of their course is not operating as it should. Having realized that they all share the view that things could be better, they may decide to organize themselves in order to try to improve the situation. They may call a meeting of students and appoint a chairman or spokesman. They may decide to draw up a petition and approach their course director in the hope that such action will help to resolve the problem. The students in this example are organizing their behaviour in order to achieve a common goal and objective.

In a similar way, other forms of organization have developed. It is possible to view work organizations as comprised of people who share common goals or objectives. Some writers on organizations view them as goal-orientated and rational, and some have tried to classify organizations according to their predominant values or purposes – e.g. economic, political, social, educational. Other writers regard perceptions of organizations which emphasize shared or common goals to be a gross oversimplification of reality. Many of the goals and values which are held by people in organizations are conflicting and contradictory. For example, people in a particular department of a company may use the department to ensure the advancement of their careers rather than the overall benefit of the company. Thus, individuals have their own goals for money, status, etc., and their function in an occupation may be merely a means of achieving those goals.

People may also experience value conflict because they belong to two or more organizations at the same time. A manager, for example, may be a member of a trade union or professional association, and may find conflict between the values he holds as a manager and those he holds as a member of a trade union or professional association. In this way organizations are comprised of complex and conflicting values which are held by people.

In studying organizations it is important that the overlapping nature of organizational life be understood. One's experience of work organizations affects other aspects of life; and one's experience in other organizations affects one's experience of work. Equally, a good deal of work-related experience is determined by the economic environment within which organizations operate. For example, it has been said that the fundamental goal of any business organization operating within a market environment must be its own survival. Survival, however, is easier for some organizations than for others, because of differences in the degree of protection from market forces (see Appendix 3.1, page 78, for an indication of the range of market structures). The greater such immunity is the more likely it is that other goals and objectives will be superimposed upon those which are directly related to survival, and the more dissimilar organizations are in this respect the greater will be the differentiation in experience for those employed by them.

Many of these organizational matters will be taken up in subsequent chapters, but initially it will be useful here to abstract from them in considering some of the basic features of the market for people as employees. This will provide an overview of the system and a useful reference point for complications to be dealt with later. In the subsequent sections of this chapter we can then note some important characteristics of the employment market and imperfections which attach to it, and, finally, examine reasons why wage payments vary as between different occupations.

1.2 A simple pricing and allocation model

As Heineman and Yoder (1965) point out, simple models of markets are frequently criticized because they use assumptions which appear to be unrealistic in particular cases. But it is important to realize that this view is a consequence of a misconception of the purpose of such models, which is not to explain what happens in any specific market but rather to emphasize major characteristics of *all* markets. Precisely because they involve drastic simplifications, such models are also useful as a first approach in reducing complicated situations to manageable proportions. In effect, they provide a small-scale map of a large area; to get more information about particular parts of the area, larger-scale maps of them are needed which provide a closer perspective and considerably more detail.

The main function of a market is to allocate resources and, in the process, to establish prices for such productive inputs as labour and for the goods and services produced. It is, therefore, usual to distinguish between factor markets (in respect of inputs such as labour, capital and raw materials) and product markets. In either case, however, imperfections arise which hinder the free functioning of the market, so that resources are not properly allocated or prices efficiently set. To attempt to introduce and handle all these imperfections at once would be not only counterproductive, but also largely impossible. Indeed, we need some initial method of showing what these imperfections are and what effects they have. One such method would be to construct a model which excluded all imperfections, analyse the way it works and then compare it with real markets. This would serve two purposes: on the one hand, it would show what to expect when a market functions perfectly; and on the other, it would allow of the separate introduction of any additional factors which were of interest in providing more detailed information.

The model of a perfectly competitive market for labour services can be constructed by making the following assumptions:

(1) Employing organizations
    (a) having perfect information of all aspects of the market;
    (b) are individually too small to have any significant influence on the market as a whole;
    (c) attempt to maximize profits and behave rationally;
    (d) do not combine with one another to affect input prices and utilization.

(2) Employees
    (a) have perfect information of all aspects of the market;
    (b) are perfectly mobile in occupational, industrial and geographical senses;
    (c) react positively to differentials in earnings;
    (d) do not combine with one another;
    (e) are homogeneous[2].

If all these conditions are met, the resultant market would price and allocate human resources with maximum efficiency and without frictions of any kind.

To see the way in which the market would operate, consider *Figure 1.1*, where the left-hand diagram represents organization A and the right-hand diagram represents organization B. In each case the labour supply curve (S_L) is positively inclined, which indicates that an increase (decrease) in supply requires an increase (decrease) in the real wage rate (w). The organization's demand curve for labour represents (as will be explained later in this chapter and more fully in Chapter 3) the contribution to output made by each extra employee, and therefore, at

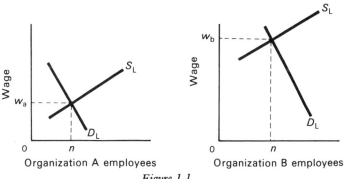

Figure 1.1

any given wage, it indicates the profit maximizing level of employment, since profits are reduced at levels before or after this point[3].

The wage rate offered by organization B (w_b) is clearly greater than that offered by organization A (w_a). Because of assumption (2a), people employed by the latter will be aware of the differential ($w_b - w_a$), and assumptions (2b) and (2e) ensure a transfer of employees from A to B in response. As this movement begins to take place, w_b will decline and w_a will rise, so that the two wage rates approach each other as a consequence of changes in supply. The final outcome is shown in *Figure 1.2*, in which

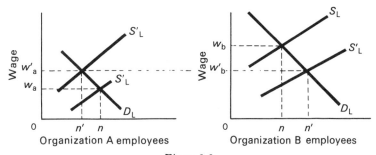

Figure 1.2

the initial supply and demand functions are reproduced. The movement in supply away from organization A shifts its supply curve from S_L to S'_L, raising the wage from w_a to w'_a; similarly, organization B's supply curve shifts from S_L to S'_L and the wage falls from w_b to w'_b. The market eventually reaches an equilibrium position in which wages are equalized ($w'_a = w'_b$). Each organization hires the number of people it desires at the market-determined wage rate and there is no longer any incentive for people to switch employers. Moreover, because of assumption (1a), organizations always have the information necessary to satisfy assumption (1c); and since wage rates equal the addition to output, not only are wages equal in equilibrium, but also the last person employed in any organization or occupation adds the same amount to total output as the last person employed in any other organization or occupation. This is an important point, since it demonstrates the necessary condition for achieving maximum output from any given input quantity; output can always be increased by reallocating existing resources whenever their output contributions are different as between alternative uses.

It is also worth noting that within this model any new entrant to the labour market will, given a *Figure 1.1* situation, offer his or her services to organization B. Assumption (2a) ensures that the individual has knowledge of the wage differential, while assumption (2c) determines the organization entered. We have, therefore, provided answers to all the questions posed in the second paragraph of this chapter. In doing so, however, we have abstracted from many considerations which might be important in particular circumstances. Indeed, the rest of this book can be seen as an elaboration of these details, but, as Cartter and Marshall (1967) point out, 'The real labour market differs from a perfect market in degree, but not necessarily in kind'[4]. Real markets may adjust more slowly and less perfectly, and the empirical verification of the mechanism may be complicated by imperfections of various kinds. For example, mobility may be insufficiently high to bring about the required shifts in supply; or monopoly elements on either side of the market may, at least in the short run, prevent wages reaching the competitive levels necessary for efficient functioning of the market. Moreover, it must be realized that the more detail required from a model the more complicated that model tends to become. However, with the overview provided by the elementary model developed in this section, we can now briefly consider some of the factors which characterize the market for labour services and which produce the need for more detail.

1.3 Characteristics of the market for labour services

The features to be discussed in this section which are attached to the employment relationships occurring between people and organizations can be grouped in various ways. Because of their interconnectedness, overlap occurs between one set of factors and another. While this has been circumvented as far as possible in order to avoid repetition, it should be kept in mind that these individual factors do not occur in isolation.

1.3.1 Personalized factors

Perhaps the most obvious but furthest-reaching consideration attached to the provision of labour services is that it is the only instance in which what is sold has to be delivered personally by the seller. It is this more than anything else which makes the labour market different from other markets. Combined with this fact is the second fundamental consideration that, in most cases, the subsistence of the seller depends wholly on this market return. There is here, therefore, a basis for conflict between people and organizations, since, for the former, wages are the means of substance and, therefore, subject to upward pressure, while, for the latter, wages are a cost of production and therefore subject to downward pressure.

These considerations make the labour market very different from financial or commodity markets and have many far-reaching implications, some of which will form the basis of subsequent chapters. At the moment it will suffice merely to stress the importance of occupational decision-making for the individual. In some cases potential ability may restrict occupational choice severely, but in other instances, and progressively as ability becomes greater, it is crucial for the individual to make efficient job choices. Failure to do so will result in the individual not entering those occupations where his probability of success is greatest or where potential future earnings are highest. In this context, 'future earnings' refers to income over the whole period of labour force participation and we are considering not merely the relative level of earnings in any given period, but also their comparative stability. It is well accepted that in the short term some jobs may involve work of an intermittent or seasonal nature and that this must be compensated for by higher earnings. Over the longer term, we are concerned much more with uncertainty than with foreseeable changes in demand and that attached to some jobs may be less volatile than others. Again, some occupations may provide a relatively better base for switching to others when the need arises, so that, in this case also, lifetime earnings are that much greater than in other employments.

1.3.2 Social factors

The attitudes and norms of society have a considerable role to play in determining the kind of people available for employment, the length of time for which they are available and even the money rewards which they receive. In the latter respect, according to the 'iron law' theory of wages developed by Malthus[5] in the late eighteenth century, in the long run there was a natural tendency for wages to approximate to their subsistence level, below which malnutrition and starvation (still strong characteristics of the greater part of the world's population) begin to occur. In more economically advanced and therefore wealthier countries the concept of a 'just', 'fair' or 'minimum acceptable' wage level may be

reinforced by society, sometimes in the form of minimum wage legislation. This may become necessary if, as in *Figure 1.3*, the equilibrium
wage (w_e) in a competitive market is below the level acceptable to
society, say w_m.

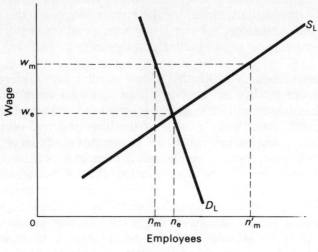

Figure 1.3

It is evident from *Figure 1.3* that problems may arise if w_m is
maintained by legislation. Since $w_m > w_e$, the market will be pushed into
extended disequilibrium and the level of employment will be reduced.
At the equilibrium wage rate of w_e, the employment level is n_e, but if the
wage is held at w_m, the employment level will fall to n_m, so that $n_m n_e$
workers become unemployed. Of the total excess supply of $n_m n'_m$, there
are $n_m n_e$ workers displaced from this particular market plus $n_e n'_m$ who,
while possibly in employment elsewhere, would prefer to work in this
market at a wage of w_m.

An alternative approach to minimum wage legislation is to guarantee
the income of workers by making separate payments from public funds
equal to the difference between the acceptable minimum and the
equilibrium wage (i.e. $w_m - w_e$). This method has the advantage that
each separate labour market is allowed the opportunity of finding its own
equilibrium level and therefore the total allocation of human resources
throughout the economy may be that much more efficient. On the other
hand, this system has the disadvantage that recipients of such payments
often feel degraded and their social and economic value may suffer as a
result.

While the type of occupation to which such a system is likely to be
applied may frequently have low public esteem, other employments are
accorded a high status. High status jobs often carry high wages, but it is

not clear whether the high status causes or follows the high wage. Is a particular occupation given a high status ranking because the wage happens to be high? Or does society ensure that those employments which are highly esteemed are also highly rewarded in financial terms? Moreover, the problem may be complicated by considerations of responsibility. It is generally accepted that people with more responsibility should receive greater pay and many status jobs may appear to involve a relatively high degree of responsibility. The converse, however, is not true.

Legislation on minimum wages has been mentioned as one example of society's impact on the relationships between people and organizations. But, as will be discussed in subsequent chapters, society seems to use the law in many ways as a regulatory tool. It has been used, for example, to prevent organizations using discriminatory hiring policies, to control employment of the young, to establish trade union negotiating rights, to foster health and safety at work, and so forth.

A variety of other social factors impart important characteristics to the market for labour services. It must be recognized, for example, that the career prospects and life chances of individuals entering the employment relationship tend to be unevenly distributed throughout the work population. Thus, class, race and gender play a disproportionate role in determining the likely employment prospects of the individual worker. Non-work factors, such as family background, friendship networks, religion and education, play an important role in influencing the resources and expectations that an individual brings to the workplace. These, in turn, are likely to be modified by subsequent experience within and outside the employing organization. An important factor in this process is the influence that various interest groups exert over the expectations, resources and life chances of various categories of members, and we shall return to a consideration of the impact of these and other social processes on the employment relationship throughout this book.

1.3.3 Organizational influences

The primary purpose of some organizations is to produce goods and services, while others exist to exert an influence on the business and employment relationships which develop, and this is reflected in the goals which each pursues. In the latter category we can include trade unions, employers' associations and government agencies of various kinds.

If the overall aim of business organizations is taken to be survival, then, within a market context, other goals will assume lesser or greater importance accordingly as the organization immunes itself to market forces. An organization operating in a highly competitive environment will have comparatively little scope for developing subsidiary objectives; as the degree of control over the market is extended through monopolization (in an individual market) or conglomeration (through the production of goods for many different markets) or multinationalism (by operating in several countries), freedom to follow other goals becomes greater.

Survival in competitive situations demands a high degree of efficiency. Indeed, the desire to escape from such competition may become an objective of the organization which leads it to seek greater control over its market environment in the ways just indicated. Other objectives which arise as a consequence may include growth of the organization, expansion of market share, extension of managerial rewards and power, and so forth.

Any individual goal of an organization can be seen as the end which it selects and sanctions and to which it applies energies and resources in a constructive and purposeful manner. The end result is invariably a compromise and subject to pressures from management, owners (shareholders) and the workforce, especially when organized into trade unions. Being a compromise, it has many components which are related to formal and informal organizational objectives, product characteristic aims, derived objectives (which have no immediate connection with business aims), shareholder and workforce expectations. Some of these objectives may be complementary and others conflicting. Consequently, and notwithstanding a degree of commonality between them, individual work experience can vary significantly between different organizations, depending on the impact of the external environment, the goals which are determined in relation to the strengths of different interest groups, the organization's structure, and so forth.

By structure of an organization we mean patterns of relationship among roles within it. These patterns comprise relatively enduring and often repeated forms of behaviour which can be classified as being either formally or informally produced. A formal structure is planned and operates via official codes, rules and communication channels with the intent that it will be used by the organization's members.

An informal structure is unspecified, unwritten and unplanned. While it can arise out of, and in reaction to, a formal structure, it is not necessarily related to a formal structure. Initially a trade union may develop as an informal structure (although it is likely to because formalized as part of its subsequent development) within a business organization; it may set its own goals and norms independently of, and sometimes in opposition to, management objectives. A task of management will then be to fit the formal structure to the informal structure in the process of collective bargaining.

Trade unions are protective organizations of people who combine together for the purpose of securing improved conditions of employment. In medieval times there was no need for employed workers to have separate organizations and recognized crafts were catered for by guilds, membership of which included both masters and journeymen (i.e. skilled craftsmen). Since the latter could expect to progress to the former category in due course, the interests of both coincided to a high degree. But the changes brought about by the Industrial Revolution from approximately the second half of the eighteenth century onwards caused these interests to diverge[6]. Moreover, the modern form of labour force was being created as the enclosure of agricultural land forced more and more people to depend for their living on the sale of labour services to the newly emerging capitalists.

Unionization has developed differentially at different periods and among different types of workers. The first British trade unions were largely restricted to combinations of craftsmen and, mainly owing to anti-union legislation and the hostility of employers[7], it was not until the second half of the nineteenth century that unionization broke away from the ranks of artisans and began to spread to various types of semi-skilled and unskilled workers. Similarly, in more recent decades, the growth in union membership has largely been accounted for by its spread to white collar workers. *Table 1.1* provides data on labour force size and trade union membership during the present century.

While the market environment of workers is connected with the development of trade unions, it is sometimes argued that employers' associations are formed as a response to the creation of unions. Heineman and Yoder (1965) note, however, that employers' associations have not always waited for the expansion of unions and that their activities have included a number of interests not connected to their negotiations with unions. Nevertheless, employers' associations usually include labour negotiations as a principal area of concern and frequently seek to produce a higher degree of monopsonistic (i.e. buying) power than would be available to a single employer. Moreover, just as trade unions in Britain are represented collectively by the Trade Union Congress (TUC), so many employers subscribe to the Confederation of British Industry (CBI). These two bodies are useful in a number of ways to those who support them, and not least in the extent to which they constitute effective pressure groups on government. In representing the collective interests of their members, they may be successful in effecting or preventing changes in, for example, national legislation which affects bargaining positions.

It is useful to note at this point that one of the ways in which the existence of employers' and workers' organizations complicates analysis of the market for labour services is in respect of wage determination. At

Table 1.1 Trade union membership, labour force and unemployment

Year	Labour force	Change p.a. (%)	Union membership	Change p.a. (%)	Union density (%)
1892	14 126		1 576		11.2
1901	16 101		2 025		12.6
1911	17 762		3 139		17.7
1913	17 920		4 185		23.1
1917	18 234		5 499		30.2
1920	18 469		3 348		45.2
1923	17 965		5 429		30.2
1933	19 422		4 392		22.6
1938	19 828		6 053		30.5
1945	20 400		7 875		38.6
1948	20 732	+1.3	9 326	−0.3	45.2
1949	20 782	+0.2	9 348	+0.5	44.8
1950	21 055	+1.3	9 289	−0.3	44.1
1951	21 177	+0.6	9 535	+2.6	45.0
1952	21 282	+0.4	9 588	+0.6	45.1
1953	21 352	+0.5	9 527	−0.6	44.6
1954	21 658	+1.4	9 566	+0.4	44.2
1955	21 913	+1.2	9 741	+1.8	44.5
1956	22 180	+1.2	9 778	+0.4	44.1
1957	22 334	+0.7	9 829	+0.5	44.0
1958	22 290	−0.2	9 639	−1.9	43.2
1959	22 429	+0.6	9 623	−0.2	42.9
1960	22 817	+1.7	9 835	+2.2	43.1
1961	23 112	+1.3	9 936	+0.3	42.9
1962	23 432	+1.4	10 014	+1.0	42.7
1963	23 558	+0.5	10 067	+0.5	42.7
1964	23 706	+0.6	10 218	+1.5	43.1
1965	23 920	+0.9	10 325	+1.0	43.2
1966	24 065	+0.6	10 262	−0.6	42.6
1967	23 807	−1.1	10 190	−0.7	42.8
1968	23 667	−0.6	10 193	0.0	43.1
1969	23 603	−0.3	10 472	+2.7	44.4
1970	23 446	−0.7	11 179	+6.8	47.7
1971	22 231	−0.9	11 127	−0.5	47.9
1972	22 303	+0.3	11 349	+2.0	48.7
1973	23 592	+1.2	11 444	+0.8	48.5
1974	23 689	+0.4	11 755	+2.7	49.6
1975	23 852	+0.7	12 193	+3.7	51.1
1976	24 032	+0.4	12 386	+1.6	51.5
1977	24 186	+0.6	12 707	+2.6	52.5

Source: Various but mainly Price and Bain (1976).

the risk of oversimplifying, there are two schools of thought: one holds that relative wages are determined wholly by market forces of supply and demand and the factors which underlie them; the other considers that relative wages are the result of power forces as represented by bargaining organizations. Clearly, adopting this 'either or' standpoint means that the views are mutually exclusive, but it should be recognized that there are considerable difficulties in producing conclusive empirical evidence for either argument.

Business operates within a framework of law and is retained by organizations which also operate within the law and have specific functions by operating checks and balances. As indicated earlier, two types of organization in which we are particularly interested are employers' organizations and trade unions. In addition, the Advisory Conciliation and Arbitration Service (ACAS) is also important in a British context.

Trade unions in Britain have a long and chequered history. Although they began to appear earlier, their legality and growth dates from 1825 with the repeal of the Combination Act of 1799, which gave trade unions immunities to act in 'restraint of trade' in the pursuance of trade disputes. Their immunities were extended in various pieces of legislation often following the decision of judges in curbing union powers and activities.

The latest piece of legislation extending trade union immunities was the Trade Union and Labour Relations Act 1974 and the Amendment Act of 1976, which can be amended so as once again to reduce trade union immunities, a to-and-fro situation which has gone on for over 150 years.

Trade unions in Britain have over 12 million members and the density of trade union membership in relationship to the workforce is now about 52 per cent (see *Table 1.1*), although the density of trade union organization is very uneven between the unions. In some sectors of industry it is virtually 100 per cent, while in other sectors, especially where few workers are employed in small firms, it is between 10 per cent and 25 per cent There are no sectors of employment (except the police service, where membership of a trade union is incompatible with the contract of employment) where there is no trade union organization or a trade union catering for the specific group of 'white collar' or 'blue collar' workers.

Employers' organizations grew up in Britain in response to the growth of trade unions. Today there are several thousand individual employers' organizations in the Engineering Employers' Federation because of its strength and professionalism. Employers' organizations are now co-ordinated by the CBI.

ACAS plays a considerable part in restraining both employers and trade unions. It advises, conciliates and provides arbitration if it is requested. It is the state institution which fulfils the role of a 'fire brigade' in industrial relations.

The activities of ACAS are defined and determined by the Employment Protection Act 1975. The powers are spelled out in the sections of the Act and the general duty is formulated thus in section 1(2) of the Act:

The Service shall be charged with the general duty of promoting the improvement of industrial relations, and in particular of encouraging the extension of collective bargaining and the development and, where necessary, reform of collective bargaining machinery.

1.3.4 Market imperfections

A perfect market is one which is free from any kind of impediment which would hinder the free operation of the forces of supply and demand. 'Perfect' is therefore a purely technical term relating to the efficiency with which a market system operates; the term has nothing to do with the desirability or otherwise of such a system.

Communication and the transmission of information is of central importance in the labour market. If people and organizations are unable to obtain information about events in the market, they cannot react to them and resources may consequently be misallocated. Similarly, an employing organization cannot function properly without adequate internal means of communication. The consequences will be much the same if, for example, an employer is unable to obtain information which will allow him to distinguish between more and less productive workers either within the organization or in the external labour market from which recruits are obtained. Again, human resources may be misallocated if people do not receive information sufficient to distinguish between higher-paying employers and occupations.

Monopoly and monopsony elements also produce market imperfections, the former relating to selling power and the latter to buying power. Trade unions, for instance, are sometimes represented as monopoly sellers of labour, while firms in isolated geographical areas where other employers are absent are likely to possess considerable monopsony power. In either eventuality, wages and employment levels will be different from those occurring in markets free of these imperfections.

Any restriction on the ability of people to move between occupations, industries or geographical areas is likely to constitute a serious market imperfection. The degree of seriousness will tend to vary considerably with time and place, but one or other form of this impediment is usually present in labour markets. For example, it is often difficult for some people to enter occupations which require a high level of skill, not because they lack the necessary potential, but rather because they cannot finance the training costs and periods involved. Again, it is often argued that society is divided into, say, four or five socio-economic groups and that movement and interaction between them is considerably limited. Thus, members of one group do not compete with members of other groups. This fragmentation view of the labour market can be taken even further, so that we obtain separate markets for fitters, patternmakers, electricians, etc. These individual markets become quite separate to varying extents, so that fitters do not compete with moulders, pattern-makers do not compete with electricians, and so forth. At least in the short run, training and experience requirements produce what Cairnes described as 'noncompeting groups' which result from a low elasticity of substitutions.

The effects of these and other types of imperfections are likely to vary in severity as between different groups and countries, and over different periods in time. In analytical terms, they also cause difficulties by reducing the observed degree of association between factors which are expected to be causally related. One common problem, for example, is that, while expected changes do occur, they may take place only after a period of time has elapsed. If one does not allow for this, or considers the wrong period, empirical results may be poorer than otherwise. The problem may be compounded by the fact that, out of the number of reactions which do occur, some will take place in one period and some in another.

1.4 Factors underlying supply and demand schedules

Some of the more important aspects which characterize the relationships between people and organizations having been discussed, it is now useful to outline the factors which are important in determining the supply of, and demand for, labour services. With the simplified model thus established, subsequent chapters can then discuss various aspects in greater detail.

1.4.1 Supply of labour services

It was mentioned earlier that a crucial labour market consideration is that the seller of labour services must deliver himself to the point of sale. Because of this requirement a second factor arises. Whereas the supply of any other productive input depends solely on the financial induce-ment, the supply of labour services depends also on the non-financial or psychic income attached to any employment. This non-pecuniary income may be either positive (as when an occupation offers some form of job satisfaction such as accompanies the acquisition and exercise of a skill) or negative (as when dangerous, dirty or disagreeable aspects are attached to a job). The sum of financial plus non-financial advantages less the sum of financial and non-financial disadvantages is referred to as net advantage. Equilibrium then requires that net advantages between jobs be equalized. This can be expressed by writing

$$U(F_a, N_a) = U(F_b, N_b) \tag{1.1}$$

where U is the utility (or satisfaction) to be obtained from financial (F) and non-financial (N) income in any two jobs a and b.

It is evident that equilibrium does not now imply the equalization of monetary earnings, since an adequate supply may be obtained because a low financial reward is sufficiently offset by a high psychic return. Conversely, relatively high financial earnings will be required in some jobs in order to compensate for their disagreeable nature.

The relative non-pecuniary aspects of alternative employments tend, however, to be quite stable in the short to medium term. In many cases employers would find them difficult to manipulate as a variable affecting supply. Hence, employing organizations may concentrate on monetary payments and, except over the longer term, supply becomes a function of financial rewards.

So far supply has been thought of in terms of numbers of people, but for some purposes it is more relevant to measure supply in hours. In this case it does not necessarily follow that an increase in the wage rate will cause an increase in supply; indeed, a wage rise may produce a fall in the supply of hours. The reason is that, as real income rises, people tend to consume more goods, including leisure, which may be regarded as a normal good[8]. Obviously, if more time is taken in leisure, there are fewer hours available for work. As with any other commodity, a change in the price of leisure involves both an income and a substitution effect. Thus, at a wage rate of, say, £3.00 per hour, the cost of each hour taken in leisure per week is £3.00. If the wage rate is increased to £4.00 per hour, each hour of leisure is now more expensive and less leisure will be taken – i.e. there is a substitution effect which increases the number of hours worked. But the increased hourly wage rate also raises the real income of the worker, so that he can buy more of all goods, including leisure. Hence, more leisure is bought and less time is spent working, so that the income effect reduces the supply of hours. Whether the net outcome is a rise or fall in total hours worked clearly depends on the relative strengths of income and substitution effects. The possible outcomes are shown in *Figure 1.4*, where the initial portion of the supply curve (S) has the familiar positive slope, the substitution effect (E_s) being greater than the income effect (E_y) (e.g. as the real wage increases, the income effect tends to rise in strength, so that eventually it outweighs the substitution effect and further increases in the real wage reduce the number of hours worked each week[9]).

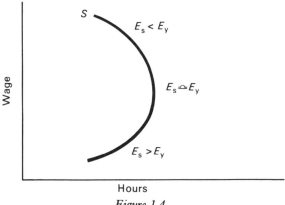

Figure 1.4

This backward-sloping supply curve was first noted by Brentano in the *Economic Journal* in 1912, but the earliest estimates of the relationship between hours worked and hourly wage rates were made by Douglas from United States data for the period 1890–1926. Although the results should be treated with caution, he found strong negative correlations in 14 out of 15 industries studied and only one (weak) positive correlation. A number of more recent studies have also indicated a backward-sloping curve.

It must, however, be recognized that individual labour supply decisions are not necessarily the result of decision processes involving only purely personal factors. For example, Rees (1979) points out that it is 'an oversimplification to view decisions on whether or not to be in the labour force as a choice between work and leisure, where leisure includes only recreation and time for such personal needs as eating and sleeping. Most of the men and single women under age 25 who are not in the labour force are full-time students, and going to school or college is certainly not leisure. Most married women not in the labour force are full-time housekeepers for their families, and keeping house is hard work'.[10] Leisure (as defined above) is clearly an important factor, but we must recognize that the domestic production of goods and services (such as that engaged in by a housewife or a member of the labour force when not so working) is a crucial alternative to both work and leisure. This line of thought also leads to the conclusion that family or household income may in some respects be a more important determinant of labour supply than individual earnings. Consequently, from a household point of view the three variables of major importance are leisure, family income and domestic productive activity. The way in which these different activities are distributed between household members depends partly on preferences but also on the relative market prices which confront each member of the family. 'Hence an increase in one member's earnings may not result in a reduction in his hours of work but a reduction by another member. An increase in the wage rate offered to one member of a household makes his consumption of leisure and production of domestic goods more costly to other members of the family.'[11]

Evidently, then, the employment experience of one family member may affect the labour market participation rates of other members. This is the thinking behind the 'added worker hypothesis', which argues that a cyclical fall in aggregate demand which causes the usual breadwinner to be unemployed may induce additional members of the family to enter the labour market to protect household income. Now it may be expected that the fall in demand reduces not only family income, but also the real wages of those in employment. Hence, in the former respect, if market work is an inferior good (for which demand falls as income rises), there is an income effect which increases participation rates, while in the latter case the change in real wages produces a substitution effect resulting in reduced market activity. The added worker hypothesis therefore suggests a predominantly stronger income effect, so that changes in the labour force are countercyclical.

An alternative view is provided by the 'discouraged worker hypothesis', which argues that the unemployment occurring in periods of depression causes some people to become so discouraged as to either withdraw from the labour market or fail to enter it. In this case, changes in the labour force will be procyclical and the substitution effect will outweigh the income effect.

A number of tests have been made to these hypotheses using multiple regression analysis[12]. Time series data have been used by some analysts (e.g. Strand and Dernburg, 1964), and cross-sectional data by others (e.g. Bowen and Finegan, 1965), one result of which has been to indicate that the two hypotheses can be present simultaneously in different families. On balance, and while the added worker effect appears strong for some low income families, when all households are taken together the evidence is in favour of a stronger discouragement effect, so that labour force participation and the trade cycle are positively related.

Over the long term, participation rates for women have increased significantly, as *Figure 1.5* indicates. A number of factors have contributed to these changes, not all of them easy to quantify. Partly because of legislation and changing social attitudes, sex discrimination in Britain has declined and the acceptability of women in employment has risen. Average family size has declined, so that the period for which women are

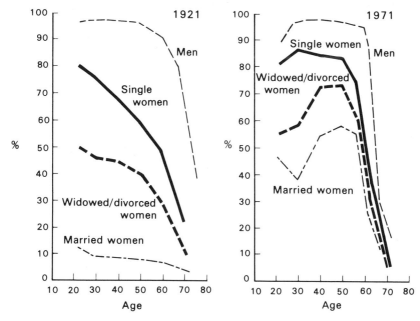

Figure 1.5 Economic activity rates (from *Economic Progress Report*, No. 56, November 1974)

tied to the house has fallen and more time is available for labour market activity. For that amount of time which is devoted to non-market activity in the home more capital-intensive methods of domestic production have become available in the form of automatic washing machines, microwave ovens, etc., reducing the time needed for various activities and increasing that available for involvement in the labour market. The value of female work in the market has also risen owing to the increased level of education of women.

Another aspect of supply requires mention at this point (although it will receive more detailed treatment in the next chapter). This concerns the supply of human capital, an important part of which is the supply of skill. Skills, ability and even knowledge are referred to as types of human capital, because, in much the same way as physical capital (in the form of tools, plant, machinery), they are capable of yielding future services and can be used in the process of production. Such attributes are commonly acquired through education and training processes and cannot therefore be obtained without both financial and psychic costs. Equally, there are benefits attached to the possession of human capital. These may partly take the form of non-financial advantages due, for example, to the exercise of skills, but pecuniary returns are also expected to be greater, because those who have more human capital will tend to be more productive than those who have less.

The supply of human capital is clearly subject to lengthy gestation periods and, in more extreme cases, upwards of 15 years may be required to produce certain types of specialist skills. Consequently, the process of adjustment in the market becomes more complicated and can be expected to follow a cobweb cycle. An example is shown in *Figure 1.6*, from which it is clear why the term 'cobweb' is applied. In *Figure 1.6(a)* the supply and demand schedules are S_{hc} and D_{hc}, respectively. Suppose the wage rate to be at w_a: employing organizations will demand n_a workers but supply will be at n'_a, resulting in an excess of $n_a n'_a$. For all

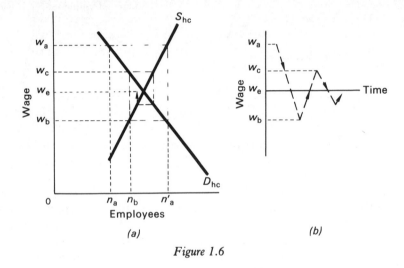

Figure 1.6

workers to find employment the wage must fall to w_b. But at w_b fewer people will come forward for training, so that, at the end of the next training period, supply will fall to n_b. When n_b workers eventually enter the market, the excess demand (of $n_b n'_a$) will push up their wage. At a wage of w_c more people will be attracted for training, so that in the next period supply will increase. Adjustment continues in this fashion until, in the present case, an equilibrium wage rate is reached at w_e. For markets which converge on equilibrium in this way, the cobweb model is referred to as being stable and the wage fluctuations decrease over time as indicated in *Figure 1.6(b)*. It is, of course, possible to have an unstable situation in which the fluctuations become progressively greater over time and the market moves further and further from its equilibrium point[13]. An unstable situation can be produced in *Figure 1.6* by introducing a flatter supply curve so that there is an increase in its relative elasticity (see Appendix 1.1 on this concept).

1.4.2 Demand for labour services

When an organization takes on an additional worker, the sale of the extra output which is produced raises the revenue of the firm. Similarly, the employment of an extra person raises the costs of the enterprise. Profits can obviously be increased whenever the engagement of an extra worker adds more to total revenue than to total cost. It will, therefore, always be profitable to expand the labour force if the addition to cost is less than the addition to revenue; it will be profitable to reduce output if the converse holds.

Over some ranges of output it is likely that the change in cost will be less than the change in revenue as production expands; but eventually the change in cost will become greater than the change in revenue. Any organization wishing to make the maximum amount of profit will need to find the point between these relationships at which the change in cost equals the change in revenue. If we represent these small or *marginal* changes in cost and revenue by MC and MR, respectively, the general condition for profit maximization (as explained in Appendix 1.2) is that marginal cost must equal marginal revenue:

$$MC = MR \tag{1.2}$$

This general condition must clearly apply also to any separate type of input. If the labour market is competitive, the marginal cost of hiring an extra worker is the wage (W). Hence, $W = MC$. To distinguish it from the general case, we may call the addition to revenue attributable to the last worker employed the 'marginal revenue product' (MRP). Hence, $MRP = MR$. Therefore, Equation (1.2) can be rewritten as

$$W = MRP \tag{1.3}$$

For reasons to be explained in Chapter 3, over the relevant range the MRP attributable to each additional worker will be declining in the short run, so that plotting its values at different employment levels will produce a curve similar to that displayed in *Figure 1.7*. In fact, the MRP curve is the firm's demand curve for labour. This can be seen by considering the organization's employment decision for some given wage rate w_0 as set by the market. If n_1 workers are employed, the last worker adds w_1 to total revenue (i.e. $MRP = w_1$). Since w_1 is in excess of the wage being paid (w_0), more is added to revenue than to cost and total profit must rise. Specifically, profit rises by $w_1 - w_0$. Total profit is increased further, albeit at a declining rate, if more employees are engaged up to, say, n_2 workers. In this case the last worker adds w_2 to total revenue, adds w_0 to total cost and therefore profit rises by $w_2 - w_0$. Clearly, total profit will continue to rise with employment until n_0 workers are hired and the MRP of the last person engaged equals the

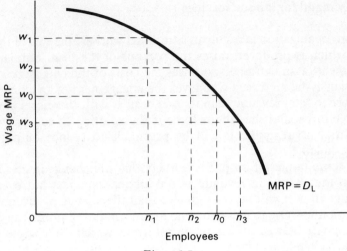

Figure 1.7

current wage rate. It is equally clear that any expansion of the workforce beyond n_0 must reduce total profit. At n_3 the marginal revenue product of the last worker is equal to w_3 but, since the wage paid is w_0, total profit falls by $w_0 - w_3$.

For a wage rate of w_0, the optimum employment level for a profit-maximizing firm is n_0, where MRP is brought into equality with the wage rate. If the wage rate fell to w_3, the optimum employment level would rise to n_3; at w_1 it would be n_1, and so forth, with the level of employment rising only if the wage rate falls. Hence, at any given wage rate the MRP curve indicates the corresponding employment level and therefore constitutes the firm's demand curve for labour.

1.5 Wage differentials between occupations

A good many factors have been introduced in this chapter which are important from a variety of perspectives. In this final section a few of them will be used to illustrate how a particular problem can be approached and an answer provided while generating some additional information pertinent to the people–organization relationship.

Why is it that employing organizations pay different wage rates to different people in different occupations? To provide a complete answer to this question would require the inclusion of so many variables that the task would become extremely difficult. But it is not necessary to include every possible cause of wage differentials, since many of these will be of very minor importance and others will occur infrequently. Hence, we can begin by selecting only the more important influences and those which are more commonly active. In order to introduce these selected variables, we can employ a useful methodological device by utilizing the model developed in Section 1.2, where the only cause of wage differentials is market disequilibrium. This approach is useful for two reasons: in the first place, it emphasizes that in the real world, where markets are but rarely in equilibrium, observed differentials are partly due to incomplete market adjustment; secondly, the approach allows any other cause of a differential to be introduced and its effect clearly analysed without the very difficult task of handling several different variables simultaneously.

Many alternative influences could be introduced but, if we take the demand side as given, Adam Smith probably covered most of the major factors when he said that the supply price (i.e. the wage for which people are willing to work) varies with (1) the pleasantness or unpleasantness of a job, (2) the degree of trust or responsibility, (3) the instability of employment, (4) the probability of success or failure in a job and (5) the cost of learning a job. An analysis of the individual effects of these factors, which would cause wages to be different even if all markets were in equilibrium, can carry us a long way towards explaining occupational differentials. For example, suppose that jobs differ only in respect of their relative short-run employment stability, so that over, say, a year certain jobs will involve several weeks of unemployment (due to perhaps seasonal fluctuations in demand). Wage rates (i.e. hourly or weekly payments) for these occupations must be greater than others to compensate for periods when earnings are zero; otherwise people would enter only those jobs where employment is more stable and earnings over the year are higher. Again, enough has probably been said in Sub-section 1.4.1 to show that, other things equal, jobs with high non-pecuniary incomes will entail lower financial income, and vice versa.

In specifying his five factors Smith was, of course, taking a number of other things as given, but these can be introduced and their effects analysed as desired. Thus, we might show that earnings may be greater in some jobs because of various types of market imperfections. People who could fill some jobs may not do so because they are not aware of the existence of higher wage rates in those jobs; hence, there is no increase in supply and wage rates are not reduced. Similarly, if higher wage rates are available only in a different geographical region, attachment to one's home environment may restrict geographical mobility and, hence, maintain higher differentials elsewhere. Again, the division of society into non-competing groups through inequalities of educational opportunity or other reasons will perpetuate higher differentials than would otherwise be the case.

Educational or training opportunity is of the greater importance the less dependent people are on genetic inheritance for their level of productivity. Hence, King (1972) points out that, with the first four of Smith's factors held constant, the fifth provides a long-run theory of occupational wage differentials. In broad terms, if one's job requires training and others do not and if such training is paid for by workers, post-training wages will be higher than in other jobs because of the return employees will obtain on their investment. Trained workers will be more productive than unskilled labour; consequently, when equated to marginal products, the wages of skilled people will be greater than those of unskilled workers.

The whole question of education and training is so important that the next chapter is devoted to it. In a market economy a worker tends to be paid equal to the valuation placed on him by employing organizations. That value depends to a large extent on his productive capabilities, which, in turn, are affected by the education and training received. Hence, the lifetime earnings of a worker rise with the level of education and training undergone both before and after entry to the labour market. From the employer's side, all kinds of skill, ability and knowledge are required in people hired for productive purposes. Some of these attributes are developed in people through educative processes prior to market entry, and the education sector is therefore important because it partly determines the quality of labour which organizations must hire initially. Education and training continue to be important after people have been hired, however, because it is through such processes that any deficiency as between the supply of and demand for skills is remedied.

Questions

1. Give examples of capital-intensive methods of domestic production.
2. What factors did Adam Smith consider to be most important in determining the supply price of workers?
3. Suggest reasons why occupational mobility may be greater or less in some countries than in others.
4. Give examples of occupations for which the supply of human capital involves (a) short, (b) medium and (c) long gestation periods.
5. In the light of income and substitution effect analysis, how would you expect a reduction in income tax to affect hours worked?
6. Draw an unstable cobweb diagram and compare it with a stable cobweb diagram. What causes the difference in stability?
7. Discuss cases in which it is more appropriate to measure occupational differentials in (a) wage rates, (b) earnings.
8. Explain why 'The real labour market differs from a perfect market in degree but not necessarily in kind'.

9. Discuss the view that the most practical tool available to the manager of an organization is a good theory.
10. Using the model of Section 1.2, analyse the effects on supply of one job requiring a greater amount of human capital than any other.
11. From the explanation provided in Appendix 1.2 use the information given in *Table Q.1* below to calculate average and marginal costs and revenues and profit over the range of output indicated. Ensuring that the scale used for the output axis is the same in each case, construct two graphs in the manner of Appendix 1.2 and determine the profit maximizing level of output in each case. (Note that the same result should be obtained from each graph.)

Table Q.1 Weekly cost, revenue, output schedule

Output	Fixed cost	Variable cost	Total cost	Average cost	Marginal cost	Price over average revenue	Marginal revenue	Profit $(\mathcal{J}R - TC)$
1	20	20				10		
2	20	28				10		
3	20	34				10		
4	20	39				10		
5	20	42				10		
6	20	44				10		
7	20	47				10		
8	20	51				10		
9	20	56				10		
10	20	63				10		
11	20	74				10		
12	20	90				10		
13	20	110				10		
14	20	135				10		

Notes

[1] The term 'behavioural' will be used throughout to indicate either or both psychological and sociological aspects.

[2] Note that assumption 2(e) is not strictly necessary but is included at this stage for convenience.

[3] See, for example, the discussion in the companion volume *Organizations: Structure and Policy* (Butterworths, in preparation), Chapter 3.

[4] Cartter and Marshall (1967), Chapter 8, page 203.

[5] See Cartter and Marshall (1967), Chapter 9, for an explanation of Malthus' theory. Very briefly, an increase in real wages leads to greater procreative activity. The subsequent rise in labour supply depresses wages, and, if they fall below subsistence level, the population and labour force contract. The latter may also occur because the geometric growth rate of population exceeds the arithmetic growth rate of food supply. The reduced supply of labour raises real wages again. Thus, over the long period, real wages fluctuate about their subsistence level.

[6] See Pelling (1963) for a brief discussion of the emergence of British trade unions.

[7] See Pelling (1963), page 15.

[8] A normal good is defined as one for which demand increases as income increases. Its income elasticity of demand is therefore positive.

[9] For a fuller analysis, see McCormick (1969), Chapter 1, or Rees (1979), Chapter 2.

[10] Rees (1979), page 3.

[11] McCormick (1969), pages 41–42.

[12] For an explanation of the statistical terms used in this paragraph see, for example, the companion volume mentioned in Note 3.

[13] For a discussion of the cobweb model see, for example, Lipsey (1975), Chapter 12.

References

Bowen, W.G. and Finegan, T.A. (1965). 'Labour force participation and unemployment', in Ross, A.M. (Ed.), *Unemployment Policy and the Labour Market*, University of California Press, Berkeley, Los Angeles

Cartter, A.M. and Marshall, F.R. (1967). *Labour Economics: Wages, Employment and Trade Unionism*, Richard D. Irwin Inc.

Heineman, H.G., Jr. and Yoder, Dale (1965). *Labour Economics*, 2nd edn, South Western Publishing Co.

King, J.E. (1972). *Labour Economics*, Macmillan, London

Lipsey, R.G. (1975). *An Introduction to Positive Economics*, 4th edn, Weidenfeld and Nicolson, London

McCormick, B.J. (1969). *Wages*, Penguin, Harmondsworth

McCormick, B.J., Kitchen, P.D., Marshall, G.P., Sampson, A.A. and Sedgwick, R. (1974). *Introducing Economics*, Penguin, Harmondsworth

Meacham, S. (1977). *A Life Apart. The English Working Class 1890–1914*, Thames and Hudson, London

Pelling, H. (1963). *A History of British Trade Unionism*, Penguin, Harmondsworth

Price, R. and Bain, G.S. (1976). 'Union growth revisited: 1948–1974 in perspective', *British Journal of Industrial Relations*, **XIV**, No. 3

Rees, A. (1979). *The Economics of Work and Pay*, 2nd edn, Harper and Row, New York

Strand, K.T. and Dernburg, T.S. (1974). 'Cyclical variations in civilian labour force participation', *Review of Economics and Statistics*, **46**

Appendix 1.1: Elasticity

Elasticity is a concept which is used to relate a change in one variable to the resultant change in another variable. It can, therefore, be employed where any two variables are causally related. Thus, in respect of price and demand, the coefficient of price elasticity of demand (η_d) is defined as

$$\eta_d = \frac{\text{percentage change in quantity demanded}}{\text{percentage change in price}}$$

$$= \left(\frac{\Delta q}{q} \cdot 100\right) \div \left(\frac{\Delta p}{p} \cdot 100\right)$$

$$= \frac{\Delta q}{q} \cdot \frac{p}{\Delta p}$$

which can be rearranged for convenience as

$$\eta_d = \frac{\Delta q}{\Delta p} \cdot \frac{p}{q} \tag{A1.1.1}$$

where Δ = change, q = quantity demanded and p = price. Assume the demand curve to be as represented in *Figure A1.1.1*. The last expression

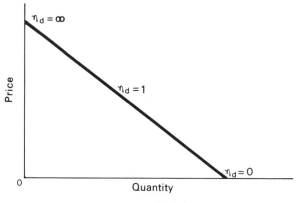

Figure A1.1.1

for the elasticity coefficient is useful because it emphasizes that its value depends both on the original price and quantity and on the steepness of the demand curve. $\Delta p/\Delta q$ measures the slope of the demand curve; it is constant in the case of a linear demand curve and therefore its inverse $\Delta q/\Delta p$ is also constant. Thus, if the demand curve is non-linear, the elasticity coefficient varies over its length, because both $\Delta q/\Delta p$ and p/q are varying, but for linear demand curves η_d varies over its length *only* because p/q changes (since $\Delta q/\Delta p$ is constant). In fact, the coefficient increases in (absolute) value from zero (where the demand curve cuts the horizontal axis) to infinity (where the demand curve cuts the vertical axis); halfway up its length it has a unitary value.

This last, unitary, value separates cases of elastic demand from those of inelastic demand. Demand is said to be elastic with respect to price if $\eta_d > 1$, so that the percentage change in quantity is greater than the percentage change in price; demand is price-inelastic if the percentage change in quantity is less than that in price, so that $\eta_d < 1$. (It should be noted that, strictly speaking, in the case of demand, one would expect a negative sign on the coefficient, since quantity and price vary inversely. For supply the value will be positive, since quantity and price then vary in the same direction.)

In some cases $\eta_d = 0$, $\eta_d = \infty$ or $\eta_d = 1$ over the whole of the curve. These cases are shown in, respectively, parts (a), (b) and (c) of *Figure A1.1.2*. In *Figure A1.1.2(a)* the change in quantity for any change in

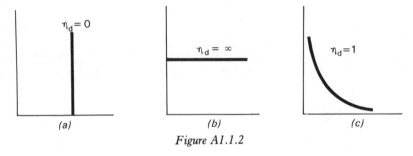

Figure A1.1.2

price is zero and therefore the elasticity coefficient is zero. As the demand curve shifts from a vertical to a horizontal position, the percentage change in quantity becomes progressively larger for any given change in price and approaches an infinitely high value. In *Figure A1.1.2(c)* the demand curve is a rectangular hyperbola and the value of the area under the curve $(p \cdot q)$ is the same at every point; hence, the percentage changes in price and quantity are always the same.

Appendix 1.2: Marginalism

Information about the total value of a variable (such as production or revenue) is clearly necessary for many purposes, but it is often useful and illuminating to consider also changes in the value of variables. When these changes are small, they are referred to as marginal changes. This form of analysis began to develop from about 1870 as a means of specifying the necessary and sufficient conditions for achieving the maximum value of a variable (*Palgrave's Dictionary of Political Economy*, Vol. 2, Macmillan, 1925).

For example, a common application of the marginalist method is to profit maximization. Given the constraints which operate (such as the technological relationships in production, the quantities which consumers are prepared to buy at different prices, etc.), the conditions for achieving maximum profit can be defined by considering changes in revenue and cost. For readers with an appreciation of calculus, a marginal rate is the first derivative of a function. (As will be seen, however, first-order conditions are necessary but not sufficient and second-order conditions are also needed which relate to changes in marginal rates.) For these and other readers, a marginal rate is shown, in graphic terms, by the slope of the total function. Thus, in *Figure A1.2.1*

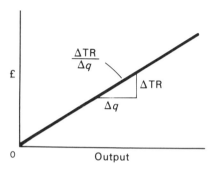

Figure A1.2.1

the rate at which total revenue changes (ΔTR), or marginal revenue, is constant because the function is linear and the slope or gradient of a straight line is the same at any point. The slope is given by the ratio of the change in revenue to the change in output (Δq) – i.e. ΔTR/Δq.

If a function is not linear, the slope or marginal rate is different at different points on the curve. In *Figure A1.2.2*, for example, lines are drawn tangential to a total cost curve at five points. The slopes of these tangents indicate the slope of the total cost curve, or marginal cost, at each of the points. Thus, marginal cost (or the slope of the total cost curve) is greater at point c_1 than at c_2 because the line at c_1 is steeper (has a greater slope or gradient) than the line at c_2. Similarly, the value of marginal cost is smaller at c_3 than at c_2. Hence, between c_1 and c_3 marginal cost is falling; on the other hand, between c_4 and c_5 it is rising. It should also be noted that between c_3 and c_4 marginal cost reaches its lowest value.

Marginal cost can be estimated in *Figure A1.2.2* from the ratio of the change in total cost (ΔTC) to the change in output, much as before – i.e. ΔTC/Δq. However, since the function is not linear, in this case the

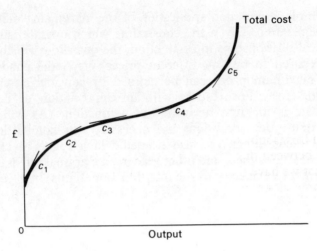

Figure A1.2.2

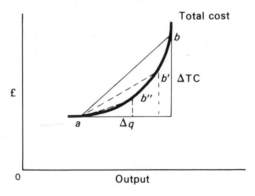

Figure A1.2.3

estimate will only be approximate. This is illustrated in *Figure A1.2.3*. The delta sign, Δ, indicates discrete rather than very small changes and this leads to some degree of error. Thus, if we take the change between points a and b, $\Delta TC/\Delta q$ approximates the slope of the curve at point a. It actually gives the slope of the line between a and b. If we take a smaller range (say from a to b'), ΔTC and Δq become smaller and the line ab' is nearer to the slope at a. For smaller changes still, such as between a and b'', the error is reduced further.

We can now show how marginal revenue and marginal cost can be used to determine the level of output at which total profit (q) is at a maximum. The two functions are reproduced together in *Figure A1.2.4*.

We can clearly exclude any rates of output below q_1 and above q_2, since in these cases total cost is greater than total revenue. Since total profit at any level of output is measured as the vertical distance between the TR and TC curves, we need to find the point between q_1 and q_2 where this difference is greatest. In terms of the graph, the location can be approximately determined by measuring the distance with a rule. Alternatively, if a rule is placed along the lower side of the TR curve and then moved parallel downwards until it is just tangential to the TC curve, and this is indicated by the line ab, we locate point c. The vertical difference between the TR and TC curves is found to be greatest at this point. What we have then done is to find a point on the TC curve which has the same slope as the TR curve, which is to say that at point c

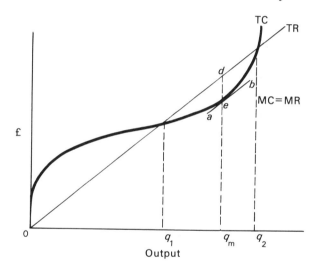

Figure A1.2.4

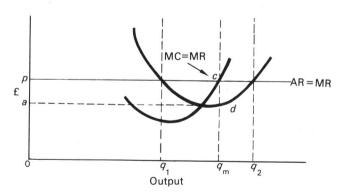

Figure A1.2.5

marginal cost (given by the slope of the TC curve) is equal to marginal revenue (given by the slope of the TR curve). This is quite a general result and defines, for any firm producing individually in any type of market structure, the condition that marginal cost (MC) must be equal to marginal revenue (MR) for maximum profit to be made.

The same result can be demonstrated by drawing the marginal and average cost and revenue curves instead of the total curve, and this is generally preferable because the graph is more flexible. As *Figure A1.2.5* indicates, the average cost curve, as derived from the total cost curve in *Figure A1.2.4*, is U-shaped. This shape depends on the behaviour of marginal cost and, in general, when a marginal quantity is falling, the associated average quantity will also be falling; when a marginal quantity is rising, the associated average quantity will also be rising; when a marginal quantity is constant, the associated average quantity will also be constant. The first two of these propositions are demonstrated in *Figure A1.2.5* by the average and marginal cost curves and the third by the average and marginal revenue curves.

With the output axes drawn to the same scales, the profit maximization level of output is shown to be the same in *Figure A1.2.5* as in *Figure A1.2.4*, at q_m. The average cost of producing each of the q_m units is dq_m, while the price or average revenue obtained is cq_m; average profit per unit of output is therefore dc and total profit consequently given by the area $apcd$ which is equal to total revenue (area $0pcq_m$) minus total cost (area $0adq_m$). Any reader unhappy about these general relationships should work through the numerical example provided in Question 1.11 at the end of Chapter 1.

An output level of q_m in *Figure A1.2.4* is indicative of the firm's short-run equilibrium position – i.e. in terms of profit it can never do better than equate MC and MR. Long-run equilibrium for the industry will also require AC = AR, so that there are neither excess profits to attract increases, nor losses to promote decreases, in supply.

Chapter 2

Demography and education: structure and quality of the workforce

2.1 Introduction

There are many different approaches to the study of people in organizations. Novelists, historians, geographers and scientists all contribute something to our understanding of human behaviour. However, in this chapter we are looking at people as 'human resources'. People can be regarded as human resources, because in a complex society people work to provide goods and services which are necessary or desirable for life. For this reason the size and structure of a population is important. The provision of human resources is thus a necessary input for the economy, but for centuries scholars have recognized dangers of population growth to a size where society is unable to provide sufficient goods and services for the maintenance of life.

The first part of this chapter considers the complex relationship between the economy and the size of a population. We shall then consider the main features and factors which determined the size of the British population. The second part of the chapter considers the nature and importance of our education system, as one of the aims of education is to provide people with relevant knowledge and expertise that can be used in employment. Education thus affects the quality of 'human resources' that are provided for the economy. Thus, the final part of the chapter is concerned with the effects of education and training on productivity earnings and related matters.

2.2 Population and the economy

In his famous exposition of *The Wealth of Nations* in 1776, Adam Smith (1723–1790) suggested that the size of a population was an indication of the prosperity of a country. He believed that in a society where the demand for labour was high and where there were tendencies for real wages to increase, there was likely to be an expanding population. Adam Smith's view of the 'wage fund' theory suggested ways to achieve a healthy economy. To state his views very simply, Smith believed that the surplus which was produced could be used unproductively on the purchase of services or it could be used productively to purchase new machines. In their turn the machines would provide work for more people. Thus, he advocated the 'ploughing back' of the surplus as a means to further growth and as a 'fund' for wages. He also believed that if people were prosperous, they would have more children, and thus a growing population was an indicator of a healthy economy. He admitted that prosperity could encourage the production of too many people. However, if this occurred, an excess of people on the labour market would cause real wages to decline and in the face of declining prosperity fewer children would be born. Thus, the '. . . demand for men, like that for any other commodity, necessarily regulates the production of men; quickens it when it goes to slavery, and stops it when it advances too fast' (Smith, 1776).

Adam Smith's views were developed in great detail and with many qualifications. He realized that poverty did not necessarily lead to a reduction of births, and he was aware of regional differences in labour markets which were not compatible with his model. However, many people now share the view that economic factors affect the size of population. Smith also tried to explain the size of population by reference to the (economic) values held by people. Equally, today it is impossible to understand population changes in Great Britain without knowledge of the wider values of our society. For example, the prevailing religious beliefs and attitudes towards working mothers may affect decisions to have children.

In 1798 the Reverend Thomas R. Malthus (1766–1834) published his first essay on *The Principle of Population*. His views were based on the claims that:

> (1) 'the power of population is indefinitely greater than the power in the earth to produce subsistence for men' and (2) 'population when unchecked increases in a geometrical ratio. Subsistence increases only in an arithmetical ratio . . .' (Malthus, 1798).

The significance of these views can be illustrated by considering a hypothetical population of 100 people. In about 30 years that population could double to 200. In 60 years it could double again to 400, and in 90 years could double again to 800, and so on. While the population is expanding by geometrical ratio, the means of subsistence, mainly food supplies, increases more slowly. A field of potatoes may produce 100 tons of potatoes. Over 30 years its production may improve to 200 tons, and over 60 years to 300 tons. Because of these different rates of growth, Malthus believed that population would grow more rapidly than the means of subsistence and eventually starvation would occur. As long as the force for population growth was greater than man's capacity to increase his food supply, Malthus believed that 'the law of diminishing returns' would apply. In the former example each additional person (or unit of labour) would produce fewer potatoes from the field. Because Malthus believed that the level of subsistence was ultimately limited, he believed that 'famine, vice and misery' operated as checks on population growth by increasing the death rate. He later felt, however, that 'moral restraint' would also be needed to check the birth rate.

Malthus still has his supporters, for there have been instances where growing populations have starved because food supplies could not be increased. Neo-Malthusians continue to express concern about population growth, particularly in a world context. Some attempt to specify the size of existing resources and how long these will supply the population. However, the discovery of new resources and new technological developments give hope to those who are more optimistic about population issues. They would stress how difficult it is to estimate limits to resources and technological developments. Who, for example, 100 years ago, would have believed that Britain would be extracting oil from under the North Sea in 1981? In his interesting account of changes in the world population Carlo M. Cipolla (1979) stresses the importance of technology. He adopts a historical and global perspective, and outlines how mankind has transformed energy by developing different technologies at different times. Cipolla stresses the part played by technology in determining economic and population conditions. However, there must be social demand for new developments or, expressed another way, the

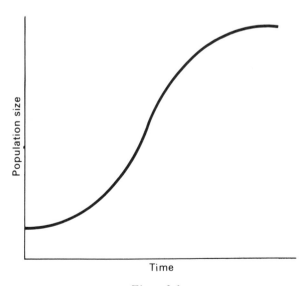

Figure 2.1

social climate and value system must permit of or encourage such changes in technology. The belief in the need to find new sources of energy gave impetus to the discovery and extraction of North Sea oil.

Some theorists have tried to learn from animal experiments. In 1925 an American scientist, R. Pearl, experimented by confining fruit-flies to a specific territory and providing them with a constant supply of food. Pearl recorded the population changes of his flies over time and described his results in terms of a logistic curve (*Figure 2.1*). The fly population increased until it reached the maximum level that could be supported by the constant food supply. Pearl argued that human populations followed the same pattern as his flies. Increased mortality, reduced fertility, etc., would regulate the size of populations to appropriate levels. Cipalla (1979) indicates that this belief has many weaknesses, because incomes and resources are unequally distributed among people, and man has the ability to increase his sources of food and energy. There are difficulties in applying the logistic curve to human populations, but Learmouth and Connors (1975) suggest that, if the model applies, the evening out of the curve is likely to arise from the dissemination of information and the discussion of population issues which change expectations and beliefs.

2.3 The population of Great Britain and the Demographic Transition Model

Demography is the study of the conditions of human life, as shown in statistics of births, deaths, diseases, etc. Demographers are often concerned to establish the general direction or trend of population changes. They view the population in a dynamic way, because it changes over time.

The Demographic Transition Model (*Table 2.1*) describes the changes which have taken place in the British population over time. It 'seeks to describe the changes in birth and death rates which occurred in the first

Table 2.1 (from Learmouth and Connors, 1975)

	Birth rate	Death rate	Total population
Stage 1	high	high	relatively stable over long periods
Stage 2	high	rapidly declining	radically increasing
Stage 3	low	low	relatively stable

societies to pass through the Industrial Revolution' (Learmouth and Connors, 1975). In Stage I of the model the birth rate and death rate are relatively balanced, although there are likely to be periods when a high birth rate and a low death rate are interrupted by famine and disease. It has been suggested by Learmouth and Connors that Britain experienced

Table 2.2 UK population changes and projections

	Population at start of period (millions)	Average annual change (thousands)				
		live births	deaths	net natural change	net civilian migration and other adjustments	overall annual change
Census enumerated:						
1901–1911	38.2	1091	624	467	−82	385
1911–1921	42.1	975	689	286	−92	194
1921–1931	44.0	824	555	286	−67	201
1931–1951	46.0	785	598	188	+22	213
Mid-year estimates:						
1951–1961	50.3	839	593	246	+6	252
1961–1966	52.8	988	633	355	−15	339
1966–1971	54.5	937	644	293	−71	222
1971–1972	55.6	862	661	202	−30	171
1972–1973	55.8	808	672	136	−4	132
1973–1974	55.9	752	664	88	−78	10
1974–1975	55.9	721	671	50	−71	−22
1975–1976	55.9	689	681	7	−22	−15
1976–1977	55.9	655	660	−5	−28	−33
1977–1978	55.9	664	665	−	−17	−17
1978–1979	55.8	718	673	45	. . .	. . .
Projections:*						
1978–1981	55.9	727	689	38	−31	7
1981–1991	55.9	856	710	146	−39	107
1991–2001	57.0	857	712	145	−40	105

* Projections based on mid-1978 estimate of total population.

Source: Office of Population Censuses and Surveys; General Register Office (Scotland); General Register Office (Northern Ireland) (all published in *Social Trends*, No. 10, HMSO, 1980).

Stage I before 1876. Stage II of the model was marked by a fall in the death rate as the result of better hygiene and control of diseases. In Britain the crude death rate fell between 1876 and 1931. After 1931 Stage III was reached, as the death rate became comparatively stable and low, while the birth rate, although somewhat variable, was much lower than it had been in 1870. If the Demographic Transition Theory is correct, countries which experience industrial and economic development similar to those experienced by Britain are likely to find similar demographic changes. It is helpful to examine the present structure and size of the British population with knowledge of the pattern changes which have taken place.

The total size of any population is determined by births, deaths and migration. It is also related to the sex and numbers of people born in the previous generation. Since 1811 (and until recently) the population of England and Wales has been growing, but in 1811 the mean annual rate of intercensal increase was 1.43, while in 1961 it was 0.54. The pattern has been similar in Scotland, but between 1921 and 1931 a small decline took place (see Kelsall, 1979). *Table 2.2* indicates the major population changes which have taken place in this century. It is worth noticing that between 1976 and 1978 deaths were greater than the number of live births. However, projections based on a mid-1978 estimate of total population indicate a steady increase during the remaining years of the twentieth century. It is also worth noticing how the birth rate has fluctuated throughout this century. A high birth rate tends to be followed by another period with a high birth rate about 25 years later, as each generation reaches its probable 'phase of reproduction'.

Table 2.3 shows more clearly how the total number of live births has fallen since 1951. The writer of *Social Trends* (Anon., 1980) comments that the '. . . year 1978 saw the first annual increase (4 per cent) in the number of live births since 1964. Most of the rise represents an increase in the rate of child bearing: only a small part is due to increasing numbers of women in childbearing age.' Between 1961 and 1978 the number of illegitimate births increased from 46 000 to 61 000, so that illegitimate births now account for nearly one-tenth of all births. Women and men (in 1977) tend to be older when they get married (compared with the situation in 1951) and they tend to wait longer after marriage before having their first child. Births have fallen in all social classes, with most couples limiting themselves to two children or fewer. However, the families with three or more children are far more likely to have fathers with partly skilled or unskilled occupations than fathers with professional occupations.

This century has also seen a reduction in the death rate (see *Table 2.4*). Male mortality continues to be higher than female mortality at all ages, and there has been a substantial decline in infant mortalities.

Table 2.3 Live births in Great Britain: totals and rates

	Total live births ($\times 10^3$)	Crude birth rate (live births per 1000 persons all ages)	Age specific birth rates* per 1000 women aged:						
			15–19	20–24	25–29	30–34	35–39	40–44	all ages (15–44)
1951	768	15.7	21	126	135	90	47	14	72.5
1956	798	16.0	27	148	152	90	47	13	78.2
1961	912	17.8	37	173	178	104	49	14	90.0
1966	946	17.8	48	177	175	98	46	12	91.1
1971	870	16.1	51	155	155	78	33	8	84.2
1972	804	14.8	48	142	143	70	29	7	77.5
1973	750	13.8	44	132	136	64	25	6	71.8
1974	710	13.1	41	124	130	60	22	5	67.6
1975	672	12.4	37	116	123	59	20	5	63.7
1976	649	11.9	33	111	120	58	18	4	61.0
1977	632	11.6	30	105	119	59	18	4	52.8
1978	661	12.2	30	108	124	64	20	4	60.7

* Births to mothers aged under 15 are included with the 15–19 group. The 15–44 group contains all births.

Source: Office of Population Censuses and Surveys as published in *Social Trends*, No. 10, HMSO (1980).

Note: The crude birth rate can be misleading, particularly when the percentage of older people in the population is increasing.

Migration is the third factor which affects the size of the total population. The agreed international definition of an immigrant is used for demographic purposes – i.e. 'someone who having lived abroad for at least twelve months, declares an intention to reside in the UK for at least twelve months'. The definition of an emigrant is the converse of that (Anon., 1980). Since 1962 there has been a greater outflow of people from than inflow of people into this country. However, between 1973 and 1978 the number of people in Great Britain who were of New Commonwealth and Pakistani (NCWP) ethnic origins increased by about 25 per cent. The age structure of those who are wholly of NCWP ethnic origin is very different from that of the population as a whole. The latest estimates of the NCWP population were made by the Registrar-General in 1976, and these show far higher proportions of younger than older people among the NCWP population. One may, therefore, expect

Table 2.4 Standardized death rates (per 1000 population) in Great Britain: by age and sex

Year	Age						All ages
	Under 1	1–14	15–44	45–64	65–74	75 and over	
1930–1932							
Males	79.5	3.7	4.0	17.5	58.7	167.5	20.7
Females	59.7	3.3	3.4	12.9	43.4	138.7	16.4
1950–1952							
Males	34.5	0.8	1.9	16.0	55.3	160.7	17.6
Females	26.5	0.7	1.5	9.0	34.8	124.4	12.1
1960–1962							
Males	26.0	0.6	1.5	14.9	54.7	148.6	16.4
Females	19.9	0.4	1.0	7.7	30.4	110.2	10.4
1966							
Males	22.4	0.6	1.5	14.6	54.6	146.8	16.2
Females	17.1	0.4	0.9	7.4	28.9	103.6	9.9
1971							
Males	20.2	0.5	1.4	13.8	52.1	137.5	15.2
Females	15.4	0.4	0.8	7.3	26.4	95.4	9.1
1975							
Males	17.4	0.4	1.3	13.3	51.1	140.4	15.1
Females	13.8	0.3	0.8	7.2	25.7	95.4	9.0
1976							
Males	16.3	0.4	1.3	13.4	51.4	144.4	15.3
Females	12.1	0.3	0.8	7.3	26.1	98.7	9.2
1977							
Males	16.0	0.4	1.3	13.0	49.3	135.8	14.6
Females	12.4	0.3	0.8	7.1	25.1	92.8	8.8
Percentage change 1966–1977							
Males	−29	−33	−13	−11	−10	−7	−10
Females	−27	−25	−11	−4	−13	−11	−11

Source: Population Censuses and Surveys: General Register Office for Scotland as published in *Social Trends*, No. 10, HMSO (1980).

Table 2.5 Sex and age structure of the population of the UK in millions

	Males								Females								
	under 16	16–29	30–44	45–64	65–74	75–84	85 and over	all ages	under 16	16–29	30–44	45–59	60–74	75–84	84 and over	all ages	all persons
Census enumerated:																	
1901	6.6	4.8	3.6	2.7	0.6	0.2		18.5	6.6	5.2	3.9	2.4	1.3	0.3		19.7	38.2
1911	6.9	5.0	4.3	3.2	0.7	0.3		20.4	6.9	5.4	4.6	2.9	1.5	0.4		21.7	42.1
1921	6.6	4.9	4.3	4.1	0.9	0.3		21.0	6.5	5.5	5.0	3.6	1.9	0.5		23.0	44.0
1931	6.0	5.4	4.5	4.6	1.1	0.4		22.1	5.9	5.7	5.2	4.2	2.4	0.6		24.0	46.1
Mid-year estimates:																	
1941	5.4	5.5	5.5	5.0	1.4	0.5		23.3	5.3	5.5	5.8	4.6	3.0	0.8		24.9	48.2
1951	6.1	5.0	5.5	5.6	1.6	0.7		24.4	5.9	4.9	5.7	5.1	3.5	1.1		26.1	50.5
1961	6.7	4.9	5.3	6.4	1.6	0.7	0.1	25.7	6.4	4.8	5.3	5.5	3.9	1.2	0.2	27.3	53.0
1971	7.3	5.6	4.9	6.5	2.0	0.7	0.1	27.1	6.9	5.4	4.8	5.2	4.5	1.4	0.4	28.6	55.7
1981	6.8	6.0	5.3	6.2	2.2	0.8	0.1	27.2	6.4	5.6	5.2	5.0	4.4	1.6	0.4	28.7	55.9
Projections:*																	
1981	6.4	6.1	5.5	6.1	2.2	0.9	0.1	27.3	6.1	5.8	5.4	4.8	4.5	1.7	0.4	28.7	55.9
1986	6.1	6.4	5.7	5.9	2.1	1.0	0.2	27.5	5.8	6.1	5.6	4.6	4.4	1.8	0.5	28.8	56.3
1991	6.4	6.2	6.0	5.9	2.2	1.0	0.2	27.9	6.0	5.9	5.9	4.7	4.2	1.8	0.6	29.1	57.0
1996	6.9	5.6	6.2	6.3	2.1	1.0	0.2	28.3	6.5	5.3	6.1	5.1	4.0	1.8	0.6	29.4	57.7
2001	7.0	5.2	6.5	6.3	2.0	1.0	0.2	29.5	6.6	5.0	6.4	5.3	3.9	1.8	0.6	29.6	58.0

* Projections based on mid-1978 estimate of total population.

Source: Census of Population Reports: Population Projections 1978–2018 – Office of Population Censuses and Surveys, published in *Social Trends*, No. 10, HMSO (1980).

that greater numbers of these ethnic minorities will enter the employment market in the future.

Thus, Great Britain has experienced a declining death rate and now has a low birth rate. The reason for these changes can only be suggested. It may be that children are now regarded as economic liabilities rather than assets or that the cost of housing has reduced fertility. The movement towards 'female emancipation' has made it acceptable for women to decide how many children they want, and when (if at all) they wish to have them. In 1978 just over 60 per cent of all married women were 'economically active' (i.e. employees, self-employed or registered unemployed), according to the General Household Survey.

The sex and age structure (see *Table 2.5*) of the population is important, for it indicates how many people will be entering the labour market at a particular time. Projections in *Table 2.5* indicate that in 1986 there will be an increased number of males and females aged 16–29. This has important implications for the employment market and for planning in the further education sector. *Table 2.5* also shows that in the younger age groups there are rather more males than females, while among the elderly there are more women than men. By the year 2001 the number of people aged 75+ is expected to increase substantially. Those who are retired form part of the economically inactive section of society (along with students, those who are permanently unable to work and those keeping house), which is supported by those who are 'economically active'.

Over 60 per cent of all females (aged 16–59) in 1978 were 'economically active' and the next ten years will probably (according to projections quoted) bring greater numbers of young people on to the labour market. There will also be more people of NCWP origins entering employment and more old people to be supported and cared for.

2.4 Education and the quality of the workforce

A minority of British children are able to commence their education by attending a nursery school, but by 1974 the number of nursery places in the public sector had increased to 85 000 from 31 000 in 1961. Most children commence in primary school at the age of 5 or slightly under, but the number of children attending primary schools declined by 5 per cent between 1974 and 1978, and it is expected that there will be further 'falling rolls' during the 1980s. The major educational change which occurred during the 1970s was the growth of comprehensive secondary schools. As *Table 2.6* indicates, by 1978, 76.8 per cent of those attending a maintained secondary school in England were at a comprehensive, 92 per cent of those in Wales and 92.5 per cent of those in Scotland.

Table 2.6 Pupils in secondary education in England and Wales, 1971 and 1978

	1971 (%)	1978 (%)	Thousands
(a) Maintained secondary schools in England			
Middle deemed secondary	1.9	6.7	258
Modern	38.0	10.0	386
Grammar	18.4	5.1	196
Technical	1.3	0.3	12
Comprehensive	34.4	76.8	2956
Other	6.0	1.1	44
Total pupils (%)	100.0	100.0	
(thousands)	2953	3851	3851
(b) Maintained secondary schools in Wales			
Middle deemed secondary	0.1	–	–
Modern	22.3	4.5	11
Grammar	15.4	3.2	8
Comprehensive	58.5	92.0	222
Other	3.7	0.3	1
Total pupils (%)	100.0	100.0	
(thousands)	191	242	242

Source: Department of Education and Science, Welsh Office, adapted from *Social Trends*, No. 10, HMSO (1980).

Comprehensives were developed in response to feeling that the tripartite system was unfair. The tripartite system provided grammar, technical and secondary modern schools for those over 11 years of age, according to the type of abilities which they were thought to demonstrate. Children from middle-class backgrounds populated grammar schools in large numbers. In addition, many felt that the testing of abilities at 11 years of age was wrong and that potentialities could not always be predicted at that age. It was believed that comprehensive schools would offer all pupils the benefit of a wider curriculum, that 'social mix' would be better and that children of manual and unskilled parents would have better educational opportunities.

Thus, DES circular 10/55 encouraged local authorities to reorganize secondary education in a way that would facilitate the transfer of pupils between streams. Current figures appear to suggest that there have been few changes in the proportion of pupils who gain five or more 'O' level or 'A' level passes at GCE since 1970/71, but there has been a steady increase in the proportion of pupils gaining fewer than 5 'O' level GCE passes or CSE qualifications. Measuring output in terms of examination results is only one indicator of the performance of people leaving school. Many others who leave school may not be motivated to take examinations, or may be unable to perform well in them. One has no real way of knowing whether the present-day unqualified school leavers are better or worse than those who left ten years ago.

Between 1976/67 and 1977/78 the percentage of boys entering further education changed very little. In 1966/67 18 per cent of all boys leaving school entered full-time further education. By 1977/78 the figure stood at 17.8 per cent. However, over the same period the actual numbers of male students in full-time further education increased from 55 000 to 70 300. Over the same period there was an increase in the percentage of girls entering full-time further education from 2.1 per cent in 1966/67 to 25.8 per cent in 1977/78. This percentage increase represents a numerical increase from 61 000 to 96 400 girls entering further education. In this respect the quality of the female labour forces may be improving and this may enable women to improve their employment prospects.

The number of full-time and sandwich students on non-advanced courses in major establishments of further education in the UK almost doubled between 1967/68 and 1977/78. By the latter date (since 1967/68) the total number of full-time students undertaking first degree courses in the UK grew by nearly 70 per cent. In addition, not only do more young people have some sort of qualification compared with older people, but also the level of qualification attained has been rising (*Figure 2.2*). By this type of measurement there appear to be improvements in the quality of the workforce. There are also additional benefits which accrue to individuals who undertake further or higher education.

In 1977 the results of the General Household Survey reported that over half of all males aged 20–64 with a university education had earnings in excess of £5000, whereas only about 10 per cent of those who ended their full-time education with elementary or secondary school earned over £5000 in 1977. Few will be surprised to read that higher education is more common among non-manual workers, employers and managers, and professional people, than it is among different types of manual workers.

Estimating the likely demand for higher education during the 1980s is difficult. In 1978 the Department of Education and Science produced a discussion document called *Higher Education into the 1990s*. The actual population who will be 18 years of age and over in the 1980s is known, and it is expected to increase in the first half of the decade. However, the

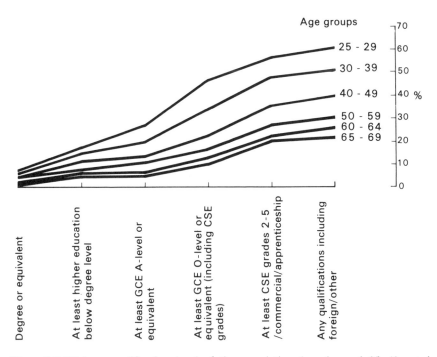

Figure 2.2 Highest qualification level of the population (people aged 25–69 not in full-time education) of Great Britain, 1977 and 1978. Total sample size (= 100 per cent): 25–29 = 4.1; 30–39 = 8.0; 40–49 = 6.9; 50–59 = 7.3; 60–64 = 3.3; 65–69 = 3.2. Source: General Household Survey combined data for 1977 and 1978, published in *Social Trends*, No. 10, HMSO (1980)

proportion who will become eligible for higher education by virtue of obtaining relevant qualifications is not known. Equally, it may be difficult to predict how many people will want to enter higher education. The DES describes the age participation rate (APR) as the number of home entrants below 21 expressed as a percentage of the 18-year-old group and the qualified leaver rate (QLR) as the number of qualified leavers expressed as a percentage of the 18-year-old group.

The APR stood at 6.9 per cent in 1960/61 and steadily increased to 14.2 per cent in 1972/73. Since then it has declined to 13.1 per cent in 1977/78 (*Table 2.7*). Thus, although the 1980s will bring more people in the 18-plus age groups, estimates of the numbers entering higher education depend on forecasts of the qualifications achieved and the APR. In March 1979 the DES revised its estimates of the demand for higher education in the 1980s. It continues to expect the APR to increase because of: (1) the new opportunities on higher education courses; (2) the consolidation and spread of comprehensive secondary education; (3) the experience of increased participation in full-time education among 16–18-year-olds; and (4) the message to be learned from the employment market – i.e. that, in general, higher qualifications mean better chances of employment. In 1979 the DES appeared to favour further consideration of a policy which would expand higher education to cater for increased demand resulting from 'the hump'. If this policy is adopted, the question arises of how resources will be used after 'the hump' has passed. Many hope that an increase in the participation rate of young

Table 2.7 The relationship between QLR and APR in higher education

	1969–1970	1973–1974	1977–1978
QLR	13.2	14.9	15.5
APR	13.7	14.0	13.1

Adapted from *Future Trends in Higher Education*, DES (1979).

Table 2.8 Figures provided by the Minister of State for Education and Science as part of a written statement to the House of Commons in February 1979 (from Jones and Williams, 1979)

	Mature home entrants (thousands)	As a percentage of all home entrants to HE
1970–1971	27.3	21.0
1971–1972	29.2	21.6
1972–1973	28.1	20.8
1973–1974	29.6	22.0
1974–1975	30.5	22.4
1976–1977	33.0	23.5
1977–1978 (provision)	33.8	24.6

home entrants or adults will offset the demographic decline. The number of mature students in higher education has steadily increased over the past 8 years (see *Table 2.8*), and the continued demand for places at The Open University gives some indication of the buoyant demand from adults for higher education.

There are other opportunities for adults to continue learning. Many firms provide a wide range of training opportunities for their employees and these activities are co-ordinated by 27 Industrial Training Boards. Under the Employment and Training Act 1973 the Department of Employment established the Manpower Services Commission (MSC). The MSC works through the Industrial Training Services Division

(TSD). The Employment Services Division operates JobCentres to help the unemployed, while the TSD promotes industrial training in sectors not covered by ITBs and runs the Training Opportunities Scheme (TOPS) for adults who wish to change or improve their skills. In 1977/78 over 73 000 completed TOPS courses of different types.

The MSC is largely concerned to ensure an adequate supply of trained manpower, although the availability of qualified workers also depends on the education system in general. In the remainder of this chapter, therefore, we shall consider the importance of education and training in relation to the productivity of the individual at work.

2.5 Education, productivity and earnings

Because of its capacity to satisfy many different individual and societal needs, education must be regarded as a multidimensional product. Particularly in a business context, however, the single most important aspect of education is arguably its relationship with employment. In this connection, it is important not only because of its association with the productivity and earnings of the individual, but also because of its crucial role in influencing the flexibility of the workforce, response to change and, as a final outcome, the aggregate rate of economic growth, upon which so many other private and social objectives depend.

When one considers the relationship between education and employment, it is necessary to draw attention to the fact that there are two different views on the matter: the human capital view and the screening view. As indicated in Chapter 1, the human capital school of thought applies a common definition of capital to certain human attributes. Thus, capital, as a produced means of production, is a good capable method yielding a flow of future services. People are therefore regarded as investing in themselves if expenditures give rise to future services and raise earnings potential above what it would otherwise have been. Such expenditures may be made on education, health, diet, labour market information, and so forth, with the result that productivity and earnings are thereby increased. Hence, the concept of investment, defined as the process of capital accumulation, is applicable to people as much as to the transformation of physical matter. This is in no way to suggest that people are to be treated as nothing more than inanimate objects, but merely that there are certain human attributes which can usefully be analysed by applying to them the concept of capital.

Education is one type of human capital. Consequently, if an educational process produces in the individual knowledge, skills and abilities which were either not there originally or would otherwise not have been developed, it can be regarded as a process of (human) capital formation to the extent that productivity, and therefore earnings potential, is now enhanced. Moreover, if people are paid approximately in line with their relative productivity, then we should expect to find that the more highly educated have greater lifetime earnings than the less educated. This is the relationship which has been found to exist: whether measured by years of schooling or by level of qualification obtained, there is a high correlation between the amount of education received and the level of earnings over the working life-cycle.

But other things also correlate highly with earnings: sex, race, social background and age are commonly quoted examples. While not seeking to deny the observed relationship between education and earnings, those who subscribe to the screening view of education would argue that the causal relationship is quite different from that held by human capitalists. A broad indication of their position would be that education (by which term they usually mean higher education) is not a productivity-augmenting process but is rather an elaborate screening device which filters out those people who have particular characteristics regarded by employers as desirable in those being hired for certain occupations. In its extreme form, the screening theory sees additional increments of education as adding nothing to the level of productivity of the individual but merely acting as signals to prospective employers that such people are on average more productive than others.

Information about individual abilities is useful to an employing organization, since, if people differ in this respect, total output can be increased by identifying workers according to ability and assigning them to appropriate jobs. Productive ability may be determined in other ways, but if education can effectively be used as a screening device, it provides employers with a cheap and convenient tool of personnel selection. In essence, when a firm hires workers, it takes a sample from the population of available workers. That population has a certain heterogeneity with respect to required traits; hence, there is some probability that an employer will choose people without the desired characteristics. The use of education as a screen allows an employer to divide people into more homogeneous groups and thereby reduce the probability of making a wrong choice.

On the other hand, there may be an incentive for workers to invest in signals (such as educational qualifications) which indicate their greater productivity. For example, if labour market information is sufficiently imperfect for employers not to know individual marginal products, any worker will receive a wage equal to the average marginal product for the group. In such a situation, the more productive worker is subsidizing the less productive and the former have an incentive to make their higher value apparent to employers.

Theoretical contributions to the screening theory have been made by Arrow (1973), Spence (1973, 1974) and Stiglitz (1975), among others, and the interested reader may consult Taubman and Wales (1974) in conjunction with Layard and Psacharopoulos (1974) and Wolpin (1977) for some empirical evidence. In this book, however, the human capital view will be adopted as the more viable interpretation of education as a process which, like training, creates and develops productively useful skills, abilities and knowledge. Increments of human capital in these forms, therefore, raise productivity above what it would otherwise be. The effect is illustrated in *Figure 2.3*.

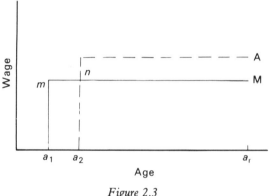

Figure 2.3

Assume that one individual leaves school at the legal minimum age of a_1, enters employment and receives no subsequent training of any kind. Abstracting from any physical or mental depreciation which may occur as a result of the ageing process, the marginal product of the worker will remain constant and equal to the wage rate at a level represented by the age–earnings profile marked M. Alternatively, additional schooling could be undertaken for the period a_1–a_2 which would raise the level of marginal product on entry to the labour market above that of the minimum age school-leaver, so that productivity and earnings now follow the A profile. The area between the two profiles from labour market entry at a_2 to retirement at a_r represents the additional financial benefits which accrue as a result of the additional investment made in human capital during period a_1–a_2.

This investment cannot be made without incurring costs. Following Becker (1964) and others, we may divide these costs into two types. The first type consists of any direct outlays made by the individual on such items as tuition fees, travelling, books, etc. The second and (certainly for most British students) the quantitatively more important element is the indirect or opportunity cost involved. This consists of the income which could have been earned but which is foregone by remaining in full-time education. This wage rate is £m per period in *Figure 2.3*. Consequently, and assuming that the student receives no other related income, the opportunity cost earnings are given by the area a_1mna_2, since this is the amount which could have been earned by entering the labour market at age a_1.

A similar stylized profile emerges if the effect of on-the-job training is considered, as in *Figure 2.4*. Employment commences as before at age a_1 and, if an unskilled occupation is entered which involves no training, the profile appears as that labelled U, which is horizonal at a wage rate of £w. In the alternative skilled occupation, training takes place over the period a_1a_2 and its effects on marginal product and earnings are shown,

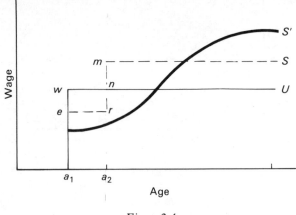

Figure 2.4

for simplicity, as a once-for-all shift in the profile, as indicated by that labelled S. Given a trainee wage rate of £e, the opportunity costs then appear to the trainee as the area *ewnr*, with the benefits again being represented by the difference between the S- and U-profiles after age a_2. The profile for the occupation which involves training takes on an extreme concaved shape; more continuous productivity and wage changes, however, may produce a profile nearer to S'.

Some implications can now be drawn from human capital theory about the relative and absolute behaviour of earnings over the working life-cycle. An age–earnings profile will tend to be higher the greater the investment in education and training prior to labour market entry. The lower the amount of post-entry investment in education and training the flatter will be an age–earnings profile; in the limit, with zero investment, the profile will be horizontal. Profiles will rise the more steeply the greater the amount of investment and will continue to rise the longer the investment period. Although it is an empirical finding rather than an implication, it may also be noted that Mincer (1962) found formal schooling and on-the-job training to be positively associated – the more one has of the former, the more one is likely to receive of the latter. Hence, schooling and training on the job are complementary activities rather than substitutes. But age–earnings profiles can fall as well as rise, and this can be attributed to either physical or human capital depreciation or to some combination of the two. In the former case, physical effort becomes more difficult to maintain as age advances; in the latter case, skills and knowledge acquired during or before the early years of employment may become outdated as a result of later developments and the effects of technological change.

Unemployment may also occur as a result of technological change, and lifetime earnings are thereby depressed as certain forms of human capital are made obsolete. Technical progress appears to occur at an increasing rate of change and, therefore, the unemployment which it produces tends to become a greater problem over time. However, as Cartter and Marshall (1967) point out, this can be at least partly met by designing training and educational courses to include the acquisition of skills and knowledge which are of wider applicability than the initial area of employment of the trainee. Hence, '. . . fewer and fewer schools of business administration today emphasize functional training in advertising, accountancy, production, or marketing, for these fields are changing so rapidly that one's education is likely to be obsolete before

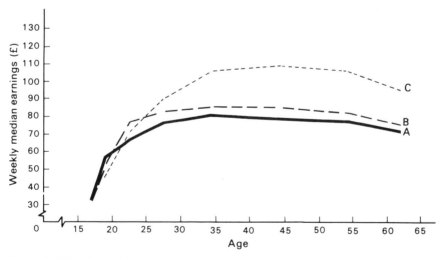

Figure 2.5 Earnings of full-time males, 1978. A: Painting, repetitive assembly, product inspecting, packaging and related work. B: Processing, making, repairing and related work (metal and electrical). C: Professional and related in science, engineering, technology and similar. Source: *New Earnings Survey*, Part E, 1978 (see Appendix 2.1)

graduating. Rather, emphasis is now being placed on a better general understanding of economic theory and principles, of behavioural science and communications, of systems of quantitative controls and on the development of analytical skills which will be relevant to many different situations and changing business practices.' Generality in training thus tends to promote future flexibility in the workforce, allows organizations to make a more effective response to technical change and provides workers with a greater degree of protection against the incidence of unemployment over working lifetime.

Human capital theory, then, carries certain implications for, among other things, the behaviour of age–earnings profiles. The extent to which these theoretical expectations are met empirically can be judged by inspecting *Figure 2.5*, the data for which were obtained from the New Earnings Survey and relate to 1978 for three broad categories of workers. The three groups are intended to broadly represent (1) the unskilled and semi-skilled, (2) the skilled and (3) those workers with higher level skills. Thus, pre-entry educational attainment and post-entry training can be expected to increase as we move from group 1, through group 2 to group 3. Moreover, the profiles exhibit all the characteristics previously discussed and are typical of the age–earnings relationships usually observed.

2.6 Rate of return on investments in human capital

One method of evaluating an investment is to estimate its expected rate of return. This is quite straightforward and is complicated only to the extent that it reverses our usual manner of looking at changes in financial values. Most people are used to estimating a change in value from the present to some future date. For example, we may place a £100 deposit with a building society and wish to arrive at its value in a year's time when interest is paid at some given rate. Estimating the rate of return on a human capital investment involves the reverse procedure, because what we now need to estimate is the present value of sums to be received in the future and not the future value of a sum deposited in the present.

In the case where a deposit is made, we may lend some amount V to a building society and expect it to acquire a value of E after 1 year when the interest rate is i. Hence,

$$E = V + iV \qquad (2.1)$$

which for convenience can be rewritten as

$$E = V(1+i) \qquad (2.2)$$

However, because a present value calculation reverses this process, we need to convert i into a rate of discount and divide by it instead of multiplying. Thus, dividing each side of equation (2.2) by $(1+i)$, we obtain

$$V = \frac{E}{(1+i)} \tag{2.3}$$

V is now the present value of E when E is to be received one period into the future. For example, equation (2.1) or equation (2.2) tells us that if we lent $V = £100$ at an interest rate of $i = 10$ per cent, at the end of 1 year we would receive $£100 + (0.10)(100) = £110$. On the other hand, equation (2.3) gives the information that £110 to be received in a year's time has a present value of $£110/(1.10) = £100$. In other words, evaluating an investment means working back from expected future values to present values, whereas in the case of a loan we are converting present values into future values.

For present purposes we may let E represent the expected additional earnings which are associated with a human capital investment, so that we are estimating its present value. However, additional earnings will accrue, not just in one year but in a succession of years. Just as £100 lent for 2 years will be worth more at the end of that time than £100 lent for 1 year, so £110 to be received in 2 years' time has a lower present value than £110 receivable in 1 year's time. Its value is $E = £110/(1.10)^2 = £110/1.21 = £90.9$ and, in general, the denominator is raised to an extra power for each year involved. Thus, if E-values are to be received in each of three future years,

$$V = \frac{E_1}{(1+i)} + \frac{E_2}{(1+i)^2} + \frac{E_3}{(1+i)^3} \tag{2.4}$$

To economize on notation where a large number of years is involved we can use the Greek capital sigma (Σ) to indicate that the sum of a number (n) of E-values is being taken. If t designates particular years, we can write

$$V = \sum_{t=1}^{n} \frac{E_t}{(1+i)^t} \tag{2.5}$$

where $\displaystyle\sum_{t=1}^{n}$ is read as 'the sum between $t = 1$ [the first year] and n [the last year]'. To carry out a specific calculation, equation (2.5) is written out as in equation (2.4) and the appropriate values substituted. Since i and the Es have known values, V can easily be determined.

In many instances, of course, the costs of the investment (C) are also spread over a number of years and these have to be deducted from the earnings, so that equation (2.5) becomes

$$V = \sum_{t=1}^{n} \frac{E_t}{(1+i)^t} - \sum_{t=1}^{n} \frac{C_t}{(1+i)^t} \qquad (2.6)$$

Now we wish to find the interest rate of return on the investment and this is a particular value of i. Specifically, it is the value of i which makes the sum of the discounted additional earnings equal to the sum of the discounted costs. If we use r to represent this particular value of i, we have

$$V = \sum_{t=1}^{n} \frac{E_t}{(1+r)^t} - \sum_{t=1}^{n} \frac{C_t}{(1+r)^t} \qquad (2.7)$$

or, more conveniently,

$$V = \sum_{t=1}^{n} \frac{E_t - C_t}{(1+r)^t} \qquad (2.8)$$

since we are dividing the Es and Cs by the same denominator. Equation (2.8) can then be expanded in the manner of equation (2.4) and the appropriate values substituted.

A numerical example may help to clarify the procedure. Assume that training for a job takes place over 2 years and that the direct and indirect costs amount to £500 and £675 in the first and second years, respectively. Assume that after training additional earnings accrue over the next 3 years of £500, £700 and £650. We then have

$$\frac{-500}{(1+r)} + \frac{-657}{(1+r)^2} + \frac{500}{(1+r)^3} + \frac{700}{(1+r)^4} + \frac{650}{(1+r)^5}$$

and a value for r must be found which will make the sum of these amounts equal to zero. This value can be found by trial and error (and using a computer for a large number of periods). For example, at 10 per cent $(1+r) = 1.1$, $(1+r)^2 = 1.21$, and so on. Thus,

$$\frac{-500}{1.1} + \frac{-675}{1.21} + \frac{500}{1.33} + \frac{700}{1.46} + \frac{650}{1.61}$$

$$= -454.5 - 557.8 + 375.9 + 479.4 + 403.7$$

$$= -1012.3 + 1259$$

$$= 246.7$$

from which it is clear than an r of 10 per cent is too low. An r of 25 per cent gives

$$\frac{-500}{1.25} + \frac{-675}{1.56} + \frac{500}{1.95} + \frac{700}{2.44} + \frac{650}{3.05}$$

$$= -400 - 432.7 + 256.4 + 268.9 + 213.1$$

$$= -832.7 + 756.4$$

$$= -76.3$$

which is too high. In this way the required r-value can be determined as 20 per cent. This gives

$$\frac{-500}{1.20} + \frac{-675}{1.44} + \frac{500}{1.73} + \frac{700}{2.07} + \frac{650}{2.50}$$

$$= -416.7 - 468.7 + 289 + 338.2 + 260$$

$$= -885.1 + 887.2$$

$$= 2.1 \simeq 0$$

With the negative and positive sums adding approximately to zero, the internal rate of return on the investment is determined as 20 per cent.

Whether this investment is worth undertaking or not can only be decided by comparing its rate of return with the yields which could be obtained by using the funds in the best alternative way. Blaug (1970) suggests that for British households the best alternative is the yield on units trusts (i) which have realized a real rate of return of about 8 per cent after tax. If $r > i$, the investment can be judged profitable.

A number of adjustments need to be made to the data, however, before an effective comparison can be carried out. First of all, it should be emphasized that the E-values in equation (2.8) are the *additional* earnings after training and not total earnings. Secondly, the internal rate of return calculation should be made only after some allowance has been made for the effects of economic growth on real income, since cross-sectional data will usually be used; to take this into account, earnings have to be increased at some compound rate over the relevant periods. In addition, an allowance needs to be made for income tax – it is income net of tax which is relevant for private internal rates of return. Also, some adjustment may be made for the fact that not all of the increase in earnings is attributable to the investment in education. The proportion which is thus attributable is sometimes referred to as the 'alpha factor' (α) and it is expected that $0 < \alpha < 1$. Most estimates suggest $0.60 \leqslant \alpha \leqslant 0.75$ (see, for example, the discussion by Vaizey, 1973, of different

Table 2.9 Private internal rate of return estimates

Author	Period	Adjustments to data	Type of investment	Rate of return (%)
Ziderman (1973)	1966–1967	Income tax	A-levels	10
		Labour force	1st degree	23.5
		participation	Master's degree*	19.0
		Unemployment	Doctorate*	14.5
		Mortality		
		2% growth rate		
		Ability	A-levels	8.5
		(assuming that	1st degree	21.5
		$\alpha = 0.66$)	Master's degree	16.0
			Doctorate	11.0
Birch and Dalvert (1973)	1970		Teaching:	
		Survival	all male graduates	11.7
		Economic activity	all male non-graduates	6.9
			all female graduates	27.5
			all female non-graduates	26.8
		Valuation of	all male graduates	14.1
		holiday periods	all male non-graduates	9.6
			all female graduates	29.3
			all female non-graduates	29.0

* Estimated from first degree level.

estimates). Further adjustments are also sometimes made for survival at various ages and for active participation in the labour market. *Table 2.9* presents some British rate of return estimates which provide an indication of the differing types of treatment and variations in the values obtained.

Questions

1. List and describe the major factors which affect the size of a population.
2. (a) What does demographic information tell you about the nature of the British population?
   (b) What are the implications of the demographic information for the labour market?

3. State the reasons why (a) an individual and (b) society may believe further education to be valuable.
4. Explain why the S-profile in *Figure 2.4* is higher than the U-profile after age a_2 but is also horizontal after that point.
5. What factors might determine the rate of return to the educational qualification for which you are now studying?
6. Demonstrate in which cases the internal rate of return is likely to provide a better predictor of labour supply than an approach based simply on wages.

References

Anon. (1980). *Social Trends*, No. 10 (a publication of the Government Statistical Service)

Arrow, K.J. (1973). 'Education as a filter', *Journal of Public Economics*, **2**

Becker, G.S. (1964). 'Human capital. A theoretical and empirical investigation with special reference to education', National Bureau of Economic Research

Birch, D.W. and Calvert, J.R. (1973). 'How profitable is teaching?', *Higher Education Review*, Autumn

Blaug, M. (1970). *Economics of Education*, Penguin, Harmondsworth

Cartter, A.M. and Marshall, F.R. (1967). *Labour Economics: Wages, Employment, and Trade Unionism*, Irwin

Cipolla, C.M. (1979). *The Economic History of World Population*, Penguin, Harmondsworth

DES (February 1978). *Higher Education into the 1990s*

DES (March 1979). *Future Trends in Higher Education*

Jones, H.A. and Williams, K.E. (1979). *Adult Students and Higher Education*, Advisory Council for Adult and Continuing Education

Kelsall, R.K. (1979). *Population*, 4th edn, Longmans, London

Layard, R. and Psacharopoulos, G. (1974). 'The screening hypothesis and the returns to education', *Journal of Political Economy*, September/October

Learmouth, A. and Connors, B. (1975). 'Demographic Tools and Social Sciences Viewpoints', Unit 5, Block 2, *Population Resource and Technology*. The Open University. Social Science: A foundation course: Making Sense of Society

Malthus, T.R. (1798). *An Essay on the Principle of Population*, Macmillan, London, 1926 (reprint of the 1798 edition)

Mincer, J. (1962). 'On-the-job training: costs, returns and some implications', *Journal of Political Economy*, suppl., October

Pearl, R. (1925). *The Biology of Population Growth*, cited in Cipolla (1979) and Open University Unit

Smith, A. (1776). *The Wealth of Nations*, ed. E. Cannom, Methuen, London, 1950

Spence, M. (1973). 'Job market signalling', *Quarterly Journal of Economics*, **87**

Spence, M. (1974). 'Competitive and optimal responses to signals: an analysis of efficiency and distribution', *Journal of Economic Theory*, **17**

Stiglitz, J.E. (1975). 'The theory of screening, education and the distribution of income', *American Economic Review*, June

Taubman, P.J. and Wales, T.J. (1973). 'Higher education, mental ability and screening', *Journal of Political Economy*, January/February
Vaizey, J. (1973). *The Economics of Education*, Macmillan, London
Wolpin, K.J. (1977). 'Education and screening', *American Economic Review*, **65**, No. 5
Ziderman, A. (1973). 'Does it pay to take a degree?', *Oxford Economic Papers*, **15**, No. 2

Appendix 2.1: Weekly earnings of male workers, employed full-time (1978)

Age group	Painting, repetitive assembly, product inspection, packaging and related (£)	Processing, making, repairing and related (metal and electrical (£)	Professional and related in science engineering, technology and similar (£)
Under 18	33.0	32.1	
18–20	56.5	53.4	45
21–24	67.0	76.5	70.8
25–29	76.4	82.4	89.6
30–39	81.5	85.8	105.2
40–49	79.5	85.4	109.4
50–59	76.8	82.0	109.4
60–64	71.5	75.5	94.4

Source: *New Earnings Survey*, Part E, Table 128 (1978).

Chapter 3

Organizations and employment

3.1 Introduction

The educational structure and institutions of a country provide employing organizations with their initial manpower resources. An enterprise is therefore concerned first with the efficient utilization of this workforce and its relative internal deployment. Once these people have been hired, however, they are frequently developed through training processes of various kinds which have resultant effects on employment conditions. These aspects are investigated here, and in the following chapter it is then possible to focus on the internal market and arrangements within a large organization.

3.2 Utilization of externally provided manpower

There are many possible influences which affect the amount of labour an organization employs, but in most business contexts there is a fundamental concern with profitability and the efficiency from which it results. For simplicity of exposition, then, we may initially assume the existence of competitive situations in both product and factor markets and examine the behaviour of an employer who seeks to obtain maximum profitability by utilizing resources in the most efficient way.

For any productive enterprise a short-run period can be defined during which the quantity of at least one type of input is fixed. In manufacturing, for example, the fixed factor will usually be capital. Total output will then vary directly with the quantity of labour employed up to some point, after which the relationship is likely to become inverse. The situation is indicated in *Figure 3.1(a)*, which is drawn on the basis of some given amount of capital. The total product curve (TP) conforms to the law of variable proportions, which states that, with at least one factor fixed, increases in another factor will at first raise output by successively greater amounts but after some point output will increase by progressively smaller amounts. Therefore, in the short run, although we may initially expect increasing returns, after some level the variable

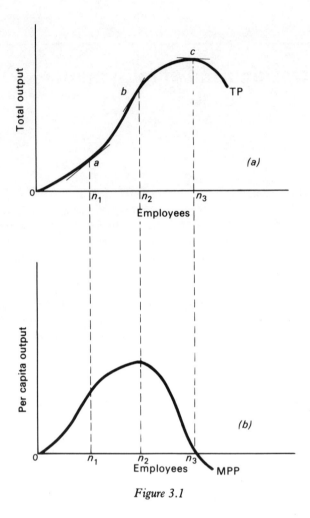

Figure 3.1

factor will become subject to diminishing returns. In the first case, at relatively low levels of employment such as n_1 in *Figure 3.1(a)*, fixed plant and machinery is used inefficiently and without the benefit of operating economies which occur at greater output levels. As production rises, these inefficiencies are reduced and each extra worker adds more to output than the one before. Further expansion of the labour force then reduces the rate of growth of output until, after a level of n_3, further additions actually reduce total output.

What is really important, therefore, is not the fact that total output increases but rather the rate at which it increases, and this depends on the changing productivity of the variable factor labour. Hence, what we are interested in is the addition to output produced by each extra worker, usually referred to as the marginal physical product (MPP). In *Figure 3.1(a)* this is represented by the slope or gradient of the total product curve. To illustrate the change in MPP, tangents are drawn at three points – *a*, *b* and *c*. It is obvious that the line drawn at point *b* is steeper than the line drawn at point *a*. Consequently, the MPP is increasing between *a* and *b*; similarly, it is decreasing between *b* and *c*. In fact, at point *b* it has reached a maximum and at point *c* it has fallen to zero, after which it becomes negative (as indicated by the downward slope of the TP curve after point *c*).

The behaviour of the marginal physical product of labour can be seen more easily if it is plotted separately as in *Figure 3.1(b)*. The section of the curve between the origin and n_2 is of little interest, because it will

Table 3.1 Labour demand data

Labour employed	*(1)* MPP	*(2)* $p_c(=MR)$	*(3)* TPP_c	*(4)* TRP_c	*(5)* MRP_c	*(6)* $R(=MR)$	*(7)* TRP_v	*(8)* MRP_v
1	34	£20	34	£680	£680	£20	£680	£680
2	33	£20	67	£1340	£660	£19	£1273	£593
3	31	£20	98	£1960	£620	£18	£1764	£491
4	28	£20	126	£2520	£560	£17	£2142	£378
5	25	£20	151	£3020	£500	£16	£2416	£274
6	20	£20	171	£3420	£400	£14.50	£2479	

p_c = constant product price in perfect competition.
MPP = marginal physical product.
MRP = marginal revenue product.
TPP = total physical product.
TRP = total revenue product.
Subscripts c, v refer to constant product price in perfect competition, and variable product price in imperfect competition, respectively.

clearly benefit any organization to go on employing more workers while MPP is rising. It is only when MPP is falling that limits to the level of employment must be considered. But to see how these limits are determined it is convenient to make use of the numerical example in *Table 3.1*.

Since we are only interested in cases where MPP is declining, *Table 3.1* ignores any possible range of increasing returns to a factor (rising MPP) and shows only decreasing returns (falling MPP). For the present, columns (6)–(8) may be ignored as we consider the effects of increasing the labour force up to a level of six employees. The MPP values in column (1) decline as employment rises and are therefore indicative of a movement down the curve in *Figure 3.1(b)* between levels n_2 and n_3.

We now need to convert the physical values in column (1) into monetary values. If the product market is perfectly competitive, the enterprise will be able to sell additional units of output at the same price (p_c). Its demand curve is perfectly elastic because changes in its own output are so small a proportion of total output that the impact on price is negligible. Hence, the price is column (2) remains constant at £20. Total physical product is shown in column (3) and is simply the cumulative additions of column (1). Column (4) gives the monetary value of column (3) and is obtained by multiplying total output at each level of employment by the constant market price, which, because it is invariant, has the same value as marginal revenue (MR). When we speak generally of the marginal revenue of a firm, we are referring to the additional income resulting from the sale of another unit of the product. Similarly, the term 'marginal revenue product' (MRP) is used to indicate the market value of the output produced by the last worker employed. It is, therefore, obtained by deducting the previous value of column (4) from the current value. For example, the MRP of the third worker is the value of total revenue product (TRP) at that level minus the TRP value when two workers are employed, viz. £1960–£1340 = £620. Alternatively, we could multiply column (1) by column (2), so that

$$MRP = MPP \cdot p_c$$

where p_c is the price of the product for a competitive firm.

It is instructive to represent these quantities graphically. In *Figure 3.2* the level of employment is measured horizontally and MPP is initially measured vertically. Plotting these values against the corresponding employment levels, we obtain the curve marked MPP. Now, if the MPP

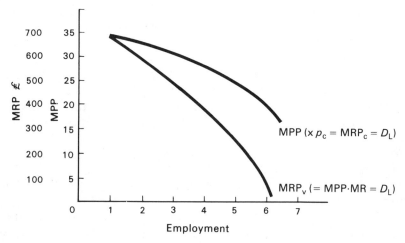

Figure 3.2 For explanation of symbols see *Table 3.1*

values are multiplied by a constant (such as p_c), the corresponding curve will remain unaltered in its essential characteristics. Hence, if we renumber the vertical axis in *Figure 3.2* so that it also measures marginal revenue product, and plot the corresponding values from *Table 3.1*, the MRP curve will lie in exactly the same position as the MPP curve.

If we now relate the MRP curve to various wage rates, it will become evident that we have in fact derived the organization's demand curve for labour. Consider a wage rate of £500 per month and suppose that two people are currently employed. The second person hired added £660 to total revenue but increased total cost by only £500. Total profit was thereby increased. If the marginal cost of labour remains unchanged and is equal to the wage rate, it will also be profitable to employ a third and fourth person, since in each case the addition to cost is less than the addition to revenue. Indeed, the level of employment can be raised to five workers – but if it goes beyond this, total profit will begin to fall. A sixth worker will cost £500 but will add only £400 to total revenue. On the other hand, if the wage rate falls to £400 per month, then it *will* be profitable to hire six people. In other words, in equating marginal cost to marginal revenue, the organization moves along its MRP curve, which is therefore its labour demand curve.

Different types of labour really constitute different factors of production. One can therefore visualize different demand functions for each separate type of worker, with employment levels varying with changes in relative wage rates. The problem for a competitive firm then arises of utilizing these various types of workers in the most efficient manner. This problem can be stated in either of two equivalent ways: it is (a) to produce a given output at the lowest cost or (b) to produce the highest output for a given cost. The problem is usually referred to as that of obtaining the *least cost factor combination*, which requires that, in order to obtain a given output, the marginal physical product of £1 spent on one type of labour must equal that marginal physical product of £1 spent on another type of labour. For example, if two types of workers are hired who have marginal physical products MPP_a and MPP_b and are paid w_a and w_b, respectively, cost minimization requires that

$$\frac{MPP_a}{w_a} = \frac{MPP_b}{w_b}$$

This condition[1] can be generalized for any number of factor inputs. Thus, with n different types of workers $(1, 2, 3, \ldots, n)$ the least cost condition becomes

$$\frac{MPP_1}{w_1} = \frac{MPP_2}{w_2} = \frac{MPP_3}{w_3} \ldots = \frac{MPP_n}{w_n}$$

3.3 Effects of other markets

If we drop the assumption of a perfectly competitive product market, the analysis of labour demand can be extended to cover monopolistic competition and pure monopoly. The essential difference in these cases is that the firm can sell additional output only if it progressively reduces the price of its product. Price is therefore no longer constant as output varies. The effect is illustrated in columns (6), (7) and (8) of *Table 3.1*. To make the difference as clear as possible, however, the values of columns (1), (2) and (3) are retained. Hence, multiplying column (3) by the variable price indicated in column (6) produces the values in column (7). But it will be noted that, since column (6) values are lower than those in column (2) after the first employment level, column (7) values are lower than those in column (4). Consequently, when we obtain MRP values in column (8), they are lower than corresponding values in column (5) and plotting them in *Figure 3.2* produces a labour demand curve which lies below, and is more steeply inclined than, that for a firm operating in a perfectly competitive product market.

The difference is important for several reasons. In the first place, it demonstrates that, other things being equal, a given wage rate will be associated with a higher level of employment the more competitive the product market[2]. At a wage rate of £500 per month the latter produces an employment level of five against one of (approximately) three. Secondly, the analysis demonstrates that variations in the elasticity of demand for the product will produce variations in the demand for labour. Hence, the less elastic the demand for the firm's product the lower will be the fall in quantity demanded for any given price rise and the lower will be the reduction in labour demand. As will be seen later, this has important implications for wage bargaining between employers and trade unions.

Oligopolistic markets in which there are few sellers have become increasingly common, and this type of situation raises an interesting possibility. Each firm is concerned to protect its own share of the market and will take the expected behaviour of rivals into account in order to at least maintain its own position. If it reduces price, it will expect competitors to follow suit to prevent a loss of sales; if it increases price, it will expect that rivals will not follow suit, because the relative fall in their prices will expand their market share. As illustrated in *Figure 3.3*, therefore, the demand curve of the individual firm will exhibit a kink at the ruling market price p: below this point its demand curve will be relatively inelastic, since price reductions will not expand sales appreciably; above this point its demand curve will be relatively elastic, since price increases will cause an appreciable fall in sales[3].

The importance of the kinked demand curve is that it produces a marginal revenue curve with an area of discontinuity over which changes in the marginal costs of production (which would include wages) have no effect on price or, therefore, on output. In *Figure 3.3(a)* the marginal cost curve may shift between c_1 and c_2 and output will remain at q with price at p. This analysis evidently implies a corresponding range of discontinuity in the labour demand curve. Thus, in *Figure 3.3(b)* changes in the wage rate over the range d_1d_2 will have no effect on the

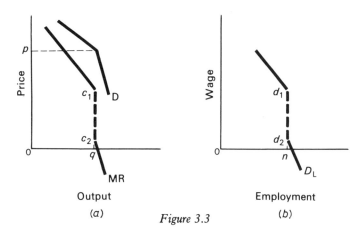

Figure 3.3

(a) Output

(b) Employment

level of employment n, since, if output is maintained at q, the organization will still require n people to produce that amount of output. In effect, the labour demand curve becomes perfectly inelastic over the range d_1d_2.

The structure of the product market can quite obviously have a significant effect on the amount of labour employed by an organization, the elasticity of demand for labour and the reaction to wage changes. No less important is the state of competition in the labour market itself. This can best be seen by first assuming a perfectly competitive product market combined with some power by an employing organization to influence wages in the labour market. Whereas the labour supply curve in a perfectly competitive factor market is completely elastic, some degree of monopsony power implies a positively inclined supply curve, as shown in *Figure 3.4*. The difference is that in the first case additional workers can be hired at an unchanged wage rate, while in the second case extra labour will only be forthcoming at an increasing wage rate. Assuming labour to be more or less homogeneous, an increase in the wage rate which is necessary to attract an additional worker will need to be paid to all previously employed workers. Hence, the marginal cost of labour is not (as in perfectly competitive labour markets) just the additional wage paid to the extra employee, but that amount plus the cost of bringing all previously employed workers up to a new level.

Consequently, the marginal cost curve lies above the supply curve, so that, while equating supply to demand in a competitive market would imply an employment level of n_c, to maximize profits the organization will equate the MRP of labour to the marginal cost of the last employee and hire only n_m workers. The level of employment is therefore less than

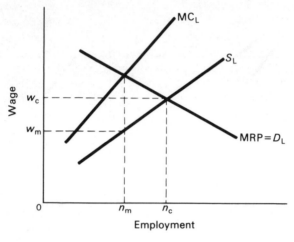

Figure 3.4

it would have been in a perfectly competitive labour market. Moreover, since only n_m workers are hired, the employer will expect to pay a wage rate of w_m instead of w_c, so that wages may also be lower than in a more competitive labour market. It is, therefore, evident that the state of the labour market itself can have a significant effect on employment and wage levels.

3.4 Demand elasticity and wage bargaining

It is convenient at this point to make a short digression on the determinants of labour demand elasticities, since an understanding of these will become important at various later stages and particularly in Chapters 10 and 11. The elasticity of demand for labour concerns the effect which a wage change has on the demand for labour. Hence, it is important in determining the extent to which a trade union can secure wage increases for its members without causing a rise in their unemployment. Conversely, the elasticity of demand for labour also affects the relative market strength of employers when facing unions in a bargaining context.

The outstanding British economist Alfred Marshall (1842–1924) identified four determinants of the elasticity of labour demand:

(1) *The elasticity of demand for labour varies directly with the elasticity of demand for the product.* Consequently, since the demand for labour is derived from the demand for the product which it produces, if product demand is elastic, the demand for labour to produce it will also be elastic; if product demand is inelastic, the demand for labour will be inelastic. In the former case the power of a trade union to raise wages without causing a severe reduction in the employment of its members is relatively weak but strong in the latter conditions. However, since the product demand curve is relatively less elastic at industry level than at firm level, this condition would suggest that a union will find it more advantageous to bargain collectively with representatives of employers than with individual firms.

(2) *The elasticity of demand for labour is the smaller the smaller the proportion of labour costs in total costs.* This condition is sometimes referred to as 'the importance of being unimportant', but it must be related to the ease or otherwise of substituting other factors as replacements. Labour costs (either in total or for a particular group of workers) may be relatively small, but if it is easy to bring in replacement factors, even a small increase in wages may lead employers to introduce them. The extent to which factor substitution is possible is determined by available technology and is not something which can be changed in the short run. It does, however, suggest the third determinant.

(3) *The elasticity of demand for labour is the less the less easily other factors can be substituted for it.* If there is a low elasticity of substitution with workers difficult to replace, the dependency of firms on labour is increased and the elasticity of demand for labour is correspondingly low. Hence, it will be relatively easy for a trade union to secure wage increases without appreciably raising the level of unemployment of its members. Conversely, employing organizations will find it relatively difficult to resist wage demands.

(4) *The demand for labour is the less elastic the less elastic is the supply of substitute factors.* Thus, even if it is technologically easy to replace labour in the process of production, the elasticity of supply of alternative factors may be so low that a union can obtain wage increases for its members at little cost in terms of employment.

These considerations relate to short-run market conditions and, in general, suggest that unions may have considerable power over such periods to raise the total earnings of workers. This is because short-run demand elasticities tend to be low, owing to the immobility of other factor inputs, and if the elasticity of demand is numerically less than 1, a wage increase will raise total earnings. (Similarly, if the elasticity of demand for labour is greater than 1, a wage increase will reduce the total earnings of trade union members.)

Over the long run, the elasticity of demand for labour will rise as it becomes possible to increase the quantity and change the form of other factor inputs. As the possibility of factor substitutions rises, so will the elasticity of labour demand. Moreover, if unions have effected wage increases, it is likely that product prices will also rise, either because wage increases are passed on or because the rise in wages increases product demand. Burkitt (1975) points out that while demand may fall, the MRP schedule can still shift to the right (because of greater revenue per unit sold), and it is not *a priori* possible to say what the longer-run effect on employment will be, since it will depend on subsequent price and demand changes and considerable time-lags in their working out. However, Burkitt argues that over the long period any depressive employment effects which result from a wage increase and a high elasticity of substitution may be overshadowed by increases in income which shift the labour demand function to the right. Union wage pressure will not then increase unemployment but, although contributing to a slower rate of workforce expansion, will raise the equilibrium wage level.

3.5 Training and manpower development

The general education system supplies new entrants to the labour market whose quality and level of productivity must be initially accepted by the organizations which hire them and to whom the foregoing analysis is directly applicable. For many workers, however, entry to the labour market is merely the beginning of a process of development made necessary because of the heterogeneous manpower demands of employing organizations who operate in different sectors, industries and markets, and who (as Doeringer and Piore, 1971, point out) are to some extent unique in terms of the technology which is being used. Most firms, therefore, have a need for manpower which is, to greatly varying extents, different from that initially provided by their external environment.

Probably more important than these static considerations are those dynamic factors which become important as soon as processes of change are allowed for. Thus, Wedderburn (1968) in summarizing a number of OECD studies puts emphasis on the type of training given to workers and its effect on the flexibility of organizations in meeting change, whether resulting from variations in the pattern of demand or from developments in technology. In either of these cases survival may well depend on the adaptability of the organization's human resources, whether employed in management or on the shopfloor. The OECD studiesshow that a degree of generality in basic training produces greater flexibility and a swifter response to change, so that periods of dislocation and retaining costs are reduced compared with cases where employers have trained their workforce in a much narrower way.

There are broadly two alternative ways in which labour can be trained – on the job and off the job. In the former case training takes place along with activity which contributes directly to production; in the latter case training and contributions to output are separated and learning usually takes place in an area specially designated for that purpose, such as an organization's training school or a college of further education. Training may also be either formal or informal, the former frequently being associated with off-the-job training and the latter with on-the-job training, although this need not necessarily be the case. Formal training involves a planned programme of learning activity for which certain objectives are made more or less explicit and their attainment tested during and/or at the end of the period. Informal training, while provided with the achievement of certain objectives in mind, is considerably less structured and usually involves learning by observation of an experienced worker (sometimes loosely described as 'sitting by Nellie') but also depends heavily on learning by doing. While one can expect the cost of formal or off-the-job training to be higher than that of informal or on-the-job training, this is not in itself an acceptable basis for deciding between alternative methods. As Thomas, Moxham and Jones (1969) point out, most decisions by firms about training are not concerned with its introduction but rather with the question of whether to replace one training scheme with another. The decision should then not merely be based on a comparison of relative costs but should take into account both costs and benefits. It is only when an adequate cost–benefit analysis has been undertaken that proper decisions can be made.

Employers provide training in the expectation that it will have a positive effect on the marginal product of the worker. Hence, a trainee will be more productive after training than before. However, according to the analysis developed by Becker (1964), given competitive conditions, benefits of training will accrue to, and the costs will be paid by, either the employer or the trainee, depending on whether training can be categorized as either general or specific. General training is a type which is useful to many employing organizations and, in the limiting case of perfectly general training, raises the marginal product of the trainee by the same amount in all such firms. Specific training raises the marginal product of the trainee more in the firm providing the training than in other firms; in the limit, completely specific training increases the marginal product of the worker only in the organization providing the training. Training costs themselves are of two kinds: direct costs, which involve actual financial outlays on such items as tools, equipment and the pay of instructors; and indirect or opportunity costs in the form of income which is lost but which could have been obtained in the absence of training. In general terms, the opportunity cost of anything is defined as the alternative foregone when acquiring it. Hence, for a firm a certain amount of saleable output may be lost if, for example, a skilled worker spends some of his time supervising a trainee instead of in productive activity.

Becker's argument is broadly that he who benefits from training will be prepared to pay its costs. In the case of general training, the marginal product of the worker will, as a result of training, rise by the same amount in many firms besides that providing it. If the labour market is competitive, any employer will be obliged to pay a worker equal to his marginal product. On the termination of training, therefore, the general trainee will be able to command the same increased wage rate in many firms. To retain the services of such a worker, the firm providing the training will thus find itself having to increase the wage rate by the full increase in marginal product. In other words, the employer will be unable to capture any of the benefits from training and will consequently not be willing to pay its costs. But the worker, whose post-training wage rises to equality with his higher marginal product, will be prepared to pay the cost of training because he receives all the benefits.

Although there have been cases in the past when trainees have made actual financial payments to employers who have undertaken to train them (e.g. for training in the law), Becker argues that general trainees will pay the cost of their training by accepting a wage below the level of their marginal product during training. The difference between the trainee wage and marginal product is determined by the total cost of training.

Where training is completely specific, the productivity of the trainee improves only in the organization providing the training. Even after the full training period the trainee's marginal product in other organizations will not have increased at all but remains at its original level. To these other enterprises such training is irrelevant, and the wage which they are willing and obliged by the market to pay remains at its original level. Consequently, the organization which trains a worker in specific skills need pay no more after training that it did before in order to retain the services of that employee. As a result, all the benefits of training accrue to the firm and the worker receives none; the former, therefore, will be willing to pay the cost and the latter will not.

The uncertainty attached to an organization's investment in training is greater than that incumbent upon its investment in physical capital. Changes in consumer demand or technology may render either obsolete, but a firm's outlays on people may also be written off because they leave for alternative employment. A firm is likely to experience some degree of labour turnover and each person quitting involves writing off a past investment. To cut down on such losses, Becker argues that the firm may increase the post-training wage. Since specifically trained employees are being paid below their marginal products, the organization has scope to make such an increase and, in effect, it passes on to the worker some of the benefits of training. However, since the high post-training wage is now likely to attract more potential trainees than before, not only are quit rates cut down, but also a surplus of people for training develops. The organization will find it possible to reduce the wage paid to those hired for training and effectively now passes some of the costs on to trainees. A situation therefore develops in which the costs and benefits of specific training are shared between firms and employees. It is not possible to make any *a priori* statement about the proportionate share of costs and benefits as between organizations and trainees, and this will presumably be determined by particular market conditions.

The training analysis developed by Becker and summarized very briefly above represented a significant theoretical advance and has many implications, particularly for the behaviour of organizations in respect of the people they employ. It has not, however, been without its critics. Eckaus (1963), for example, complains that Becker makes training completely separate from production and that this, together with the assumed perfect mobility of labour, turns commercial enterprises into nothing more than training schools in which training and production decisions are completely separate. Moreover, in order to reach a decision, the organization must compare the marginal costs and benefits of training, but Eckaus suggests that this may not be possible. The difficulty is that whenever a good is produced jointly with another product, the marginal costs of each cannot be defined – only the marginal cost of producing an extra unit of both commodities can be estimated. Eckaus suggests that this may be the case with training undertaken on the job. People learn as they produce output, and training is therefore an unavoidable joint product with the organization's usual output. Consequently, the costs of general training cannot be exactly determined and shifted onto the trainee. However, Oatey (1970) takes issue with this point of view and argues that the costs of informal skill acquisition *can* be estimated. There may be some difficult cases, but there should be plenty of instances where they can be readily estimated. For example, the costs of a newly recruited operator increasing output from 70 to 90 pieces a day in 5 days through learning from experience can be estimated by considering the loss of the 50 or so pieces more that would have been produced by a fully skilled operator working at the criterion level. If a new engineer takes 2 hours to overhaul a component where the criterion is 30 minutes, the costs of his learning from experience can be estimated in terms of the overhauls 'lost' or extra overtime worked. Equally, a determination of the possibly disastrous effects of an inexperienced manager's mistake that halts production for a few hours may well convince the company directors that management training is not quite so 'costly' after all[4]. In addition, Oatey also argues that training costs are not unavoidable, since a firm can circumvent them altogether if it chooses to recruit only fully skilled manpower.

A general criticism made by Eckaus is that many conclusions reached by Becker 'depend so strictly on the assumptions of perfect factor markets that the arguments, however ingenious, must be suspect'[5]. Oatey agrees that Becker's analysis is framed in these terms but that it can easily be adapted to the real world. This is a view supported by Blaug (1970), who reiterates Oatey's view: 'All that needs to be assumed to make Becker's theory applicable to the real world is that (a) general trainees are paid less than the going rate for performing some skilled task and that (b) specific trainees tend to be paid above the going rate in the firm providing specific training.'[6]

Oatey, however, goes on to argue that rational human capital investment decisions should be made, not on the degree of skill generality, but rather on the basis of the mobility potential of the trainee. Indeed, Becker drew attention to the importance of labour mobility in pointing to the fact that strong monopsonistic power could render all human capital investments specific. Geographical isolation, for instance, may mean that even general trainees do not move to alternative firms even though their skills could be utilized. Developing this line of thought, Oatey argues that an organization would be unlikely to undertake any form of training if it knew that all trainees would leave after training; similarly, it might pay for any type of training if it could be certain that all trainees would remain with it afterwards. Consequently, it is the mobility potential of the trainee which should be the basic investment criterion for an organization.

3.6 Manpower demand and fixed labour costs

When only skilled workers are being considered, it is appropriate to regard labour as a completely variable input which can be increased or reduced according as the demand for output rises or falls. There may, of course, be legal restrictions placed on an organization's ability to hire and fire in this manner. We shall abstract from these aspects here and leave them for more detailed discussion in Chapter 9. This will allow of a more effective investigation of the modified behaviour which certain types of labour costs promote in organizations.

In the simplest case, in which the only cost is the wage, labour is a variable input. The level of employment is determined by comparing the wage with MRP, and it changes as either of these values changes. But employers, in fact, also incur certain fixed costs in respect of their workforce which affect not only hiring and firing policies, but also turnover rates and occupational differences in the stability of employment and earnings. These fixed costs can be defined as those which do not vary proportionately with hours worked by an employee. They consist of two types:

(1) *Turnover costs*, which arise when people are either hired or fired, and include costs of recruiting and selecting workers, recalling ex-employees and any severance costs such as redundancy payments.

(2) *Employment costs*, which are independent of hours worked but incurred during the period of employment, and include payments for training, materials, tools, taxes per employee, employer's pension contributions, etc.

A consideration of these types of fixed cost will show that they are likely to rise as a proportion of total labour costs with increases in the level of skill. Advertising is likely to be more expensive for the highly as opposed to the less skilled. For example, vacancy inserts in local newspapers will suffice for unskilled labour, but for managerial workers it will probably be necessary to advertise in the national press or in specialized journals. The seniority of people selected to conduct interviews, as well as the time spent on each candidate, is likely to rise with the level of skill. In some cases (e.g. high-level managers, highly specialized personnel) outside agencies may be engaged for selection purposes. Similarly, employment costs vary directly with the level of skill. A higher level of skill will usually involve greater training costs because of the longer duration of training, higher equipment expenses or the greater amounts involved in providing personnel to give instruction. In some cases an organization may have its own school and staff of instructors.

One of the main contributors to the development of the analysis of fixed labour costs is Walter Y. Oi (1962), who begins from the predictions that general training will be paid for by workers and specific training by firms. For simplicity he assumes that the employer will pay all the costs of specific training. Oi then argues that the existence of fixed labour costs converts the workforce from a variable factor to a quasi-fixed factor, because fixed costs represent an investment by the firm in the worker. The degree of fixity (F) depends on the ratio of discounted turnover plus employment costs (C) to total labour costs ($W + C$) – i.e.

$$F = \frac{C}{W + C}$$

where W is the expected value of future discounted wage payments.

Consequently, F approaches zero as C becomes very small and approaches unity as C becomes very large: for a completely variable factor $F = 0$ and for a completely fixed factor $F = 1$.

The greater the degree of fixity, the more reluctant will a firm be to lay-off a worker when demand for the product falls because the fixed labour cost 'drives a wedge between the wage rate and the marginal value product, the relative magnitude of the wedge being measured by the degree of fixity'[7]. For a firm in a competitive position any fall in product demand will reduce the price of that good and thereby reduce the employment of a variable factor. Especially if the fall in demand is expected to be temporary, the employment of a quasi-fixed factor will not be reduced immediately, because the longer such a worker remains with the organization the greater the period over which the fixed labour costs can be amortised. Moreover, if such employees are laid off, it may prove difficult to persuade them to return when demand recovers. Oi quotes United States Bureau of Labour Statistics data to show that for 1953–1958 over 60 per cent of hirings involved new employees. Since these people would require training, the data emphasize the additional expenditure that can be avoided if skilled workers are retained during recessions.

The existence of fixed costs, therefore, helps to explain why skilled workers experience greater employment stability over the trade cycle and why organizations follow discriminatory firing policies. Moreover, Oi argues that, to protect their investments, firms may introduce pension and profit-sharing schemes and develop the practice of promotion from within rather than fill higher level vacancies with people hired from outside the organization. Discriminatory hiring policies may also be attempted in order to screen for those workers with characteristics associated with long tenure. In this respect, it is worth noting that the policies of employing organizations may be at variance with national economic needs. Worker mobility is a crucial factor in ensuring a competitive and flexible labour force which responds to changes in its environment. While they may benefit the firm, therefore, specific training and mobility-restricting policies may be less desirable from a national viewpoint. To the extent that such policies are becoming more prevalent and that outlays by organizations on fixed labour costs are increasing, it is possible that this aspect of manpower demand will assume increasing importance in the future.

3.7 Some empirical evidence

The marginal productivity theory of factor demand outlined in this chapter has been subjected to a variety of empirical tests. In some approaches the marginal product values of factor inputs have been estimated and then compared with actual income received. Other studies have sought to find evidence on the prediction that the labour demand curve has a negative slope.

The relationship between factor inputs into the productive process and the output they produce is referred to as a production function – i.e. production is a function of (or depends on) factor inputs. Probably the best-known form of this relationship is the Cobb–Douglas production function, named after Professor Douglas, who inferred its properties from empirical observation, and his colleague Cobb, who expressed them in mathematical form[8]. This equation[9] can then be used to test the theory by collecting appropriate data and estimating MRP values. It should be noted, however, that there are many difficult problems attached to this kind of exercise and therefore the results obtained must be treated with caution. In principle, however, one can either consider changes in the value of output as the level of employment changes over time in particular industries or use data for a cross-section of industries at a particular point in time. In the first case the main problem is to allow for the effects of technical progress which alter the input–output relationship, and in the second case the obstacle is that different industries are likely to have different production functions.

Cobb and Douglas estimated their function for United States manu-facturing industries using value-added data for the period 1899–1922. From this they estimated that labour's share in the value of output should have been 81 per cent. In fact, for 1909–1918 its actual share was 75 per cent. A cross-section test using Australian data for 1968 produced a close correspondence between the estimated and observed values for labour's share. Notwithstanding their caveats, Layard et al. (1971) at a less aggregate level also obtain a good Cobb–Douglas fit for the British electrical engineering industry. Thurow (1968), however, obtained results for the whole United States private sector over the period 1929–1965 which did not support marginal productivity theory. In every year the marginal productivity of capital was smaller than observed returns to capital. Conversely, labour earned consistently less than its marginal product. Thurow (1968) observes that the differences not only are large, but also vary over time. On the other hand, the fixed cost hypothesis developed by Oi and others suggests that some allowance should be made for the behaviour of hours worked over the trade cycle, since an increase (decrease) in product demand may be met by an existing labour force working more (fewer) hours rather than by an increase (decrease) in the number of employees. Allowing for this, Craine (1973) estimated a share in net national product of 68 per cent for United States labour which compared well with actual shares of between 59 and 65 per cent. Hence, while some evidence does not support the

MRP demand theory, other evidence does. Consequently, and particularly in view of the serious problems involved, one should be reluctant to come down too heavily on either side.

The effects of fixed labour costs were also tested empirically by Oi (1962). With data for the furniture, foundry and male clothing industries in the United States tests were made to discover whether the degree of fixity was associated with stability of employment. On the assumption that a high wage rate reflects a high degree of fixity, Oi found that the fixed cost view was supported.

A number of studies have also produced support for the theoretically derived downward-sloping labour demand curve. Using United States data for 1958–1969, Ehrenberg found the expected negative relationship for policemen, teachers and social workers, with wage elasticities of approximately -0.3, -0.4 and -1, respectively. Evidence was also produced to suggest that the (public sector) industry demand curve is less elastic than demand curves for separate parts of the industry, which again confirms the theoretical expectation[10]. Finally, if the labour demand curve is downward-sloping, an increase in the price of capital (r) relative to the price of labour (w) should result in a larger workforce (L) in the present period (t) compared with that in the previous period ($t-1$). In a multiple regression analysis using United States data for 1929–1965 Coen and Hickman did in fact find a positive relationship between the (logarithmic) ratio of L_t/L_{t-1} and r/w when output was held constant.

Questions

1. Give a definition of the short run which is applicable to any productive organization.
2. State, in no more than 100 words, why an organization's labour MRP curve is its labour demand curve.
3. What are the four determinants of the elasticity of labour demand as defined by Marshall?
4. What steps might an organization take to change the elasticity of demand for labour in its own favour?
5. Show how any two of Marshall's elasticity determinants may work against each other.
6. Show the effect on the labour demand curve of an increase in the demand for the firm's product. What will be the effect on the quantity of labour demanded for an oligopolist?
7. Discuss the importance of opportunity costs in your own (either full- or part-time) training.

8. Is the present course of study you are following general or specific in nature? Who should pay for its cost?
9. What differences are made to manpower demand by an organization's expenditure on fixed labour costs?
10. Discuss the empirical findings on labour demand in relation to the advisability of accepting MRP theory.

Notes

[1] For readers familiar with isoquant analysis the condition is that the slope of an isoquant must be equal to that of the isocost line. When the slope of the isocost line is given by w_a/w_b and the slope of the isoquant by MPP_a/MPP_b, cost minimization occurs, where

$$\frac{w_a}{w_b} = \frac{MPP_a}{MPP_b}$$

Whence

$$\frac{MPP_a}{w_a} = \frac{MPP_b}{w_b}$$

[2] It may be noted that this is a logical counterpart to the output analysis of the firm which predicts that price will be lower and, hence, output higher under competitive as compared with monopolistic conditions (assuming no economies of scale). The higher output in competitive markets will clearly require a greater labour force to produce it.

[3] For a more detailed exposition of the kinked demand curve theory and associated considerations see, for example, Koutsoyiannis (1975).

[4] Oatey (1970), pages 5–6.

[5] Eckaus (1963), Section IV.

[6] Blaug (1970), page 193.

[7] Oi (1962), page 541.

[8] See Heathfield (1971) for a discussion of the Cobb–Douglas and other production functions.

[9] Its usual form is

$$q = aK^\alpha L^\beta$$

where q = value added to output by capital and labour; K = capital; L = labour; and a, α, β = constants with α and β interpretable as capital and labour output elasticities. When the function is estimated by using multiple regression techniques, it is usually converted first into a linear form by taking logs, so that

$$\ln q = \ln a + \alpha \ln K + \beta \ln L$$

When actual values have been collected for q, K and L, the parameters a, α and β can be estimated.

[10] See the discussion in Section 3.3 in respect of Marshall's first determinant of factor demand elasticity. Differences in factor demand elasticities as between firm and industry level are derived from differences in product elasticity, which can most easily be demonstrated for perfect competition. For the firm in such a market, the demand curve is taken as perfectly elastic, but a very slight negative inclination would, in fact, be present. When the individual firm is considered, this can safely be neglected, but

when the difference is aggregated across the (large number of) firms in the industry, the slight deviation from the horizontal is magnified, so that the industry demand curve is clearly downward-sloping.

References

Becker, G. (1964). 'Human capital. A theoretical and empirical investigation with special reference to education' (reprinted in Blaug, 1968)

Blaug, M. (1968). *Readings in the Economics of Education*, Vol. 1, Penguin, Harmondsworth

Blaug, M. (1970). *Introduction to the Economics of Education*, Penguin, Harmondsworth

Burkitt, B. (1975). *Trade Unions and Wages*, Bradford University

Coen, R.M. and Hickman, B.G. (1970). 'Constrained joint estimation of factor demand and production functions', *Review of Economics and Statistics*, **52**

Craine, R. (1973). 'On the service flow from labour', *Review of Economic Studies*, **40**, 43

Doeringer, P.B. and Piore, M.J. (1971). *Internal Labour Markets and Manpower Analysis*, Heath, Lexington

Eckaus, R.S. (1963). 'Investment in human capital: a comment', *Journal of Political Economy*, **71**, No. 5 (reprinted in Blaug, 1968)

Heathfield, D.F. (1971). *Production Functions*, Macmillan, London

Koutsoyiannis, A. (1975). *Modern Microeconomics*, Macmillan, London

Layard, P.R.G., Sargan, J.D., Ager, M.E. and Jones, D.J. (1971). *Qualified Manpower and Economic Performance*, Allen Lane, London

Oatey, M. (1970). 'The economics of training with respect to the firm', *British Journal of Industrial Relations*, March

Oi, W.Y. (1962). 'Labour as a quasi-fixed factor', *Journal of Political Economy*, **70**

Thomas, B., Moxham, J. and Jones, J.A.G. (1969). 'A cost-benefit analysis of industrial training', *British Journal of Industrial Relations*

Thurow, L.C. (1968). 'Disequilibrium and the marginal productivity of capital and labour', *Review of Economics and Statistics*, **50**

Wedderburn, Dorothy (1968). *Enterprise Planning for Change*, OECD, Paris

Appendix 3.1: Market structures

The structure of a market can be located at any point on a continuum which ranges from perfect competition at one end to pure monopoly at the other. Two other types of market, a knowledge of which is generally useful, are monopolistic competition and oligopoly. This appendix provides a brief recapitulation of these four theoretical models. More extended discussions can be found in any introductory text on microeconomics.

A3.1.1 Perfect competition

The methodological importance of this model is considerable. It provides an analytical framework for examining the behaviour of a market in the absence of frictions and imperfections which might otherwise impede the working of market forces. Therefore, the conditions which are needed to develop the model necessarily appear severe but each is capable of relaxation in order to examine the effects of any particular imperfection.

The two basic assumptions are:

(1) There is free entry into and exit from the market.
(2) Firms are price-takers – i.e. they must accept the price which is determined at market level as a result of the collective actions of all firms and consumers. This is likely to occur if: (a) products are homogeneous; (b) there are large numbers of buyers and sellers who account for roughly equal amounts of market activity; (c) perfect knowledge exists about prices and products.

With no individual able to affect price to any measurable extent, the demand curve facing the firm appears, effectively, as being perfectly elastic at the level of market price. Average and marginal revenue are therefore equal to each other (see Appendix 1.2, pages 28–32), as indicated in *Figure A3.1.1*, which also shows three possible price levels. At p_1 excess

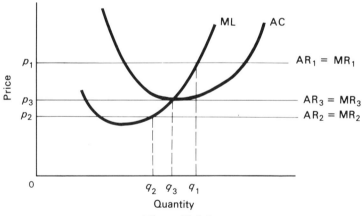

Figure A3.1.1

profits are being made, at p_2 losses are being made and at p_3 total revenue and cost are equal, so that excess profit is zero. These different price levels could be taken as indicative of the process of adjustment towards long-run equilibrium. Short-run equilibrium merely requires MC = MR, but long-run equilibrium also needs AC = AR (see Appendix 1.2, pages 28–32). Price is likely to fluctuate around p_3 before settling at that level.

A3.1.2 Pure monopoly

In this situation the entire supply in a market is produced by a single organization. The producer's and the market demand curves are therefore identical; since the market demand curve (as, of course, for the *market* in perfect competition) is negatively inclined, so is that of the

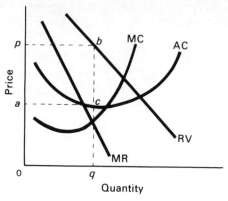

Figure A3.1.2

firm. *Figure A3.1.2* shows this and indicates that the profit-maximizing level of output occurs at q_1 (with $MC = MR$) with price at p. With $AR > AC$, excess profits are made equal to area *pbca*. Compared with the perfect competitor (*Figure A3.1.1*), it is clear that the pure monopolist can affect market price by varying his level of output.

A3.1.3 Monopolistic competition

This market is similar to the perfectly competitive one in that firms and consumers are numerous but dissimilar in that products are differentiated, information is less than perfect and non-price competition occurs. Each form consequently has a limited degree of monopoly power and the firm's demand curve is negatively inclined but more elastic than that shown in *Figure A3.1.2*.

A3.1.4 Oligopoly

Oligopoly is defined as a type of market in which there is only a small number of sellers. How many sellers is less important than the interaction between them, each being affected by, and taking into account, the reactions of competitors to changes in its own behaviour.

Of the many theoretical and empirical features of oligopoly, the theory of the kinked demand curve is of particular relevance to the present text. This takes the market price (of *p* in *Figure A3.1.3*) as given and argues that, since firms are concerned to protect, and if possible increase, their share of the market, any price increase by a single firm will not be followed by its competitors. Hence, that firm's demand curve for price increases will be relatively elastic, since sales will be lost to competitiors.

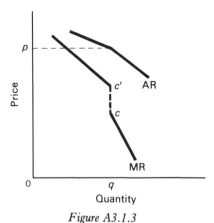

Figure A3.1.3

But a price decrease *will* be imitated by competitors, sales will not expand appreciably and therefore the firm's demand curve for price reductions will be relatively inelastic. This asymmetric reaction on the part of rivals consequently introduces a kink into the firm's demand curve at the point of market price. In turn, when the corresponding sections of the marginal revenue curve are drawn in *Figure A3.1.3*, a discontinuity occurs over the range *cc'*. The importance of this is (a) the marginal cost curve can shift over the range of the discontinuity without any change occurring in either price or output; (b) it is possible for the demand curve to shift without the usual consequences, provided that the marginal cost curve still lies between *c* and *c'*.

Chapter 4

Manpower, hiring allocation and planning by organizations

4.1 Introduction

The fundamental nature of organizations as producers of goods and services gives rise, together with the existing state of technology, to demands for people of various kinds. As the previous chapter has indicated, this demand for manpower means that the employing organization must have recourse to the general labour market in order to obtain its requirements. If it is not possible for needs to be fully met in this way, employers must accept whatever human resources the external environment provides and then change them over time in order to produce the attributes which are required. These changes are effected through training processes which themselves have important implications for the organization's demand for labour. So much has already been seen and it is now necessary to investigate not only the place of training in a wider organizational context, but also the hiring and manpower planning aspects which cannot properly be separated from it. Therefore, having considered the external environment in Chapter 2 and the nature of the demand for human resources in Chapter 3, we now turn to a number of related matters which follow from the need to utilize people in order to achieve organizational objectives.

The present chapter consequently divides into three parts, and although this division is useful and even necessary for a formal discussion, it should be remembered that in practice the topics treated here are very much interdependent. The first part of the chapter is concerned with some of the problems encumbent upon engaging people in the role of employees. This discussion of recruitment and selection problems leads, in the second section, to a general investigation of the internal allocation in policies of organizations. These matters then provide the context for the final part of the chapter, which is concerned with manpower planning at the level of the organization.

4.2 Manpower recruitment and selection

The actual process of hiring people is of crucial importance for employers. If mistakes are made at this point, it can mean a failure to meet objectives which are necessary to the survival of the organizations; at best it can mean resources wasted, not only in the process of hiring, but subsequently in training, in raw material usage, in production and in lost custom and goodwill.

In small organizations hiring may be done by the owner, general manager or even a foreman or departmental head. In larger organizations, while such people are likely to be involved, it is more probable that the overall process and much of its detail will be the responsibility of people in the personnel department who, depending largely on the size of the enterprise, will have varying degrees of specialization in such matters. While the principles involved are quite general in the sense that they apply to any organization, the expertise with which they are applied can and does vary enormously. Indeed, an important source of economies of scale is the ability of larger organizations to employ specialist staff in recruitment and selection as well as in other aspects of the personnel function.

The total manpower level will be dictated by the overall corporate plan of the organization. As will be seen later, this should be closely linked to the manpower plan, which, among other things, defines the hiring level in any given period. The overall objective is then to obtain manpower, of an acceptable quality and in the correct quantity, at the minimum cost. To get to the point where hiring is actually accomplished involves going through the sequential process of recruitment and selection. Graham (1974) defines recruitment as the process of identifying the vacancy, examining sources of supply and contacting candidates. Selection is then the second stage of reaching a decision on who to employ.

4.2.1 Recruitment

The first stage in the process of recruitment is to identify the vacancy to be filled in terms of a job description and personnel specification. A job description states the overall purpose of the job, the tasks to be carried out and the tools, equipment and other people involved.

The personnel specification (sometimes more loosely referred to as a job specification) is a detailed statement of the experience, qualifications and abilities required, taking into account any physical and social aspects of the environment which are important. In general, requirements have to be stated in behavioural terms as precisely as possible, so that not only does everyone have the same expectations, but also the correct people are hired for specific jobs. In the latter respect, for example, if a personnel specification is properly drawn up from an analysis of what is needed for a particular job, it can be used as a basis for questions when candidates are being interviewed. Moreover, from the viewpoints of analysing requirements and comparing different candidates, it is necessary to use some kind of grading system. Two such schemes are those of the National Institute of Industrial Psychology as developed by Alec Rodger, and Munro Fraser's five-point grading system:

Rodger's plan
(1) Physical attributes (e.g. health, speech)
(2) Attainments (e.g. formal qualifications, experience)
(3) General intelligence
(4) Special aptitudes (e.g. manual skills)
(5) Interests (e.g. intellectual, social)
(6) Disposition (e.g. reliability, effect on others)
(7) Circumstances (e.g. marital status).

Fraser's system

(1) Effect on others (e.g. speech, physical make-up)
(2) Qualifications (e.g. education and training)
(3) Innate abilities (e.g. responsiveness, comprehension)
(4) Motivation (e.g. objectives and ability to meet them)
(5) Adjustment (e.g. social traits, reaction to stress).

Both these systems are in use and the choice between them or competitors is largely a matter of personal preference.

The vacancy to be filled having been defined, it is then necessary to consider alternative sources of supply. As will be seen in the next section, depending on the internal structure of the organization and its manpower policies, some vacancies may only be filled from within, while in other cases hiring will take place from the external labour market.

Apart from specific policies which require it, a major reason for considering internal sources of supply is that candidates are already well known and the process is both simplified and reduced in cost. In addition, there may be considerable advantages in employing people for certain jobs who already have an intimate knowledge of the organization. Again, a policy of promotion from within facilitates the development of an internal career structure which not only allows of a more efficient utilization of individual abilities, but also tends to reduce turnover rates.

The job levels at which people from outside are hired are frequently referred to as 'ports of entry'. As will be seen later, in some cases entry ports occur only at the lowest levels, while in other cases they are widely distributed over the hierarchy of the organization. Whatever its level, however, an entry port can be fed from a variety of external sources which include other employing organizations, public and private employment agencies, and educational and training institutes, in addition to unsolicited inquiries and recommendations.

A common method of attracting a supply of labour is, of course, through advertisements in the national or local press, trade journals, and so forth. This constitutes an important channel of communication through which labour market information is transmitted. Graham (1974), however, argues that much expenditure of this type is wasted and that more attention should be paid to the type, layout and placing of the advertisement. Thus, experimentation with, say, different layouts may produce considerable variations in response rates. On the other hand, it should be self-evident that advertising in local newspapers for highly qualified manpower, or in national news media for unskilled labour, will result largely in a waste of expenditure. Ultimately, however, only the employing organization can adequately judge the relative efficiency of different forms of advertising, since the necessary data are usually only available at the source. Moreover, it should not be concluded that an efficient method of advertising is one which brings in the largest response, since, if its design has been ill-considered, many unsuitable candidates may have applied whose applications merely increase the costs of sifting wihout improving the probability of obtaining an acceptable person. An efficient advertisement is rather one which produces a relatively small number of well-qualified applicants, so that any marginal people are deterred from applying. This can be accomplished through the wording of the original advertisement or, alternatively, in some cases it may be preferred to invite requests for additional information which then provides more details of what is required. Initial or subsequent information ought to include details of pay being offered (which will need to take into account that of local or national competitors), conditions of employment, career prospects, fringe benefits, and so forth. Some of these job aspects may not vary a great deal over time but, with changes in the general level of demand for labour, response rates may vary considerably.

4.2.2 Selection

Applications may be invited either as freely written letters or on application forms which standardize information. Which method to use is not merely a matter of personal choice but may partly depend on the nature of the vacancy. In some cases it is adequate to obtain replies in a form which gives the applicant little discretion about the order and type of information, while in other cases it may be instructive to see how an applicant sets about arranging and presenting his own information.

Whatever the manner in which applications are made, they must be sifted into, say, possible marginal and unsuitable candidates. The latter may be rejected immediately, the marginals held in reserve and a short list for interviewing derived from the possibles. The short list should result from a comparison of the information provided by an applicant with the main criteria relating to the vacancy. In some cases this will be a straightforward operation; in others it may be more complex.

It is now well accepted that hiring (and training) costs correlate positively with the level of skill required, so that, as one recruits for vacancies higher and higher up the occupational hierarchy, the costs of recruitment and selection rise. In these cases, therefore, formal educational qualifications may be used as an initial filtering device (Arrow, 1973). Indeed, as we saw in Chapter 3, there are two arguments about the role of education in this respect, one of which, the human capital view, was developed in Chapter 2. The alternative view is the screening theory of education. As previously outlined, this holds, in its extreme form, that education adds nothing to the productive potential of the individual experiencing it and, by conferring different levels of formal qualifications, merely identifies for employing organizations those people who happen to be of greater productive value, with relative abilities indicated by their paper qualifications. For one reason or another, those people who are in any case more productive happen to be the ones who obtain the higher educational qualifications. It should be stressed, however, that this screening view is developed in relation to higher level jobs and, in any case, whether education is used as a screen would depend very much on particular cases.

Now, as Chapter 3 has shown, an employer can make maximum profits by equating wages to marginal revenue products. But the employer may only have information on the average product of each individual (Spence, 1973). In this case each worker receives a wage equal to the average marginal product of the group, so that relatively low-productivity workers are overpaid and high-productivity workers underpaid. It would, therefore, benefit the latter to invest in acquiring some kind of signal that would indicate to an employer that he had a relatively high marginal product and was therefore worth a higher rate of pay. An educational qualification is such a signal[1], and certain individuals clearly have an incentive to invest in acquiring them.

From the employer's point of view, if people are required with certain higher level abilities, there may be a greater probability of obtaining a person with the needed characteristics if individuals are selected for interview from among the population of those having the appropriate educational qualifications. In the screening view of things it is not that everyone without these signals does not possess the required traits, merely that everyone does not have them and they are scarcer, more difficult and more expensive to find among those without formal qualifications. Employers may therefore reduce their selection costs by using educational attainment as a filtering device which screens those not having the requisite qualifications out of jobs requiring higher level abilities.

There are a number of other interesting and sophisticated aspects attached to the screening view of education but, on the whole, the empirical tests of its validity are not encouraging. For example, certain results obtained by Taubman and Wales (1973) which may initially have appeared favourable were subsequently shown by Layard and Psacharopoulos (1974) not to be so. Also, while the former authors had claimed to show the screening effect of education on employment, Haspel (1978) reversed their conclusions by introducing, in addition to financial considerations, the non-pecuniary aspects of employment. Empirical refutation of the theory has also been produced by Wolpin (1977).

If the human capital view is accepted as a more likely interpretation of the role and effect of education, formal qualifications are used in the process of personnel selection because their acquisition not only has added to the productive capability of the individual but, depending on what has been obtained, also has done so in particular ways, developed different types of skill and produced various kinds of knowledge the values of which are likely to vary as between alternative employments.

Having drawn up a short list, different organizations may follow different interview policies, and the kind used may also vary for different types of vacancy. Individual interviews, because of their face-to-face nature, are useful in establishing rapport, although it is often admissible to have more than one representative of the employing organization so that the possibility of personal bias affecting the decision is reduced. This advantage may be furthered if an interviewing panel is used which consists, for example, of people with different interests (e.g. personnel officer, line manager). As the size of the panel increases, however, there is a tendency for effectiveness and flexibility to be lost, and this is a particular criticism of the selection board type of interview. With this approach, although more interest groups can be represented, there is a marked increase in formality and decrease in effective control over the situation. While it is quite commonly used in some areas, it frequently fails to reveal a candidate's true potentiality, either because interviewees are overwhelmed or because important lines of questioning cannot be effectively pursued. Also, compared with their behaviour in individual interviews, members of a panel may act differently and put different questions because they are conscious of the presence of colleagues. Another alternative which is particularly useful for certain types of jobs is group selection, where candidates are brought together in front of interviewers and their different performances and reactions to manufactured situations are observed. As Armstrong (1977) notes, although expensive and time-consuming, group selection methods have the advantage of being more comprehensive and of possessing 'face validity' in that they expose people to more or less real situations in response to which their performance can be analysed. Some work has also been done on assessing their 'true validity' as a predictor of job performance. While they may be superior in this to alternative approaches, they still depend essentially on the expertise of the interviewer making the assessment. However, in cases where the vacancy warrants the expenditure of additional time and other resources, several different approaches might be used, perhaps in combination with personality and aptitude tests.

Whatever form it takes, the purpose of an interview is to generate information not previously available which will result in a valid prediction of job performance. While it is also frequently used to provide information to the applicant about the organization and the nature of the vacancy, its primary use is to assist in the collection of evidence which can later be processed and evaluated. It is essential, therefore, that the interview be well structured and planned beforehand so that an optimum use of time is attained. This will be effected more easily if the personnel specification is used as a guide to qualities sought in a candidate. The interview can then be planned in order to produce the information.

Although some are designed to achieve exactly the opposite, most interviews attempt to put the applicant at ease. To this end, an informal situation may be created and initial questions designed for easy answers. Frequently an interviewer will work systematically and chronologically through the employment history of an applicant, gradually probing in greater depth to discover why past jobs were taken and left, what skills and abilities they required and how the applicant performed in them, in addition to discovering the factors which motivate him.

The psychological theory which underpins this type of approach holds that the behaviour of an individual has become stable by the time adulthood is reached. Consequently, questions about past behaviour provide information which can be taken as an indication of future patterns. However, a different view is that interviewees either with or without intent, attempt to create the most favourable impression by distorting their answers. In this case, information obtained at interviews will not provide a reliable prediction of future behaviour and situations may therefore be created by the interviewer which will facilitate the collection of more reliable data. This may involve asking the applicant to play a role, participate in discussion, etc., in order to reveal his or her true personality. However, there are doubts about the typicality of behaviour under such conditions.

The criteria on which candidates are assessed will be standardized by most organizations for cases of regular recruitment but should in any case be determined in advance. Criteria can be derived from the job specification and may be incorporated in the Rodger or Fraser grading systems discussed earlier. However, while some factors, such as experience and qualifications, are easy to assess in objective terms, other aspects, such as personality, are more difficult. It may, therefore, be useful to reinforce interviews with some kind of selection test (on personality, intelligence, aptitude and attainment) which provides more objective assessment.

Objectivity is also something of a problem where references are concerned. Organizations differ in respect of their policy on references but most will require some kind of third party comment. To the extent that a referee is able to confirm some factual aspect of an application, there is little problem. Objectivity may be in doubt, however, when character and personality judgements are involved, and these require much more care in interpretation, since they may be biased in either direction. With experience, however, a selector develops some ability to 'read between the lines'.

Logically, references should be taken up for short-listed candidates before interviews take place, since questions may arise from the comments of referees which need to be put to the interviewee. In some instances this may not be possible, and references should then be obtained after the offer of a job has been made but prior to the commencement of employment. It may also be desirable in some cases to follow up a written reference with a telephone conversation.

It is important for the organization's future efficiency in hiring to keep information, not only on different forms of advertisements and associated responses, but also on selection criteria and the extent to which they are validated by subsequent experience. In this way the most effective practices can be developed over time. Validation here, however, is extremely difficult.

The importance of obtaining maximum efficiency in the recruitment and selection of employees varies considerably in respect of different jobs. It is quite evident that the consequences may be considerable if a mistake is made when hiring, say, a manager who has responsibility for a large number of people and extensive capital equipment and raw materials. In extreme cases, inefficiency on the part of such people may endanger the existence of the whole organization. The consequences of hiring an inefficient clerk may, on the other hand, be somewhat less severe. However, there are also wider organizational policies which are important. For example, if ports of entry are maintained at every level, any vacancy can be filled from the general external labour market. But if the organization maintains entry ports only at the lowest levels, then all other vacancies must be filled by internal promotion. Thus, where people are expected to move up a hierarchy of jobs, one is not necessarily hiring a person to fill a single vacancy but must also consider longer-term implications of the extent to which individuals can be developed and reallocated within the organization. Additional emphasis is then put on efficiency in recruitment and selection, although this is merely the first step in the (perhaps increasingly) complex task of achieving the desired allocation and balance of human resources within an organization.

4.3. Manpower allocation within organizations

4.3.1 Internal allocation policies

Movements of human resources occur both between and within organizations. The first type may be referred to as events in the external labour market in the sense that they represent transactions taking place outside an individual enterprise. Movements within (especially large) organizations can, however, become so complex that a separate system is developed to deal with them and to decide such matters as promotions, demotions, transfers, layoffs and retirements. This system may constitute what is in effect an 'internal labour market', so called because it is concerned with problems of human resource allocation within the organization. Consequently, the development of such systems constitutes one way in which labour markets may become segmented or, in Kerr's (1954) terminology, 'balkanized'. Although they may be connected in various ways and at different points, such markets also tend to have varying degrees of independence from the external labour market. According to Dunlop (1966), therefore, an internal labour market is an administrative unit within which the pricing and allocation of labour is governed by a set of administrative rules and procedures.

Internal and external human resource markets are connected in one way through the 'entry ports' of the organization, which are the jobs for which people are taken on from outside. While the structure of internal labour markets in individual organizations varies considerably, most tend to have a vertical arrangement with entry ports set at low levels and all other vacancies filled by promotion from within. A worker may then progress up the 'job ladder', which consists of a sequence of jobs through which individual workers progress to higher levels. While hiring standards at entry ports may vary with the level of general unemployment, alternative wages, and so forth, lay-offs and promotions depend on fairly fixed standards which are based on seniority and ability (although the relative weightings given to these factors may vary). Moreover, the rules for discharge and hiring are usually specified in collective bargaining contracts made between the organization and trade unions and are included in manuals issued for the guidance of management. The internal wage structure is similarly defined. The greater the rigidity with which these rules are implemented the greater the difference between internal and external markets; the more flexible these rules are the more responsive the internal market to external events and the less it can be said to exist as a separate entity.

4.3.2 Causes of internal labour markets

The rules and operations of internal labour markets apply to all types of workers, whether blue collar, white collar, production, clerical or managerial employees. There is, however, a tendency for blue collar markets to be centred on an individual plant and for markets for managers to be spread across all plants owned by an organization. There may also be differences in the stress placed upon ability and seniority when promotion is determined.

Whatever the particular type of employee, Doeringer and Piore (1971) argue that internal labour markets have their roots in: skill specificity, on-the-job training and custom.

Skill specificity
Whereas Becker (1964) uses the term 'specificity' in relation to the type of training given, Doeringer and Piore use it to define the type of skill acquired through training. A completely specific skill is unique to a single job classification in a single enterprise; a completely general skill is requisite for every job in every enterprise[2]. As in Becker's analysis, however, an increase in specificity raises the proportion of training costs paid by an employer[3] and therefore increases turnover costs. This provides an incentive for organizations to increase labour retention periods and offer inducements to prevent workers leaving for other employers.

On-the-job training
It is possible that this type of training is on the whole more important for blue collar workers, and, at least in the past, it has provided the major part of required skills. Even when opportunity costs have been taken into account, its frequently informal nature makes it a relatively cheap method of training (although, because of the difficulty in costing, it may appear cheaper than it actually is). Indeed, in some cases there may be no viable alternative to on-the-job training and it is certainly encouraged by the presence of skill specificity. This tends to reduce the number of people who are likely to be in training at any one time, however, and

precludes large-scale standardized forms of training being introduced. To the extent that on-the-job training is specific, and to the extent that employers do not recover its cost from employees during the training period, the cost of such training may be an important influence on the employer's attitude to the development of internal labour markets. If unrecovered cost outlays have been made on trainees and such people leave the organization for alternative employment, human capital investment costs have to be written off. Becker (1964) suggests that turnover can be reduced by allowing workers to receive part of their higher marginal products (which result from training). This will then also allow some of the costs to be passed on. However, if this does not solve the problem (perhaps because trainees have time discount rates which are too high and which therefore cause them to place relatively little value on future earnings), it may become necessary to introduce other measures designed to reduce voluntary quits, such as job rights through seniority.

Custom
Customary practice results from a set of unwritten rules which have developed more or less gradually over time and which have a regulatory effect on work-related matters such as discipline, promotion, and so forth. It creates an area of known, acceptable and expected behaviour patterns which provides an atmosphere of stability valued by both workers and employers. Custom, which may be codified as a result of trade union pressure, may also facilitate the creation of social groups as a result of contact within the organization which generate unwritten rules and customary law. Some of these rules may relate to the pricing and allocation of labour and may also be the cause of certain rigidities which hinder the operation of market forces. On the other hand, economic consideration cannot be ignored indefinitely, and conflict between custom and efficiency requirements can lead to economic failure. To avoid this, some flexibility is needed so that new practices, repeated a sufficient number of times, can displace outdated customs.

4.3.3 Allocative structure

In the view of Doeringer and Piore, the allocative structure of internal labour markets depends on three factors: the degree of openness, scope and rules for determining priorities. These characteristics determine the type of structure which exists within organizations and therefore the way in which labour resources are allocated.

Degree of openness
Internal markets vary in the degree to which they are open to the influence of the external labour market. The degree of openness can be

measured by the proportion of entry (and exit) ports and the criteria for entry.

Ports of entry
These may result in either (1) closed internal labour markets where hiring takes place only at the lowest level and where all other jobs are filled by internal promotion; (2) open internal labour markets where all jobs are filled directly from the external labour market. Clearly, an internal labour market may exist at any point between these extremes and variations in this respect occur also as between different types of workers. For example, internal markets for clerical workers tend to be more open than for blue collar workers, which is presumably related to the greater degree of skill specificity which is claimed for the latter. On the other hand, there is a tendency for a policy of promotion from within to be followed in respect of technical and managerial labour wherever this is possible.

Criteria for entry
This may be expressed in a variety of ways, including educational qualifications, aptitude tests, and so forth, which are used to assess the quality of applicants. Entry standards are usually set by the management of the organization but are, in general, responsive to variations in the degree of tightness or slackness of the external labour market. As full employment at a macro-economic level is approached, recruitment becomes more difficult and required entry standards are then likely to be reduced. The opposite tends to happen in periods of relatively high unemployment.

Scope
The scope of an internal labour market is expressed in geographical and occupational terms. Sub-divisions often occur within these boundaries which define the internal structure of each market. For example, jobs are frequently grouped together into 'internal mobility clusters' within which promotion and demotion occur, and such clusters are then connected to entry ports. Jobs within a mobility cluster are related to one another through skill or the level of job content. Alternatively or additionally, the relationship may be through a common function or department (e.g. maintenance). However, mobility clusters may extend in both vertical and horizontal directions, the former being defined in relation to the skill content of jobs and the latter by the number and variety of jobs and the extent of specialization at any level of skill.

Rules for determining priorities
Rules are established in internal labour markets to determine the way in which workers are ranked and given priority in respect of movement

within mobility clusters. Thus, promotion is usually decided on the basis of ability and seniority, although – and particularly where on-the-job training is important – these factors tend to be highly correlated with each other. Seniority may also be used for ranking purposes where lay-offs are concerned, although in this and in cases of downgrading, 'bumping rights' are established between workers which determine the sequence in which workers displace one another when being laid off or downgraded.

The relative rights of individuals in particular jobs are sometimes referred to as 'property rights'. Seniority (usually defined in terms of the length of continuous service with the organization) is probably the most generally used determinant of job rights and is frequently employed in respect of promotions. 'Competitive seniority' is used to determine who is transferred or laid off in addition to who is promoted. In respect of discharges, for example, many organizations operate a 'first in–last out' policy. More senior workers may bump workers with less seniority throughout the whole plant or organization. On the other hand, the analysis of seniority in determining promotions is more complex, partly because not all workers have either the desire or abilities for level jobs. Some organizations, for example, use a competitive bidding system, whereas others use much less formal means.

4.3.4 Benefits and disadvantages of internal labour markets

It is claimed that the existence of an internal labour market produces conditions of greater security for workers and improved opportunities for promotion. In addition, there is at least apparently greater fairness of treatment because of the rules which are established and which govern the internal labour market. On the other hand, it is argued that in order to secure these benefits people may be willing to accept lower wages than, presumably, could be obtained in other organizations which do not operate internal labour markets. In the short term, therefore, those subject to internal labour markets may receive lower wage rates than other workers; any net benefit in terms of earnings will then depend on the relative incidence of unemployment between the two types of employees over working lifetime.

The benefits to the employer arise from several potential sources. If workers have a preference for internal labour markets, then organizations operating such systems should experience lower turnover rates. If quit rates are reduced, then training outlays will be reduced and, to the extent that such costs are not passed on to workers, training investment losses will be avoided. Equally, reduced turnover will also mean lower expenditure on selection and recruitment, not only in respect of new entrants, but also for vacancies filled by internal promotion, since the characteristics and capabilities of existing employees are well known.

There is also a debit side for organizations operating internal labour markets. If the general qualificational level of people in the labour market is rising over time (as one might expect), then the organization's labour force will always tend to be less qualified than labour currently available. Any additional training required will also tend to be greater for internal as compared with external labour, to the extent that such training is general.

Where internal labour markets exist, there is much greater importance to be attached to recruitment and selection, since existing rules and customs mean not only that it is more difficult to get rid of inefficient workers, but also that people are being engaged for their potentiality in a sequence of jobs rather than in one job; a policy of promotion from within implies that initial selection is more crucial than it is in organizations with entry ports at all levels. The difficulty in finding people from within the organization who have the requisite abilities for senior posts may be particularly severe. Moreover, management is likely to experience difficulties if existing rules and customs are contravened in order to remedy mistakes made in the past. On the other hand, as the size of the managerial hierarchy increases, there is a tendency for the application of rules of thumb to become more common, so that flexibility and necessary responses to external events are reduced. This is possibly reinforced by trade unions which codify unwritten laws into collective agreements, limit the flexibility of customary practice and raise the cost of management violation of accepted behaviour.

Limitations on flexibility mean that an organization's ability to accommodate itself to external change is reduced. Since flexibility and planning are to some degree substitutes, the less flexibility an organization has the greater the need for planning. But even where flexibility is relatively high, the general efficiency and adaptability of an organization can be improved by planning for its future manpower needs. We turn next to a consideration of this general area.

4.4 Manpower planning

An increasing number of organizations follow policies of systematically planning their future manpower position. While this practice is not followed in all organizations, it is a highly desirable activity, since it facilitates the achievement of general corporate objectives and promotes the efficient utilization of human resources. Much planning has in the past tended to rely on ad hoc methods and entrepreneurial flair. However, while it is not essential for company plans to be written down,

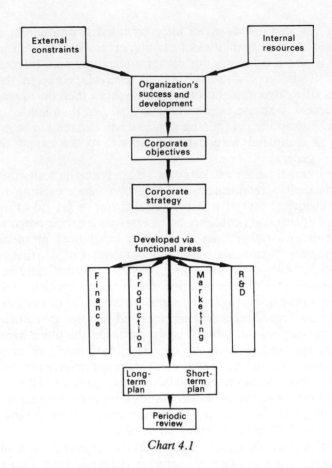

Chart 4.1

the growth in the size of organizations has been accompanied by more formal and comprehensive planning.

To put manpower planning within the company into some kind of perspective, *Chart 4.1* summarizes the main aspects of the corporate planning process. However, as Newton points out (in Margerison and Ashton, 1974), the link between the two is not always strong and they are often treated virtually as separate systems. The effect of this on the efficiency of personnel management need not be continuously disadvantageous but may be quite serious at particular times. As Donald points out: 'Initially, manpower planning may be accepted as a personnel management aid when it would be more appropriately considered on the basis of the whole business, i.e. considering whether it will be profitable to introduce manpower planning.'[5]

Manpower planning results broadly from the need to meet possible future surpluses and shortage of labour and attempts to reduce inefficiencies in the utilization of human resources. It therefore attempts to

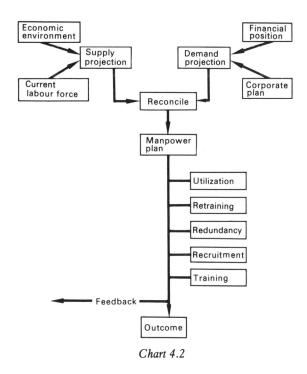

Chart 4.2

forecast the types and quantities of labour required and estimates the extent to which these needs can be met. As a result, it then becomes possible to determine policies in respect of recruitment, redundancy, training and retraining which are needed to achieve the overall corporate plan. The manpower planning process is summarized in *Chart 4.2.*

All manpower policies within the organization need to be co-ordinated in relation to the corporate plan and differences between projected manpower supply and demand reconciled. As Bell (1974) points out, the overall objectives of the organization stand the best chance of being attained when they have been translated into personnel activities so that the right person is fitted into the right job at the right time. However, this does not imply a once-for-all planning operation which, having been completed, can be left alone. In a sense, a manpower plan is never completed, because it will need continuous modification, as when, for example, changes occur in the external environment and in corporate aims and objectives. Again, changes may take place in the effective current labour force because of variations in its utilization (through, for instance, improvements in productivity or turnover) which will affect the supply projection and, hence, the extent of difference between future manpower needs and availability. Thus, the individual components of the plan cannot be seen in isolation, and if changes subsequently occur in only one section, it will often be necessary to trace through and estimate the extent of any knock-on effects. Thus, Wild and Lowes (1977) emphasize that to ensure consistent implementation of personnel policy it is necessary to maintain close links between all departmental managers and the personnel section.

On the supply side, account will need to be taken of both internal and external labour availability. Supply from inside the organization will depend on such factors as wastage (e.g. through voluntary quits, retirement, retraining), changes in productivity and working hours, etc., and on the extent and type of internal labour markets. External supply will depend on changes in either or both local and national labour markets. In the former case, the expansion and contraction of competitions in the labour market may be important in addition to relative financial and non-financial job aspects. For management and more highly qualified manpower recruitment is likely to be from the national market, where population trends, government education policies, etc., may be of relevance. (Some relevant aspects here were discussed in Chapter 1.) Government macro-economic policies are also likely to have an impact at both local and national levels, because they affect the recruitment situation both directly and indirectly. In the former case, if expansionary fiscal and monetary policies are being followed, there will be a general increase in the demand for labour which will make recruitment that much more difficult. In the latter case, the general expansion (or contraction) of aggregate demand will be felt by one's own organization, with a consequent increase (or decrease) in labour demand and, other things being equal, a larger reconciliation item to deal with as part of the plan.

As we have seen previously, the supply of some types of manpower within the organization can be increased through retraining pro- grammes. This is particularly useful if such activity can be seen as part of a development programme or if performance in the job to which supply is being increased will benefit by being filled with a person who has an intimate knowledge of the organization. Retraining may also provide an alternative to redundancy and may become necessary as a result of technological change which destroys some skills while creating a demand for others or significantly alters the content of jobs.

Internal transfers, in addition to quits, retirements and general expansion, also give rise to the need for hiring new recruits. Where people with given types of general skills (in Becker's, 1964, terminology) are required, the organization has two broad alternatives: either it can take on unskilled people and provide the necessary training or it can hire people who already possess the required skill. Which option is chosen will depend on relative costs and benefits, which may be different at different times. For example, in a period of generally low demand hiring ready skilled labour may be an attractive proposition. But when demand is already high, it may be possible to increase the supply of skilled labour only by attracting it from other firms by offering higher wages which are then exceeded by competitors as a situation of wage drift develops. It may then be preferable to hire, say, unskilled school-leavers who can be put through a training programme.

Particularly in cases where training is lengthy, the need for planning future manpower requirements is underlined, since it may take several years to increase supply. Thus, while apprentices do make useful contributions to output during their period of training, it takes between 4 and 5 years to produce a formally qualified craftsman and learning on the job is likely to continue long after this time. However, the extent to which long-term manpower planning can be undertaken will be determined initially by the corporate planning period. Even if this extends over, say, a 5 year period, it is likely that the later stages of the plan will become less detailed and this will have implications for the manpower plan. While the short-term plan (with a horizon of perhaps 1–2 years) may attach numbers to recruitment, training and other intended actions, the long-term plan is likely to be more strategic and indicative in nature.

In general, the difficulties and inaccuracies attached to manpower planning (as to most other forms of planning) increase with the time horizon of the plan. In some cases the problems may originate with people in other areas of management who believe manpower planning to be impossible or unnecessary or whose attitude is at best one of scepticism. Difficulties with greater substance may arise when forecasts of economic and other changes have to be made or if the organization is located within a relatively volatile industry. In the latter case, for example, the accelerator theory of investment tells us that changes in demand will, in general, be greater in the capital goods industry than in the consumer goods industry. Or the industry may depend for its survival on a fast rate of technical change, as, for example, in the chemical industry. Alternatively, the industry may be heavily affected by political decisions. Other problems may arise because the requisite data for establishing dependable relationships for forecasting are not available – either from within or outside the organization. Despite these difficulties, however, there is as much need to plan in respect of manpower as of other resources, and many of the problems encountered are not fundamentally different in nature from those encountered in other planning operations.

Through manpower planning, however formal or informal it may be, the organization determines its future human resource needs. The potential employee then first comes into contact with the organization as a result of the recruitment and selection processes which follow as a consequence of the planning operation. Having accepted an offer of employment, the individual subsequently finds himself within the organization, and it is to this situation that we turn in the next chapter.

Questions

1. List the major stages attached to the hiring process.
2. Suggest an alternative grading system to those proposed by Rodger and Fraser.
3. Describe and justify the type of interview situation you would arrange for hiring a new: (a) electrician, (b) sales manager.
4. Why do organizations evolve internal labour markets?
5. Taking into account their effects on movements both within and between organizations, discuss the advantages and disadvantages of internal labour markets.
6. Define manpower planning.
7. Is manpower planning an activity which can be recommended to organizations? Justify your views.
8. Discuss the alternatives to manpower planning and their practical implications.
9. 'Training is an alternative to manpower planning.' Discuss.

Notes

[1] Spence distinguishes between 'signals', which are productivity-related attributes capable of being manipulated by the individual (e.g. educational attainment), and 'indices', which are given and unalterable (e.g. race, sex, age).
[2] Doeringer and Piore (1971), page 14.
[3] See Chapter 3 for a brief summary of Becker's arguments.
[4] Doeringer and Piore also apply their analysis to craft internal labour markets, which are not of direct interest here.
[5] Margerison and Ashton (1974), Chapter 2, page 15.

References

Armstrong, M. (1977). *A Handbook of Personnel Management Practice*, Kogan Page, London

Arrow, K. (1973). 'Education as a filter', *Journal of Public Economics*, 2

Becker, G. (1964). 'Human capital. A theoretical and empirical investigation with special reference to education', National Bureau for Economic Research

Bell, D.J. (1974). *Planning Corporate Manpower*, Longmans, London

Doeringer, P.B. and Piore, M.J. (1971). *Internal Labour Markets and Manpower Analysis*, Heath, Lexington

Dunlop, John T. (1966). 'Job vacancy measures and economic analysis', in *The Measurement and Interpretation of Job Vacancies: A Conference Report*, National Bureau for Economic Research, New York

Graham, H.T. (1974). *Human Resource Management*, Macdonald and Evans, London

Haspel, A.E. (1978). 'The questionable role of higher education as an occupational screening device', *Higher Education*, 7

Kerr, C. (1954). 'The balkanization of labour mobility', in Bakke, E.W. *et al.* (Eds), *Labour Mobility and Economic Opportunity*, Technology Press of MIT, Cambridge, Mass.

Layard, R. and Psacharopoulos, G. (1974). 'The screening hypothesis and the returns to education', *Journal of Political Economy*, September/October

Margerison, C. and Ashton, D. (Eds) (1974). *Planning for Human Resources*, Longmans, London

Spence, M. (1973). 'Job market signaling', *Quarterly Journal of Economics*, **87**

Taubman, P.J. and Wales, T.J. (1973). 'Higher education, mental ability and screening', *Journal of Political Economy*, January/February

Wild, R. and Lowes, B. (1977). *The Principles of Modern Management*, Holt, Rinehart and Winston, New York

Wolpin, P. (1977). 'Education and screening', *American Economic Review*, **65**, No. 5

Chapter 5

The individual in the organization[1]

5.1 Introduction

As members of organizations, we all develop an understanding of what organizational life is like, why organizations function the way they do, what makes a good supervisor, what is a 'cushy number', etc. Behind such understanding lurk a number of often implicit assumptions about the nature of man and the factors that influence his behaviour. For example, it is commonly held that strict supervision of the workforce is an unavoidable feature of organizational life. This supposition is under-pinned by the belief that the worker is basically indolent, untrustworthy and incapable of self-direction and control. Assumptions such as these are consequential, for they influence the way in which work is designed, allocated, controlled, performed and rewarded.

The adoption of a social scientific perspective facilitates the formal consideration of assumptions such as these and helps us to distinguish more clearly between the necessary and the contingent features of organizational life. In short, the adoption of a social science perspective will go some way in enabling us to grasp an understanding of the forces that shape the behaviour of the individual in an organization.

There is no unified body of knowledge that we could point to and call social science; rather the social sciences represent a collection of different viewpoints or perspectives. It is important to gain some appreciation of these perspectives and their differences, for they have influenced the way in which behaviour in organizations has been studied. Thus, we observe that in adopting one perspective we are necessarily ignoring others – e.g. to view individual behaviour as merely reflecting the 'script' that the organization provides is to ignore the ways in which individuals actually construct and manage their behaviour. In Chapter 4 we restricted our analysis to a consideration of individuals as a resource in the internal labour market. In this chapter we shall focus on the behaviour of individuals in organizations in terms of four distinct perspectives: individual psychology, social psychology, social systems and social action (see *Figure 5.1*). After outlining their distinctive features, we shall select a number of key aspects of behaviour in organizations for more

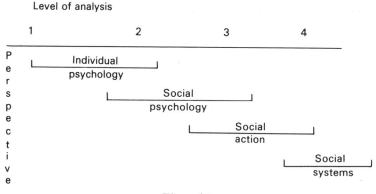

Figure 5.1

detailed consideration. Finally (in the light of the foregoing discussion), we shall consider a number of different approaches to the design of organizations.

5.2 Approaches to organization design

5.2.1 Perspectives in social science

(1) *Individual psychology*
   This perspective focuses on psychological processes such as conditioning, perception and motivation, which are assumed to reside in the individual, in terms of general laws of functioning. Thus, in relation to motivation, psychologists have been concerned with formulating general principles of motivation which operate in every individual, independent of context.

(2) *Social psychology*
   Social psychologists focus on the processes through which individuals influence one another's behaviour. They emphasize the importance of considering the social context in which an individual is situated – e.g. the ways in which membership of a group affects an individual's behaviour.

(3) *Sociology*
   Sociologists also study man in his social context. In pursuing this interest they have characteristically followed two distinct paths, one emphasizing the role of contextual factors in constraining man's behaviour (social systems), and the other highlighting the processes

through which man organizes his activities and thereby 'makes' society (social action perspective).

The division of labour among the social sciences is by no means clear-cut and at the margins it is becoming increasingly difficult to separate one from another. We can, however, distinguish four relatively different levels of analytical interest which roughly correspond to the main divisions of labour between the social sciences.

(1) The individual.

(2) The individual as a group member.

(3) The individual as occupying a position within a specific organization.

(4) The organization as being composed of a collection of roles which individuals perform.

Both psychologists and social psychologists have in the main developed a piecemeal approach to the study of behaviour in organizations focusing on more general features of individual behaviour found in organizations – e.g. motivation, leadership and decision-making. Sociologists, however, in addition to focusing on particular topics such as power, control and organization structure, have sought to develop a number of comprehensive frameworks for examining behaviour in organizations.

Before considering some key foci of concern, we shall briefly examine two influential examples of this tradition.

5.2.2 Social system[2]

This approach comes in many forms but its basic features are as follows:

(1) Organizations 'viewed' as structured bodies designed to achieve specific goals. Emphasis on closeness of 'fit' between what the organization requires of an individual and his actual performance.

(2) Focus on the interrelationship between the constituent parts of the organization (e.g. sales and production departments).

(3) At its core is the idea that a social system exists within an environment. The organization is thus an open system both receiving from and contributing to its environment (see *Figure 5.2*). This relationship is monitored and controlled by a feedback mechanism which operates to keep the organization on course after the manner of a thermostat.

A simple system has the following structure (e.g. production system):

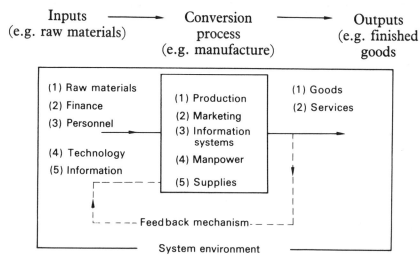

Figure 5.2 Open systems model of industrial organization

Inputs undergo some process of transformation to produce outputs, and the effects of the outputs are monitored in order to modify future inputs. For example, as Appendix 3.1 (pages 78–81) suggests, different types of product markets (e.g. competitive, monopolistic) modify the system environment and produce different information through the feedback mechanism.

An organizational analyst adopting this framework would probably proceed as follows:

(1) Identify boundaries of system and sub-systems.
(2) Identify and determine the nature of relationships between the various systems and the sub-systems – e.g. production and supplies.
(3) Identify inputs, outputs and conversion process.
(4) Trace the flow of resources through the organization.
(5) Consider how satisfactory a given pattern of relationship is in terms of the 'needs' of the organization as defined by those in control.
(6) Consider how effective (again as defined by those in control) the organization is in monitoring its environment and the ease with which it can adapt to change.

The virtue of this approach lies in its ability to focus on, and render accessible, the complex network of interrelationships that persists in organizations. The objection lies not so much in what it says as in what it ignores. In viewing the organization as a social system it necessarily ignores other features – for example, the distribution of power within an organization and the possibility that different interest groups may emerge pursuing strategies independent of those prescribed by top management. It also ignores the different identities that individuals bring to organizations and the varying commitment to organizational goals. Finally, there is an unwarranted commitment on the part of the analyst to the managerial point of view to the exclusion of other frames of reference.

While the behaviour of individuals may be seen as a reflection of the organizational rules and prescriptions, it is equally valid to suggest that behaviour in organizations represents the outcome of the interaction of individuals attempting to realize their own 'agendas'. A concern with these aspects is to be found in the social action approach.

5.2.3 Social action approach[3]

This approach seeks to understand organizational life from the point of view of those actively engaged in it rather than take as given the view portrayed by management. It rejects prescription in favour of analysis. It emphasizes the importance of considering the way in which individual members interpret particular situations, for just as organizations or analysts have developed different perspectives for analysing organizations, so members themselves can and do see organizational life in different ways. So, if we want to understand the behaviour of individuals, we must take into account the significance that any particular event or situation has for them. We cannot assume, as those adopting a social systems perspective do, that all individuals will share the same interests and values.

An organizational analyst adopting this approach would examine the following interrelated areas:

(1) The way in which work is organized, allocated and performed, the typical patterns of behaviour that members expect of one another and the extent to which these expectations are shared or conflicting.
(2) The characteristic pattern of members' involvement, the varying degrees of commitment to the organization.
(3) The typical strategies that members use to achieve their interests – e.g. the strategies of professional associations as compared with trade unions (see Chapter 6 on pressure groups).
(4) The relative capacity of members to impose their scale of relevances, interests and values on others.
(5) The source of changes in the patterns of involvement and commitment of members.

Instead of assuming that the behaviour of individuals in an organization represents the unthinking acceptance of the 'script' provided for them by those who draw up the rules, this approach allows us to establish the degrees of commitment to the rules and the ways in which members interpret and use them. It emphasizes the inherently political nature of behaviour in organizations.

The virtue of this kind of approach is that it can take into account both those forces 'inside' the individual and those present in the work situation, and thus focus on individual differences, personal variability and differences in work situations.

The discussion will now be directed to a consideration of some of the key aspects of the interrelationship between individuals in organizations.

5.3 Some key aspects of interplanning

5.3.1 Motivation

The study of motivation is concerned with examining the internal mechanism which governs choice among alternative courses of action – the internal decision-making process. Vroom (1964) has defined motivation as 'the process governing choices made by persons or lower organisms among alternative forms of voluntary activity'. In this subsection we shall consider the basic elements of this process.

One of the most influential theories of motivation is that developed by A. Maslow. He argues that man has a set of universal needs arranged in a predetermined hierarchic order (see *Figure 5.3*) such that only those

5 Individual's needs for fulfilling one's own potential.
4 Individual's need for self respect and the respect of others.
3 Individual's need for friendship and affection.
2 Individual's need for security.
1 Individual's need for life support systems — food, water, air and sleep.

Figure 5.3 Maslow's hierarchy of needs

needs which remain unsatisfied actually motivate behaviour – 'a satisfied need is not a motivator' (Maslow, 1960). Thus, to paraphrase Maslow, man only lives by bread alone when there is no bread. While the model does provide a basis for a general understanding of the process of motivation, it does not take us very far in accounting for individual differences and personal variability in behaviour. Further, 'studies offer little support for the view that the needs of managers in organisations are arranged in a multi-level hierarchy' (Lawler and Suttle, 1972).

Many of the early writers on motivation assumed that there is 'one best way' to motivate individuals, whether it be the 'carrot and stick' approach developed by F.W. Taylor or emphasis on 'social needs' by the human relations school. But such universalistic accounts completely ignore variability in individual behaviour and the utterly bland fact that the same individual can respond in different ways to the same phenomena at different times. One theory which does recognize variability is that developed by Victor Vroom (1964). Vroom argues that behaviour is situated within a field of differing forces acting on the individual. Three major forces are identified as influencing an individual's behaviour:

(1) The individual's 'wants' (e.g. to earn more money, to be accepted by his workmates).
(2) The perceived relationship between a particular course of action and goal attainment (e.g. relationship between production of 'grommets' and level of wages).
(3) The extent to which an individual believes he can influence that relationship (e.g. if a person believes his individual efforts will have very little impact (on the process leading to goal attainment), he is unlikely to expend more effort).

Individual behaviour, then, depends on the nature of these 'forces' and the attractiveness of a particular goal. According to Vroom's theory, 'people are more likely to do something, the more they think it will lead to results which they want' (Warr and Wall, 1975).

5.3.2 Working in groups

The small group is an important focus of analysis for those wishing to understand the behaviour of the individual in the organization. Individuals, by virtue of their membership of an organization, are involved in some or other small group context, e.g. workshop, administration sections, works committees, etc. A group may be defined as 'any number of people who (1) interact with one another, (2) are psychologically aware of one another, and (3) perceive themselves to be a group' (Schein, 1972). Thus, we shall not here be concerned with mere collections of people who happen to share close physical proximity to one another in a queue or waiting room, or with that mythical entity 'the organization'. The criterion of relevance is that of sustained interaction.

Figure 5.4 represents a framework for analysing behaviour in groups. It shows how characteristic patterns of processes and relationships emerge from and in turn influence the interaction between membership variables (those pertaining to the individual member) and contextual variables (those pertaining to the environment in which the group is enmeshed). These also influence and are influenced by the productivity and satisfaction of the group members.

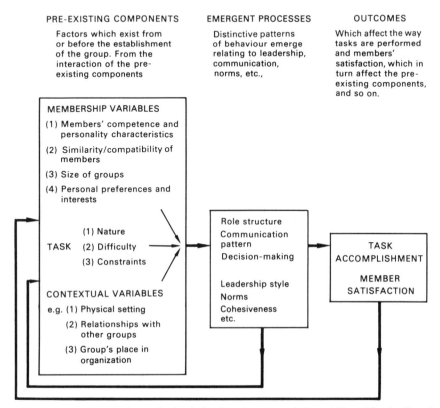

Figure 5.4 Framework for analysing behaviour in groups (adapted from Krech, Crutch-field and Ballachey, 1962)

In the remaining part of this section we shall consider just two of the processes that emerge from the interaction of group members and in turn influence the behaviour of individuals – the formation of group norms and leadership.

Group norms
A norm is a shared standard of behaviour which prescribes what is required of competent group members in terms of performance, attitudes and beliefs. The influence of group norms in determining productivity is well documented in research dating back to the Hawthorne Studies. In the late 1920s and early 1930s Elton Mayo carried out a series of experiments and observations at the Hawthorne plant of the Western

Electric Co., Chicago, USA. In observing the behaviour of one particular group, he found that the members, rather than maximizing their own individual earnings by producing as much as they were able, established a group production norm below that expected by management. The individuals conformed not to the production norms set by management but to those set by the group. Thus, the social pressure of the group clearly had a marked influence on individual behaviour. Indeed, management estimated that they were producing about 12 per cent less than they were physically capable of doing. As previous chapters have indicated, such forces carry strong implications for the organization's hiring and employment level.

Leadership
Early studies of leadership were preoccupied with the search for a generalized set of principles prescribing effective leadership and associated selection criteria. There was a tendency to emphasize either the desirability of a particular constellation of personality characteristics (e.g. extrovert, stable, fair-minded, cool, etc.) or styles of behaviour (e.g. autocratic, democratic, *laissez-faire*). It is worth recording that the position taken with respect to the 'one best way' owed as much to the personal values of the investigator as the research evidence.

As with the study of motivation, there is now a move away from such prescriptions to a treatment of leadership as a process of mutual influence between the leader and the other participant, to a consideration of the relationship between leadership styles and various aspects of the situation.

One major attempt to grapple with this interrelationship is the contingency approach formulated by Fiedler (1967). He argues that the effectiveness of contrasting styles of leadership (forceful task leadership versus relationship-oriented styles) is dependent on the favourability of the situation for the leader (the extent to which the task is clearly defined, the extent of the sanctions available to the leader and the extent to which he has the loyalty and confidence of the group). This approach is particularly useful, for it reminds us that effective leadership depends as much on contextual factors as on an individual's style or personality characteristics.

5.4 Organization structure

Organizations are composed of individuals, but the behaviour of individuals in organizations is not merely the outcome or sum of their own idiosyncrasies or personal preferences. When an individual enters the internal labour market of an organization, his individual preferences are subject to a number of controls which more or less successfully limit his behaviour. While some of these controls may be ignored without fear of sanction, complete disregard for their existence will result in expulsion from the organization. It is from the interaction of members and organizational controls that organization structure is produced. Organization structure refers to the relatively regular and stable patterns of organizational activities and relationships that persist over time. It refers, among other things, to the way in which work is allocated, jobs prescribed and controlled, responsibilities and authority distributed and performance rewarded.

Organizations are structured in various ways: some have many levels of authority with tightly prescribed rules; others are less rigidly controlled, and allow of more discretion in performing one's job. Pugh and Hickson (1973) identify five major dimensions along which structure varies:

(1) The degree to which jobs are specialized – *specialization*.
(2) The degree to which decision-making is centralized at head office – *centralization*.
(3) The degree to which procedures are documented and formalized – *formalization*.
(4) The degree to which procedures are standardized – *standardization*.
(5) The shape of the role structure, the height from the man at the top to the man at the bottom and the area under his control – *configuration*.

They stress the importance of *contextual factors* such as size, technology, ownership, location and market in shaping organization structure. We shall consider one important variable – technology.

The relationship between technology and organization structure has been an important theme in the sociological analysis of organizations. A study by Joan Woodward of 100 firms in south-east Essex, UK, revealed a direct relationship between a number of structural elements – configuration (length of line of command, ratio of managers to total personnel), specialization (nature of relationship between task functions, development, production and marketing) and technology. Her study demonstrated conclusively the futility of the search for a general body of principles applicable to all organizations irrespective of type or context. It is indisputable that the technology of a firm can have an important constraining effect on behaviour in organizations, but a theory which sees technology as determining individual behaviour is demonstrably inadequate. Why does the strike record of the British motor industry contrast so markedly with that of Germany or Japan when the technology is relatively constant?

Although technology sets limits to the way in which work is organized, it does not fully determine it, for as Trist and Bamforth (1951) show, a number of different forms of social organization are possible within the same technological system. Moreover, the 'technological implications' approach ignores the degree of 'strategic choice' open to the manager in organizing production to meet the constraints of a given technology. Child (1973), in developing this notion of 'strategic choice', directs our attention to a crucial feature of organizational life – the operation of an essentially political process in which constraints and opportunities get sifted and evaluated by those in control: the 'dominant coalition'. Thus, any analysis of behaviour in organizations must recognize the differential capacity of individuals to exercise choice with respect to their own standards of relevance and preference. While contextual factors such as technology, size, market, etc., are important constraints on behaviour in organizations, the consequential link in the chain between constraints and performance lies in the differential capacity of individuals and interest groups to set scales of relevance and standards of performance, select strategies and enforce what they consider to be an appropriate structuring of activities (i.e. the asymmetrical distribution of power).

5.5. Role

When an individual joins an organization, he is allocated to a position containing a number of expectations concerning his behaviour and character. This position, whether it be that of machine operator or of sales manager, is further embedded in a matrix of other positions each with its own parcel of expectations, duties, responsibilities and rights. Role theory provides us with an analytical framework for examining this web of expectations. We can use this framework to represent an individual's passage through an organization.

On entering employment an individual is allocated a status – a position in the structure of the organization (e.g. personnel officer). Associated with each status is a role – an expected way of behaving. Thus, we talk of an individual occupying a status and performing a role within an organization structure (i.e. a collection of roles ordered in a specific and predetermined way). Roles vary in terms of their specificity and discretion. Specificity refers to the degree to which the role is pre-programmed[4]. Thus, we may observe that some organization roles (e.g. blue collar workers) are narrowly defined with detailed specifications regarding performance, while others (e.g. executives) have only broad guidelines. Discretion refers to the degree of choice open to an individual in complying with role specifications. The degree of discretion usually increases as one moves up through the role structure.

An individual through occupying a particular position is necessarily involved with a complement of other roles. Thus, a lecturer is necessarily involved with students, other lecturers and administrative staff. R. Merton refers to this complement of role relationships as a role set. This collecting device can be particularly useful in developing training schemes, in that it identifies the range and type of relationships that an individual might be expected to be involved in on occupying a particular position in the organization (e.g. in identifying the range of skills required of an industrial relations negotiator) and thus training requirements. This form of analysis also aids the identification of potential areas or sources of conflict or strain. Conflict may arise from conflicting role expectations. The classic case here is the role of the foreman, often referrred to as the 'man in the middle'. The operatives expect him to represent their interests, while management rely on him to carry out their directives. Thus, we can identify potential sources of conflict prior to an individual occupying a role. Conflict may also arise between an individual and his role (e.g. where an individual is required by virtue of his position to sack the son of a close friend or take action contrary to his own code of ethics).

Finally, a role may have built into it an element of ambiguity which may result in some uncertainty as to what the task actually entails. This uncertainty may be on the part of the role occupant or members of his role set.

Role analysis provides a useful framework for examining relationships in organizations; it allows us to identify potential areas of difficulty and conflict. We must, however, be aware of its limitations – e.g. what do we mean by 'expectations'? (Dahrendorf distinguishes at least three levels of compulsion – 'must', 'should' and 'can'.) And to whose expectations does the role refer? Moreover, an individual's attachment to the managerial system of expectations may be less than complete. Goffman (1959) shows that while some individuals may identify with a role and see it as a sincere expression of themselves, others may create a distance between their performance and their true selves. We can all think of individuals who take their role more seriously than others. The source of these different types of commitment is to be found (as we have already seen) in the orientation that members hold with respect to their work and the way in which their expectations are confirmed or contradicted in the flow of organizational life.

5.6 Power and control

Power and control lie at the very heart of organizational life, where individuals coalesce around different axes of interest and commitment. The processes through which individuals secure their interests are as various as the ingenuity of man. They vary from the coercive threat of outright physical violence and the utilitarian exchange of material goods in return for compliance, to the insidious use of symbols such as loyalty, service, 'the good of the firm' and 'the national interest'. These aspects are discussed more fully in Chapters 6 and 8.

We shall now consider a number of approaches[5] to the design of organizations in the light of the foregoing discussion.

5.7 Approaches to the design of organizations

5.7.1 Scientific management

One of the earliest attempts to formulate a formal, explicit approach to organizational design was developed by F.W. Taylor (1856–1917) with his principles of scientific management. Taylor was an engineer by training and this is directly reflected in his approach to the organization of work, which focuses on the basic physical activities involved in production. Scientific management involves the development of a special-purpose machine (the 'first-class' worker) out of a general machine (man). 'The principal objective of management', he states, 'should be to secure the maximum prosperity for the employer, coupled with the maximum prosperity of each employee.' He did add, however, that in the interests of the worker a 'wage ceiling' should be applied, since if workers 'got rich too quickly', dissipation, drunkenness and absenteeism would increase.

The principles of a 'scientific' approach to management are:

(1) The development of a true science of work – finding the 'one best way' to perform a task.
(2) The scientific selection and progressive development of the worker – selecting the right man and training him to be a 'first-class man'.
(3) The bringing together of the science of work and scientifically selected and trained men.
(4) The constant and intimate co-operation of management and men – separation of planning from operating management and workers.

The task of management is to find the 'one best way' to perform an activity using specialized experts to establish detailed job instructions, time, price and quality standards, and to closely control the flow of work and performance. The co-operation of the worker is to be secured through directly linking cash incentives to the level of individual performances.

The whole edifice is based on a particular 'model of man' – i.e. Economic Man. The main elements of this view of man have been captured by McGregor (1960) in his Theory X.

(1) 'The average human being has an inherent dislike of work and will avoid it if he can.
(2) 'Because of this human characteristic of dislike of work, most people must be coerced, controlled, directed, threatened with punishment to get them to put forth adequate effort toward the achievement of organisational objectives.
(3) 'The average human being prefers to be directed, wishes to avoid responsibility, has relatively little ambition, wants security above all.'

It follows from this model that management must formulate precise duties for each job, provide the appropriate working conditions, specify the flow and pace of work, and closely supervise its performance.

These ideas aroused a good deal of controversy at the time, being the subject of a House of Representatives Special Committee. The faults of this approach are well documented and, it is hoped, readily apparent in the light of the foregoing discussion; they arise mainly out of an inadequate understanding of human behaviour. The Hawthorne Studies were instrumental in demonstrating these inadequacies.

5.7.2 Human relations school

This approach developed out of a series of studies (1924–1926, 1927–1932) conducted at the Hawthorne plant of the Western Electric Co., Chicago, USA, by Elton Mayo and a research team from Harvard University. The aim of the study was to examine the effect of changes in physical and working conditions on output, fatigue, accidents and labour turnover. These interests were in keeping with the teachings of F.W. Taylor. However, subsequent investigations brought into question the view that there was a direct relationship between physical working conditions and production and led the investigators to develop an emphasis on social relationships at work. The model of man that emerged from these studies was a social one, not that of a lone wolf bent on maximizing his economic potential but that of someone who desired to belong to a group, to be liked. Thus, group pressure was seen as being more consequential in influencing productivity than economic incentives.

In summary the major points are:

(1) Production is not determined solely by physiological capacity but is significantly influenced by social norms.
(2) Social relationships are important to people.

(3) Workers do not always act as individuals but sometimes as members of a group.
(4) The highest degree of specialization does not necessarily lead to the most efficient form of organization.

This work has led to an emphasis in organizational design on the role of communications and participative styles of leadership and the manner in which organizational controls are used by management, rather than to a fundamental modification of the way in which work is organized.

In many ways the scientific management and human relations schools are in conflict, starting from fundamentally different conceptions of the nature of man. However, the two schools do have two (and for our purposes, consequential) elements in common.

(1) A concern with the development of a set of generalized principles and techniques applicable to all organizations irrespective of composition or context.
(2) An *a priori* and unwarranted assumption that there is no serious or fundamental conflict of interest between management's quest for efficiency (as defined by the dominant coalition) and the interests of individual members and different pressure groups (see Chapters 6 and 7).

These elements are consequential, since, in ignoring both the particular interrelationship that persists between the internal and external environments of an organization and the possibility that individuals may be less than fully committed to the goals of the organization, Taylor and Mayo forego the possibility of grasping the realities of organizational life and thus their prescriptions are from the outset fatally flawed.

5.7.3 Bureaucracy

These criticisms apply with equal force to theories of bureaucratic management and formal organization.

The theoretical model of bureaucracy was developed by the German socialist Max Weber (1864–1920). We must appreciate that Weber's discussion of bureaucracy was largely theoretical and that he was not much interested in laying down principles governing the organization of work. He did believe, however, that any organization which in practice was found to resemble the model ('pure type') that he had delineated would be efficient – a prospect he dreaded.

The main characteristics of the model are:

(1) Legal rules
(2) Salaried administration.
(3) Specialization of function.
(4) Authority of office.
(5) The keeping of written records and documents.

This model is reflected in the work of Fayer (1841–1926) and Urwick (1891–   ). It is these writers who have advocated its virtues and developed Weber's 'pure type' into theories of bureaucratic management and formal organization. However, as intimated earlier, the approach is deeply flawed.

Organizations have to cope with contingencies arising from the external environment, technology, scale, etc. – factors which vary with each organization. Thus, as Lawrence and Lorsch and Burns and Stalker demonstrate, the effectiveness of a particular organizational design such as bureaucratic management depends on the particular context in which an organization is placed. While the bureaucratic management approach is relatively effective in a stable environment, it is poorly equipped to deal with a rapidly changing environment, where a more informal, 'network' type of design would appear to be more appropriate (Burns and Stalker, 1961). Secondly, it cannot be assumed that members are perfectly motivated to achieving the organizational goals or that they will only use the rules in the way intended by those who designed the organization. Crozier (1966) and Gouldner (1954) document one important form of unanticipated usage – working to rule. Rules by their very nature define not only what is not allowed, but also the minimum standard of performance that an individual can legitimately get away with. Working to rule has proved an extremely useful form of social control for workers.

Studies by psychologists such as C. Argynis and sociologists such as R. Merton document a host of unanticipated consequences that working in this type of organization may have on individual behaviour – for example, instilling mistrust and lack of competence, stifling personal growth and developing conformity and overadherence to regulation.

5.7.4 Contingency theory

One approach that has come to grips with some of these shortcomings is contingency theory. Contingency theory is more concerned with developing 'horses for courses' than wholesale panaceas. The emphasis is on designing structures to suit the particular operational requirements of a company instead of invoking universal precepts.

This approach was developed by Paul Lawrence and Jay Lorsch in their book *Organisation and Environment* (1967), which reports the results of an empirical study. Their study, like that of Woodward, challenged the tenets of a universalistic approach, arguing instead that different ways of organizing work were appropriate for different situations. The approach is founded on an open-systems view of organizations: 'Any work organisation is an open system consisting of the patterned activities of a number of individuals and engaging in transactions with the surrounding environment' (Lawrence and Lorsch, 1969).

Lawrence and Lorsch argue that the fundamental problem of any organization lies in resolving the demand for differentiation, which flows from the increase in scale, with the 'need' for integration if the system is to function as a whole. They suggest that the most effective organizations are those which succeed in balancing the level of specialization and co-ordination to meet the demands of the environment.

Thus, in a diverse and dynamic field such as the plastics industry effective organizations have to be highly differentiated and highly integrated. In a more stable and less diverse environment, such as the container industry, effective organizations do not have to be so differentiated but they must still achieve a high degree of integration.

Contingency theory is more a loosely knit collection of propositions than a tight coherent body of theory. This is reflected in its rather piecemeal approach to organizational analysis. T. Lipton (1971) has drawn out the main elements.

(A)   Questions aimed at assessing the degree of fit between the pattern of differentiation with the organization and the environment. Burrell and Morgan (1979) call this the Congruence Hypothesis, which requires that all sub-systems be congruent with environmental factors.

    (1) Determine performance criteria – e.g. sales turnover, return on dividend capital, percentage of revenue invested.

    (2) Identify and analyse the environment – e.g. technical, economic, market.

    (3) Measure each sub-environment – e.g. degree of diversity, degree of irregularity and rate of change.

    (4) Map the organization–environment interface – those individuals or sub-units who are directly engaged in managing this boundary – e.g. marketing or supplies.

    (5) Characterize the nature of each sub-unit – e.g. degree of flexibility, self-direction, adaptability to change.

(B)   Questions aimed at discovering what mechanisms exist for integrating the sub-units. Burrell and Morgan call this the Integration Hypothesis, which requires the setting up of an appropriate mechanism for co-ordinating the activities of the various sub-units.

(6) Determine mechanism and methods used to integrate the activities of sub-units and individuals – patterns of formal authority and channels of communication.

(7) Evaluate the effectiveness of the integrating mechanism in co-ordinating the work of the various sub-units.

(C) (8) Design a new pattern for differentiation–integration.

(D) (9) Draw up schedule for change.

The contingency approach unquestionably represents an advance in our understanding of the individual in the organization. Its shortcomings arise from its overreliance on a particular model of organizational functioning – i.e. the open-system model. In electing to view organizations in this way it necessarily ignores the political processes through which performance standards are set, particular strategies selected and courses of action enforced. The writings are punctuated by an implicit managerial bias. Thus, the contingency theorists speak of 'organizational goals' and 'organizational problems' as if these were shared by all participants. They assume that the selection of different models of control is merely a technical problem (ensuring that all sub-systems are congruent with environmental factors and have the right degree of integration) rather than a stage in the conflicting relationship in their organizations. Assumptions such as these not only are ill-founded, but also rob contingency theory of much of its analytical power.

As we saw in Sub-section 5.3.2, the individual in the organization may belong to various groups within it, and the existence of pressure groups was referred to in Sub-section 5.7.2. An analysis of this latter type of group is the subject of the next chapter.

Questions

1. (a) Define what social scientists mean by the term 'social system'.
   (b) Construct a social systems model of your present course.
   (c) What theoretical and practical problems are there in employing this form of analysis?
2. Using one seminar group of which you are a member as the basis for your analysis, examine how (a) group membership influences individual behaviour, and (b) the group links the individual to the rest of the college.
3. 'Leaders are born not made.' Discuss with reference to the role of managers.

4. What factors influence the structure of organizations?
5. Using the framework of role analysis, examine the role of a foreman.
6. 'There is a body of general principles and techniques applicable to all organizations.' Critically examine this statement.
7. Consider the view that bureaucracy is the most efficient form of organization.

Notes

[1] Grusky and Miller's book of readings (1969) is an invaluable source for many of the approaches and theories discussed in this chapter.
[2] For a more detailed account see Kost, F.E. and Rosenzweig, J.E., *Organisations and Management – A Systems Approach*, McGraw-Hill, New York.
[3] See Silverman, J. (1970).
[4] This use of the term 'specificity' should not, of course, be confused with its use in relation to training.
[5] For a more detailed account of individual theorists see Pugh *et al.* (1971).

References

Burns, T. and Stalker, G.M. (1961). *The Management of Innovation*, Tavistock, London
Burrell, G. and Morgan, G. (1979). *Sociological Paradigms and Organisational Analysis*, HEB
Child, J. (1973). 'Organisational structure, environment and performance: the role of strategic choice', in Salaman and Thompson (1973)
Crozier, M. (1964). *The Bureaucratic Phenomenon*, Tavistock, London
Fiedler, F.E. (1967). *A Theory of Leadership Effectiveness*, McGraw-Hill, New York
Goffman, E. (1959). *The Presentation of Self in Everyday Life*, Doubleday, New York
Gouldner, A.W. (1954). *Patterns of Industrial Bureaucracy*, Free Press, New York
Grusky, O. and Miller, G.A. (1979). *The Sociology of Organisations: Basic Studies*, Free Press, New York
Krech, D., Crutchfield, R.S. and Ballachey, E.L. (1967). *Individual in Society*, McGraw-Hill, New York
Lawler, E.E. and Suttle, J.L. (1972). 'A causal correlation test of the need hierarchy concept', *Organisational Behaviour and Human Performance*, 7, 265–287
Lawrence, P.R. and Lorsch, J.W. (1967). *Organisation and Environment*, Harvard University Press
Lawrence, P.R. and Lorsch, J.W. (1969). *Developing Organisations: Diagnosis and Action*, Addison-Wesley, Reading, Mass.
Lupton, T. (1971). *Management and The Social Sciences*, Penguin, Harmondsworth
McGregor, D. (1960). *The Human Side of Enterprise*, McGraw-Hill, New York
Maslow, A.H. (1960). 'A theory of human motivation', in Heckman, I.L. and Huneryeger, S. (Eds), *Human Relations in Management*, South Western Publishing
Pugh, D.S. *et al.* (1971). *Writers on Organisations*, Penguin, Harmondsworth
Pugh, D.S. and Hickson, D.J. (1973). 'The comparative study of organisations', in Salaman and Thompson (1973)

Salaman, G. and Thompson, K. (1973). *People and Organisations*, Longmans, London
Schein, E.H. (1972). *Organisational Psychology*, Prentice-Hall, Englewood Cliffs, N.J.
Silverman, J. (1970). *The Theory of Organisations*, HEB
Taylor, F.W. (1947). *Scientific Management*, Harper and Row, New York
Trist, E.A. and Bamforth, K.W. (1951). 'Some special and psychological consequences of the longwall method of coal getting', *Human Relations*, **4**, No. 1, 6–24, 37–38
Vroom, V.H. (1964). *Work and Motivation*, Wiley, New York
Warr, P. and Wall, T. (1975). *Work and Well-Being*, Penguin, Harmondsworth
Woodward, J. (1965). *Industrial Organisations, Theory and Practice*, Oxford University Press

Further reading

Glen, F. (1975). *The Social Psychology of Organisations*, Methuen, London
Handy, C. (1976). *Understanding Organisations*, Penguin, Harmondsworth
Parker, S.R. *et al.* (1977). *The Sociology of Industry*, Allen and Unwin, London
Rocthlisberger, F.J. and Dickson, W.J. (1939). *Management and the Worker*, Harvard University Press
Rose, M. (1975). *Industrial Behaviour: Theoretical Developments since Taylor*, Penguin, Harmondsworth
Salaman, G. (1979). *Work Organisations*, Longmans, London
Sofer, C. (1972). *Organisations in Theory and Practice*, HEB, London

Chapter 6

Pressure groups and work organizations

6.1 Introduction

As people work in and experience organizations, so they are likely to observe or engage in political behaviour. In fact, it may not be possible fully to understand the behaviour of particular groups in an organization without knowledge of the power struggles which are occurring. Individuals may experience political behaviour through membership of a pressure group, such as a trade union; or individuals may observe groups which seek to achieve goals by gaining influence over other groups or departments within the organization. The study of pressure groups is concerned with understanding the ways in which groups seek their goals, by influencing and making demands on those in authority. Pressure groups are normally distinguished from political parties in that they do not themselves seek to hold those positions of authority (Kimber and Richardson, 1974). The study of pressure groups is a particular approach to the study of political behaviour. The early part of this chapter therefore considers the nature and importance of political behaviour. It discusses the concepts of influence, power and authority before, in the latter part, discussing pressure groups and the behaviour of pressure groups.

6.2 The nature of political behaviour

One should not regard political behaviour as the sole prerogative of governments and parties. Political behaviour is far more widespread. It is important to stress that political behaviour involves relationships between people or groups. Political aspects are part of man's wider behaviour as a whole, and it is possible to consider the political dimensions of behaviour wherever they occur. Thus, one can study political behaviour within one organization, between organizations, within society or between societies. Many writers on politics are concerned with society as a whole and care must be exercised in applying their work to organizations. In Chapter 7 we shall be considering the part power and conflict play in changing society. Here we are concerned with work organizations.

There are many different definitions of political behaviour. Max Weber (1947) stressed territorial claims, while others have focused on the universality of political behaviour, or group processes. H. Lasswell and A. Kaplan (1950) were more concerned about relationships when they wrote: 'Political Science, as an empirical enquiry, is the study of the shaping and sharing of power.' All definitions seem to suggest that political behaviour is in some way concerned with influence, power and authority. These three concepts are closely related to one another and different writers have their own ways of linking them. Although all three forms of behaviour often occur simultaneously, a consideration of each one separately may help our understanding.

6.3 Influence, power and authority

6.3.1 Influence

Influence is the process of changing behaviour. R. Dahl (1976, page 30) says: 'Influence is a relation among actors such that the wants, desires, preferences, or intentions of one or more actors affect the actions, or predispositions to act, of one or more other actors.' Influence is an important outcome of behaviour. We may not even be aware that we are influencing people. For example, a parent may be quite unaware of the influence he or she has over his or her child's vocabulary and style of speech. There may be a latent, or what Dahl calls an 'implicit', influence operating in their relationship. On other occasions the parent will manifest the intention of influencing the child's speech by deliberately correcting a phrase. An employee may be implicitly influenced by his boss to attain high standards of work. His boss may only occasionally manifestly attempt to improve the employee's work standards.

Dahl mentions (1) trained control, (2) persuasion and (3) inducement as three different means of influence:

(1) *Trained control.* Through socialization people internalize appropriate standards of behaviour. Education and training processes seek to teach people acceptable standards and methods of behaviour.
(2) *Persuasion* frequently takes place by communicating the advantages and disadvantages of a situation. Sometimes persuasion is achieved by open and rational methods – e.g. one persuades people to use protective clothing in dangerous situations by explaining that it is for their own protection and well-being. At other times persuasion may be manipulative and deliberately deceptive – e.g. an employee may deceive his boss about the time of a dental appointment in order to have more time free from work.

(3) *Inducement* involves the use of rewards or sanctions to change behaviour – e.g. management may offer more pay for better work. The use of power, coercion and physical force are viewed by Dahl as types of inducements.

6.3.2 Power

Power is involved in relationships where an individual group or groups face 'the prospect of severe sanctions for non-compliance' (Dahl, 1976) from another individual, group or groups, for not agreeing to its demands. This definition emphasizes that power is relationships between people. It is also possible to talk about the power people exercise over things – e.g. power over technology, machinery or 'the elements'. If we wish to use 'power' in this broader way, Bertrand Russell's (1938) definition of power as the 'production of intended effects' is useful. Here we are concerned with power as a particular type of relationship between groups and individuals.

Trade unions and industrial companies often seek to exercise power over each other. For example, if a trade union threatens a strike, unless the company will pay higher wages, and a strike at that time will severely affect the company's profits, the trade union can be said to be using its power over the management. Management may know that its employees cannot afford to strike for long and may use its power in the threat of loss of wages against the members' trade union. However, there are certain aspects of power which require further discussion.

Coercion and avoiding compliance
Coercion is a form of power, but the use of the term varies in literature on power. For F. Castles (1975), coercion takes place when 'the power exercised on an individual within a social relationship is not accepted as legitimate'. If we accept this definition, 'secondary picketing' would be viewed as coercion by many people. Other writers, such as Dahl, reserve the word 'coercion' to identify situations where groups or individuals are forced to undertake behaviour which makes them considerably worse off. This use of 'coercion' may be likened to 'checkmate' in chess. Whichever way the threatened chess piece moves, he can be 'taken' by his opponent. To return to our previous example of a trade union threatening to strike for higher wages at a time which would severely damage the company's financial position: adopting Dahl's use, the mangement would only be coerced (1) if it truly could not afford to pay higher wages; (2) if it could not afford shorter hours, or better conditions; (3) if a strike would lead to bankruptcy; and (4) if in the event of closure employees were not concerned about losing their jobs.

Under these circumstances management could not use any form of sanctions or rewards, and there would be no way it could move to avoid severe damage to its interests.

Power relationships involve dependency. A group which changes its behaviour and responds is dependent on the group which initiated or controlled its change of behaviour. When, for example, the government introduced legislation on new safety standards and firms responded by changing in the required way, one could regard the firms' behaviour as dependent on the government. The process of responding is known as compliance.

Power relationships often involve recipients in choosing between a range of responses. If one's boss says 'I want your report by next Tuesday or else!' one has a choice of responses. One can completely ignore the instruction, and take one's punishment in the form of his wrath and maybe loss of promotion. One may partially comply by producing an incomplete report, in the hope of improving the situation. One may choose a particular manner of compliance which may range from humility and apology on the one hand, to belligerence and rudeness on the other. If one responds to the boss's demands, one forms a dependent or power relationship, and one can be said to have complied.

P. Blau (1964, pages 188–189) suggests four circumstances in which compliance may be avoided. Blau's analysis of power is interesting because it is based on exchange theory, which regards the acquisition of resources and services which others need as a valuable source of power. 'If these resources or services can be supplied to those who must have them, under conditions in which the person cannot exchange another resource or service, then the recipients will become dependent upon the person with the resources or services' (Weissenberg, 1971).

Blau suggests that a recipient group or individual can avoid compliance (1) when the recipient can supply another service or resource in return, or (2) when the recipient can obtain the resources or services elsewhere, or (3) when the recipient can coerce the supplier to furnish the resources or services (NB: Blau follows Dahl's definition of coercion) or (4) when the recipient convinces himself that he can really do without the services or resources to be supplied. Suppose, for example, that company X threatens not to place further orders with company Y if a delivery date is not met. Company Y does not have to comply if (1) it supplies company X with other materials which are in short supply and which company X needs, or (2) company Y can obtain orders from many other companies, or (3) company Y has the means of coercing company X into waiting (e.g. it may have a monopoly of the goods or services, or the means of blackmailing the managing director of company X) or (4) company Y decides it can manage quite well without company X's orders.

Descriptions of power

'Magnitudes' refers to the amounts of power which people have. A managing director may be described as weak, or a trade union leader as very powerful. These are descriptions of power, and in practice they are very difficult to measure.

The 'distribution' of power is a way of describing the amounts of power which are allocated to different groups or individuals within a political system – e.g. a manager may be said to have more power than a worker.

The 'scope' of power is a description of the 'range of abilities within a power relation' (Potter, 1975). To add a 'scope' description to our earlier example, we could say that a manager may have more power than a worker when the worker performs activities in the work situation.

The 'domain' of power is the extent to which one power relationship affects other power relationships. The power which a manager has over a worker may affect the worker's family if, for example, there is a restriction on when the worker can take his holidays.

Types of power

There are many ways of classifying types of power. One useful method, illustrated by C. Handy (1977), is that of French and Raven (1968), who use the following types. 'Positional' power is very similar to authority. It comes from occupying a particular position or status in an organization. For example, a supervisor has certain powers emanating from his status as supervisor which are not dependent on his personal qualities as an individual. Secondly, there is 'reward' power, which in the case of a supervisor may be seen in his ability to offer overtime work. Thirdly, 'coercive' power may come from the supervisor's ability to punish, reprimand or negatively sanction an employee. Fourthly, 'expert' power may come from the supervisor (or another employee) being particularly skilled or able in performing certain skills or tasks. In addition, 'referrent' power may arise where an individual possesses attractive qualities or acts as a major point of reference and identity. Handy (1977) adds a sixth type of power to this list. He sees the power to disrupt as a particular form of power, which he calls 'negative power'.

Individuals may have different types of power and each of their powers will have a different magnitude, scope and domain. The management and workforce of an organization are often perceived to occupy different positions with different reference points and values; and they each have access to different rewards and sanctions. Frequently the power relationships between management and workforce are maintained by institutionalized forms of bargaining and negotiation. Negotiation takes place when representatives of management and workers enter discussions to resolve their differences. In negotiations both sides try to reach a solution to a disagreement that they are both able to accept. Bargaining is the process in which groups use, or threaten to use, their different types of power as sanctions on or rewards for each other's behaviour. Each side, or group, will form an opinion of the relative magnitude, distribution and scope of the other's power, and negotiations will take place from that point. These processes will be developed more fully later in this chapter.

The use of power
Groups and individuals may have different skills in recognizing and using the sources of power, to which they and others have access. They may also have different amounts of motivation to do so. One manager may wish to expand his department or improve his prospects for promotion, while another will see no point in making more work for himself and therefore will not use his power. Some writers (e.g. Handany, 1962) use the concept of opportunity cost to describe this process. A manager may decide not to use his power to expand his department, because he does not want the cost of increased work. He may, however, decide to use his power and develop his existing staff. The choice between using his power to expand the size of his department or developing existing staff may involve an opportunity cost. The use of resources will provide valuable sources of power. Groups and individuals differ in the nature and amount of resources over which they have control. Hence, they differ in the sources of power which are available to them. Wealth, human and physical resources and authority may provide valuable sources of power.

6.3.3 Authority

Authority may be defined as legitimate power or legitimate behaviour. Like power, authority refers to relationships between people. In authority relationships one group or individual confers on another group or individual the right to control behaviour. The conferring of the right to control behaviour on another group emanates from the perception of some common goal or value. For example, I may wish to be cured of my illness and a doctor wants to help me. I give the doctor the right to examine me, diagnose my complaint and recommend a treatment. I then willingly follow the doctor's instructions. Nobody needs to persuade or coerce me into following the doctor's advice, because I regard it as legitimate.

M. Weber studied the different types of authority which can exist in society. This led him to formulate three models (or 'ideal types') of authority. Authority may emanate from the charismatic qualities of a personality. A person's behaviour may be given legitimacy because of extraordinary qualities, which make him attractive to others. Charismatic authority is said to emerge at times of crisis or when there is an unstable social system. Traditional authority rests on 'an established belief in the sanctity of immemorial traditions and the legitimacy of the status of those exercising authority under them' (Weber, 1947). Weber described two types of traditional authority:

(1) Patrimonial authority existed where a ruler had absolute authority and acted like a father figure governing his subjects.
(2) Feudalism consisted of a main leader (or king) and lieutenants (or nobles) who had independent powers of their own (e.g. the right to inherit their own land).

While contemporary organizations may still depend to some extent on charismatic and traditional forms of authority, they do rely heavily on the development of rational-legal authority. For Weber, the development of rational-legal authority was a prerequisite for the development of bureaucracy, and bureaucracy was a means to the rationalization of life. Rational-legal authority rests on 'a belief in the "legality" of patterns of normative rules and the right of those elevated to authority under such rules, to issue commands' (Weber, 1947). The search for rational understanding and rational ways of legitimizing behaviour in society was paralleled by a relative decline in traditional and charismatic forms of authority.

In most work organizations those higher up in the hierarchy are given the right to control others. Commands are obeyed because the employee believes in the legitimacy of his superior to control his behaviour. However, there are occasions when an employee may question the legitimacy of a command, and this may lead to the use of power by an employee and his superior. Many disputes between employers and trade unions or professional groups involve the questioning of the legitimacy of behaviour. Any group may find that its behaviour is regarded as legitimate by some but not regarded as legitimate by others. For example, some members of a trade union may regard 'secondary picketing' as legitimate, while others do not. The legitimacy of the government's actions may be questioned by some sectors of society, while the government claims that its policies are legitimized by the majority of people in society. (Theories of conflict and change are dealt with in Chapter 7.)

6.4 The importance of understanding power and pressure groups

The first part of this section considers how a political perspective may be of value to the individual. The second part of the section describes the activities of pressure groups which are a particular type of political group. It is important to recognize that individuals use different groups to gain influence, and in this respect an understanding of pressure groups is also important for an individual's understanding of political behaviour.

6.4.1 The individual

Political behaviour is often frowned upon as if it necessarily involves duplicity or manipulation. However, it may be necessary for an individual or group to behave politically in order to achieve objectives. This can be demonstrated if we consider the importance of political behaviour to a manager. The term 'manager' is used here to refer to people in different types of organization (i.e. to professional associations and work organizations) who have been allocated authority and responsibility for the functioning of the organization.

If a 'manager' is not aware of the political aspects of behaviour, he is likely to find himself and his group (or section) controlled, in many dimensions of their behaviour. For example, he may find that committee decisions consistently go against the interests of his section. If he were more politically astute, he would have studied the agendas of the meetings in advance. He would also have discussed his desire for particular outcomes with other people, on the grounds that they may already share his views or may be persuaded to do so. He may thus have formed a group large enough to consistently sway committee decisions in his favour. Hence, he would be influencing decision-making processes in his favour, rather than allowing them to be neutral or negative in their effects on him and his section.

A political perspective should help a manager understand and interpret the behaviour of his subordinates. It may also help him to deal with other organizations, which have power to affect his organization. For example, different government bodies have powers over industrial and commercial organizations. Recognizing the nature and scope of this power, and knowing the way to respond, can ease the organization's relationship with the outside world. When Industrial Training Boards were first established, some organizations may have regarded them as a form of government interference. Many companies responded quickly to Training Boards by recognizing their power and adapting to the procedures that Training Boards demanded. The sooner a company recognized the scope of Training Board power the sooner it was able to establish the extent of its own autonomy and freedom.

A knowledge and understanding of political behaviour should help a manager to be more aware of how groups are likely to respond, and, all things being equal, he should be better equipped to deal with problems.

A political perspective should help a manager in his assessment of likely responses and reactions to his suggestions, both by groups inside and groups outside his organization. The perspective may also assist a manager in forming his proposals in a manner which is most likely to ensure their acceptance. Awareness of the political dimensions of behaviour may make a manager more astute in recognizing those sections of an organization which are enhancing their position at the expense of others. On occasions it may be necessary to check that sectional goals are not growing at the expense of overall organizational goals.

The study of 'power' may spell the difference between success or failure, and many managers will have learned to be political as a result of their experience of organizational life. Political aspects are most likely to be evident in the decision-taking machinery of organizations (e.g. plan planning, policy formation, budgetary control), in the communication systems and in the procedures which exist for conflict resolution.

6.4.2 Pressure groups or interest groups

Pressure groups were defined earlier as groups which influence and make demands on those in authority, for decisions or actions which they favour. It is, in practice, difficult to decide when a group is or is not a pressure group. The exerting of pressure may be an intermittent rather than a continuous part of a group's behaviour, and for this reason some writers prefer the term 'lobby' or 'interest group'. The literature tends to use these and a variety of other terms when describing what are referred to here as 'pressure groups'.

The study of pressure groups covers highly organized national groups, such as trade unions and professional associations, and it has also been applied to groups which are informally organized, such as those local inhabitants who exert pressure on local authorities for new road crossings. Frequently studies of pressure groups have concentrated on the way such groups exert influence on the government or local authorities. Many writers see the political system in this more narrowly defined way. Here, as already emphasized, we are primarily concerned with a broader definition of political science and with politics within organizations. Our focus is on the effects which pressure groups have on the organization, and the earlier part of this chapter describes the processes and 'sets the scene' within which pressure groups operate. Kimber and Richardson (1974, page 16) give support to this view: '. . . it is worth re-emphasising that not all pressure group activity is directed towards influencing government policy. Pressure groups feature more or less prominently in the operation of all other aspects of the political system.'

Individuals are frequently members of work organizations (e.g. factories, schools, hospitals), and members of pressure groups (e.g. trade unions, professional associations, OXFAM, The Ramblers' Association, etc.). Such pressure groups have important effects on the decision-making processes in organizations. For example, environmental pressure groups are ever watchful of companies who pollute or despoil the countryside; groups protecting consumers, the rights of women or the disabled make demands on different organizations. They may well take their cause to the government or lobby Members of Parliament, but such actions will not always be necessary. The focus of such pressure groups is to change behaviour in organizations. The latter can themselves form pressure groups. Pressure groups do not normally wish to occupy positions of authority themselves (e.g. the thalidomide pressure group did not wish to run The Distillers Company) but rather wish to influence the decisions taken by those in authority. This is the way in which pressure groups are distinguished from political parties.

The most common distinction between types of pressure group is that between sectional (or protective) groups and promotional groups. Protective pressure groups defend the interests of one particular section of the community. Generally speaking, professional associations, employers' associations and trade unions fall into this category, but they may sometimes promote causes. Promotional pressure groups promote particular causes and normally try to appeal to as many people as they can – e.g. National Society for the Prevention of Cruelty to Children (NSPCC), National Society for the Protection of Birds (NSPB). Pressure groups vary in the representation that they offer members, and there are often great differences between total membership and active membership.

Our focus is largely on protective or sectional pressure groups. There are occasions when these groups use their influence on and power over organizations in order to obtain their demands. It is also important to remember that such groups have regular representation on other consultative bodies, pressure groups, etc., where they seek to influence decision-taking. Kimber and Richardson (1974, pages 110–119) demonstrate the great variety of official and unofficial bodies on which the Trades Union Congress (TUC) is represented. The following are six of over one hundred mentioned: British Institute of Management; Duke of Edinburgh's Award; National Advisory Committee; Industrial Health Advisory Council; National Committee on Adult and Higher Education; and Women's Employment Advisory Committee. The link between the TUC and the Labour Party should also be mentioned. Twelve of the twenty-four places on the National Executive Committee of the Labour Party are reserved for trade union representatives and many Labour MPs are financially supported by the trade unions. Kimber and Richardson

(1974, pages 110–119) also demonstrate the large number of government bodies and independent organizations in which the Confederation of British Industries (CBI) is represented – e.g. The Department of Education and Science – Regional Advisory Council for Further Education; The Department of Health and Social Services – National Industrial Advisory Committee; The Welsh Council; The Home Office – Crime Prevention Committee; Keep Britain Tidy; and Fire Protection Association. Similarly, different professional associations are represented on a variety of other official and unofficial groups and organizations.

For the remainder of this chapter we now turn to a more detailed discussion of three main types of organizations which can act as pressure groups: professional associations, employers' organizations and trade unions.

6.5 Types of pressure groups

Society is permeated by pressure groups. Examples are political parties, employers' organizations, professional organizations (e.g. of doctors, accountants, lawyers, etc.), trade unions, women's organizations, civil liberties organizations and literally thousands more which exert pressures on legislation, on governments, on firms, on individuals within and without specific organizations, to influence decisions.

Pressure groups operate in many different ways, depending on the type of individual that makes up the membership and on the objective the group has set out to achieve. For our purpose and for understanding the industrial relations structure, it will be useful to examine three important pressure groups – the professional associations, the employers' associations and trade unions.

6.5.1 Professional associations

A professional association is a body which sees its objective in establishing and maintaining standards of performance by its members and organizing the entry, training and discipline of the organization in such a way that the standards aimed for are maintained. Most professional associations had a royal charter or were registered as companies. Only members of a professional organization in medicine, law, pharmacy, accounting, etc., can carry out their professional function legally and only as long as they are members of such organizations. However, since TULRA 1974 became law it is possible for a professional association, if it fulfils the requirements of the Act as far as its independence is concerned, to register as a trade union and assume the function of a trade union.

6.5.2 Employers' organizations

There are approximately 1300 employers' organizations in the UK. They range from the Engineering Employers' Federation, with over 4500 affiliated establishments with well over 2 million employees, to local ad hoc organizations covering a particular trade or industry. Many local organizations are subordinate to national or industry-wide federations. These bodies are concerned either directly or indirectly with negotiating wages and working conditions, but some also concern themselves with such issues as trading contracts and standardization of products, which are really the business of 'trade associations'.

In 1965 The Federation of British Industries, the British Employers' Confederation and the National Association of British Manufacturers formed one united body, the Confederation of British Industry, which since its formation has played an increasingly important role as an employers' pressure group fulfilling a corresponding function to the TUC.

> The CBI admits to membership employers' associations, trade associations, individual companies in productive industry and transport (including companies which are not members of employers' associations) and the public corporations administering the nationalized industries. Other companies such as banks and insurance companies may become 'Commercial Associates'. (*Donovan Report*, 1968, page 8.)

The CBI represents the great majority of employers in the UK. Organizations of employers are of more recent origin than the organization of trade unions (or combinations, as trade unions were called in the eighteenth century and early nineteenth century) and they usually arose after trade union organization had been established in specific localities or industries.

The Engineering Employers' Federation is one of the biggest and most powerful employers' organizations, to which most engineering firms are affiliated. It has district and national organizations staffed by full-time officials which tend to be parallel organizations to the unions operating in the engineering industry. (See Appendix 10.1, page 231.)

6.5.3 Trade unions

Trade unions have existed in the UK for a very long time. Some in the printing industry can trace their continued existence back to the end of the seventeenth century. In the eighteenth century trade unions were called combinations. Parliament legislated during the eighteenth century forbidding specific combinations for being in restraint of trade. In 1799 and 1800 all combinations were made unlawful by the Combination Acts of those years and remained suppressed until 1824/25, when the Combination Acts were repealed. From that time we can speak of the legal existence of trade unions and their continuous history. During the nineteenth century trade unions gradually became national organizations, and in 1868 they founded the Trades Union Congress (TUC), which has had a continued existence since then. Unions affiliated to the TUC in 1980 had a combined membership of over 12½ millions, and if trade unions outside the TUC are included, the number of trade union members is most probably in excess of 13 million.

More than half of the working population eligible to become members of trade unions are members today. Persons eligible to become members of trade unions according to the various rule-books of trade unions are persons working for any employer. Persons who are self-employed, entrepreneurs, people living off investment income, members of the police and security services MI5 and MI6 and the unemployed are not eligible to become members of trade unions (although trade union members becoming unemployed are allowed in most unions if they so wish to maintain their cards).

The trade union movement constitutes the most powerful pressure group in contemporary British society. This development has been a gradual one covering many stages reflected in many legislative changes since 1825. This change has been accompanied over the years by both growth in membership and changes of its occupational composition.

In the beginning and up to the closing years of the nineteenth century, the movement consisted mainly of 'skilled' manual workers; in the 1880s the mass of the 'unskilled', gas workers, dockers and railwaymen became organized. Later, white collar workers, teachers, civil servants and, since 1945, foremen and various managerial and technical grades joined their respective trade unions. Today more than one-third of the total trade union membership consists of white collar workers. This shift in the composition of the trade union movement has been brought about by technological change – by industries becoming increasingly science-based instead of craft-based. The electrotechnical, chemical and transport industries provide the most important examples of this change.

These developments have been linked with the growth of education, administration, service industries and distribution employing millions of workers, an increasing proportion of these grades of workers being women.

Trade unions have always operated as pressure groups in two directions – on the one hand pressurizing employers directly and on the other trying to influence the legislature, both local and national, to shape the legal and administrative environment in the interests of their members. This is why the TUC was established in 1868. Subsequently the parliamentary representation committee was formed by the TUC and in 1900 the Labour Party emerged from the parliamentary representation committee. The Labour Party was seen by the trade union movement as forming its political arm. Today half the membership of trade unions pay the political levy and are affiliated to the Labour Party. The bulk of the Labour Party finances are derived from these trade union political levies; furthermore, a large proportion of Labour MPs are sponsored by trade unions, and to be a candidate for the Labour Party trade union membership is obligatory.

In order to understand how trade unions function as pressure organizations, one must be familiar with the underlying principles of their structure. The basic organization of a trade union is the branch. This is where contributions are collected (or through which contributions are channelled) where policy questions emanating at the 'grass roots' level are discussed and formulated as resolutions, and where in many unions elections, to higher bodies and of officials, take place. Methods of administration, elections, etc., are laid down in the rule-book, which provides guide lines for the running of every trade union. The observance of the rules can be enforced by a court of law.

In some trade unions – e.g. ASTMS – general branches (i.e. branches covering a number of establishments and having in their ranks individual members) are divided into groups based on places of employment or departments. These groups have not the status of branches but are empowered to conduct negotiations at the level of a firm or a department. These groups usually elect officials and these officials function as 'shop-stewards'.

The shop-steward or workplace representative is the most important functionary produced by the trade union movement. He is the non-commissioned officer of a trade union, and it is estimated that there are about 400 000 shop-stewards operating in workplaces in Britain today (this estimate excludes health and safety representatives, who are dealt with in a subsequent chapter). The shop-steward is the link on the shop floor between the rank and file member and the outside official structure of the trade union. The shop-steward is usually elected by his work-group and is subject to immediate recall. Some trade union rule-books to this day do not mention the existence of shop-stewards.

Around the shop-stewards a widespread grass roots movement developed during World War I. Before 1914 shop-stewards were few in numbers and a trade union organization operated primarily outside the works, but with the war this situation changed.

In the past the shop-steward collected trade union contributions from the members in his department. Now contributions are very often deducted at source by the 'check off' method. Because of his close daily contact with his members, the shop-steward dealt with their grievances and complaints by taking them up with management or passing them on to his branch or full-time official to be dealt with at a higher level. The shop-steward would also be the link in the opposite direction, passing information and sometimes decisions or instructions from the branch, the executive, the TUC or (depending on his political affiliations) his party to his membership. He would also be the main recruiting agent for his union, keeping the membership in line, especially where a closed shop had been established. In a situation involving industrial action he would obviously be the person organizing pickets, organizing 'blacking' operations and sitting on strike committees. The shop-steward would invariably be involved in negotiating or bargaining with management at the primary level.

During World War I shop-stewards began to form a movement which on specific issues wrested the political initiative from the official leadership of both national unions and the TUC. The shop-stewards' movement was particularly powerful in engineering and shipbuilding on the Clyde. The shop-stewards led powerful strikes which shook the government and caused Lloyd George, the Prime Minister, to hurry to Glasgow to negotiate directly with shop-stewards and promise to deal with one of the main grievances, rents, by legislating on rent controls.

It is usual in larger enterprises, where a number of shop-stewards operate, to organize shop-stewards' committees. These committees, which may consist of shop-stewards belonging to various unions, elect a chairman and a secretary. In many large enterprises the secretary of the shop-stewards' committee acts as a 'convenor' and is usually recognized by management as the main link with the trade union movement. He engages in bargaining and very often 'trouble-shooting' and in many of the larger enterprises is engaged in full-time trade union work paid for by the employers and is receiving average earnings for his grade. Convenors are usually equipped with an office, a telephone and clerical assistance. These arrangements are widespread and unofficial – not laid down in any rule-book or national agreement.

Firms which operate on more than one site (e.g. Lucas, Ford or BL, with shop-stewards from the various sites) form an overall shop-stewards' organization with national meetings and officials and usually appoint a principal spokesman, who may fulfil the role of the main union spokesman in negotiations with management. These shop-stewards' organizations occasionally produce plans and counterproposals to the management line – e.g. the pamphlet *The Edwardes Plan and Your Job*, which led to the dismissal of the principal shop-steward at BL, D. Robinson.

Some shop-stewards' organizations are very powerful pressure groups operating at various levels within and outside the trade unions to which they belong as individuals or elected officials. They try to influence political decisions by conferences, lobbies to Parliament and demonstrations and sometimes even protest strikes (e.g. against the Industrial Relations Act of 1971). Within the shop-stewards' movement and within trade unions, pressure groups linked to outside political parties are operating, some openly and some secretly.

The Conservative Party openly arranges meetings and conferences and publishes leaflets on specific issues arising in particular trade unions and at trade union conferences, trying to influence decisions and elections to key positions by use of the press, radio and TV. The Communist Party organizes workplace branches and acts as a pressure group giving specific political direction to trade union members and political sympathizers. The Labour Party operates by organizing its active trade union members and at the official level there is the TUC Labour Party Liaison Committee. Most trade union conferences have guest speakers from the Labour Party giving a particular political slant to the proceedings. The left wing press bears ample witness to how the various pressure groups operate and explains their political motivation.

With the growth of multinational or transnational firms, shop-stewards' movements in one country tend to link up with the shop-stewards operating within the same firm in another country. Examples are the collaboration between shop-stewards of Fords in the UK and West Germany or the collaboration between Dunlop shop-stewards in the UK and Pirelli shop-stewards in Italy. While it has to be noted that the international pressure group is still in its infancy, it does represent a growing trend.

Outside the workplace the trade unions present a formidable structure. Individual trade unions are organized on a district, regional and national basis. At the various levels bodies of delegates elect officials. At the national level there are elected executives employing various national officials, among whom the general secretary or chairman is a very powerful figure concerned with national negotiations and representation of his union on government bodies or the General Council of the TUC. Parallel to trade union organization (e.g. in the engineering industry at district, regional and national level) one finds employer organizations also manned by full-time officials which try to resolve disputes on the basis of a procedure laid down in agreements between employers and trade unions.

While the TUC is the apex of the trade union movement at a national level, trade union local organizations form pressure groups of delegates from trade union branches in Trades Councils which are the local TUCs, and in that sense exert considerable influence and have specific statutory powers in nominating working people's representatives to various appeal tribunals, nominating for the panel of justices, nominating for various consumer and other bodies; employers' organizations and various pressure groups exercise similar functions on a local basis.

Trades Councils are combined in County Associations and the Associations in turn are organized in Regional TUCs to which both counties and the regions of unions send delegates. The Regional TUCs correspond to the regions into which Great Britain is divided. At the regional level the TUCs and other government and employers' organizations meet to discuss issues of mutual interest.

The various levels of TUC organization serve also as sounding-boards of policy issues which, debated and approved at local level, are then forwarded to national levels and exert influence on policies of government and other decision-making bodies.

The Trades Councils send delegates to an annual conference of Trades Councils which discusses motions submitted to it by affiliated bodies and forwards these to the TUC or to the Government of the day. This conference elects delegates to a joint consultative committee which is manned half by representatives of the Trades Councils and half by representatives of the TUC General Council. This committee enables the TUC to keep in close touch with the grass roots of the movement by an alternative route – i.e. through the executives of affiliated trade unions down through all the levels of organizations to the branch and ultimately to the shop floor.

While half the membership of TUC-affiliated trade unions (about 6 million) pay the political levy to the Labour Party, employers' organizations (e.g. the Economic League, Aims of Industry) are more closely linked to the Conservative Party. Their influence on the manifesto of the Conservative Party was evident, for example, during the 1979 election in relationship to both economic policy and trade union 'reform'. Individual firms, especially many large ones, contribute to the funds of the Conservative Party and these funds are provided from incomes of firms before tax; Labour Party funds derived from trade union contributions invariably come from individual contributions levied on members' incomes after tax.

The TUC, the CBI and the Government are represented in the National Economic Development Organization Council. This body meets usually monthly under the chairmanship of the Prime Minister and on it serve the most influential leaders of the TUC, the CBI and the Government. These meetings are extremely important and serve as a sounding-board for the policies pursued by the various pressure groups with the intention of finding grounds for consensus on matters of concern to both sides of industry. Very often consensus is achieved – especially during periods of Labour government. The Social Contract and economic policies followed by Labour met with a broad response up to the end of 1977, when the consensus broke down over pay policies. During periods of Conservative government, consensus was less in evidence and conflict became most evident over the operation of the Industrial Relations Act 1971. Eventually both the TUC and the CBI took sides against the Conservative Government led by Edward Heath.

While there are thousands of pressure groups operating at all levels, many have an ad hoc existence and others wish to achieve fundamental changes in the structure of society and its institutions. The state machine reflects the predominating interest group in society that is wedded to the operation of private property and capitalism. The state has therefore organized itself to preserve this *status quo*. This finds expression in the operations of the security services, especially MI5 and the Special Branch, which keep a very close watch over certain pressure groups – particularly those which tend to overstep the confines of legality and those which want the capitalist system replaced by a socialist one. Closely linked and supported by the various employers' organizations and large firms is the Economic League, which had an income of £760 000 in 1978. It maintains offices and full-time officials and sees its task as combating left-wing influence in industry by various clandestine methods including blacklisting of 'militants'. It seems to have close connections with the Conservative Party through Baron Hewlett, the first president of the Conservative Political Centre, who serves on the executive of the Economic League.

At this stage is should be evident that both conflict and change are characteristics of most organizations and that pressure groups of one kind or another can be important in these respects. The resolution or avoidance of conflict, the process of change and, indeed, the efficient operation of the organization all require the existence of effective means of communication. In the following chapter, therefore, we turn to a detailed consideration of these processes.

Questions

1. What do you understand by the term 'influence'? Give examples of the different types of influence which you have experienced during the past week.
2. Describe the 'magnitude', 'distribution', 'scope' and 'domain' of the power which is exercised by either
   (a) an industrial manager, known to you, or
   (b) your lecturer.
3. How do people derive 'authority' in social organizations?

4. Write down two different definitions of the term 'coercion'.
5. What, in your view, are the major characteristics of a successful pressure group?
6. What are the characteristics of:
   (a) a professional organization,
   (b) a trade union,
   (c) an employers' organization?
7. What is the role of the shop-steward in industrial relations?

References

Blau, P.M. (1964). *Exchange and Power in Social Life,* Wiley, New York
Castles, F.G. (1975). 'Power, Coercion and Authority,' Unit 27, D101, Block 8, *Power.* Social Sciences: a foundation course: Making Sense of Society, Open University, Milton Keynes
Dahl, R.A. (1976). *Modern Political Analysis,* 3rd edn., Prentice-Hall, Englewood Cliffs, N.J.
The Donovan Report (1968). Royal Commission on TU and Employers' Organisations, esp. Chs. II, III and XII, HMSO
French, J.R.P. and Raven, B.R. (1968). '*The Bases of Social Power*'. Cited in Cartwright, D. and Zander, A. (1968), *Group Dynamics – Research and Theory,* Tavistock Publications, London
Handany, I. (1962). 'The measurement of social power, opportunity costs and the theory of two person bargaining games', *Behavioural Sciences,* 7, 67–80
Handy, C. (1977). *Understanding Organisations,* Penguin, Harmondsworth
Kimber, J. and Richardson, J. (1974). *Pressure Groups in Britain,* Dent, London
Lasswell, H. and Kaplan, A. (1950). *Power and Society,* Yale University Press, New Haven, Conn.
Potter, D. (1975). 'Power, Conflict and Integration: a study guide,' Unit 25/26, D101, Block 8, *Power.* Social Sciences: a foundation course: Making Sense of Society, Open University, Milton Keynes
Russell, B. (1938). *Power, a New Social Analysis,* Unwin Books, London
Weber, M. (1947). *The Theory of Social and Economic Organisation,* translated by Henderson, A.M. and Parsons, T., Oxford University Press, New York
Weissenburg, P. (1971). *Introduction to Organisational Behaviour,* International Textbook Company, Glasgow

Further reading

Clegg, H.A. (1979). *The Changing Systems of Industrial Relations in Great Britain* (esp. Chs. 2, 3 and 5), Basil Blackwell, Oxford
Goodman, J.F.B. and Whittingham, T.G. (1973). *Shop Stewards,* Pan Management Series, Pan Books, London
Pelling, H. (1974). *Origins of the Labour Party,* University Press, Oxford
Thomason, G.F. (1978). *A Textbook of Personnel Management,* Ch. 3, Institute of Personnel Management, London

Chapter 7

Communication, change and conflict

7.1 Introduction

This chapter considers three important processes that occur in all organizations. Consideration of communications is the starting point, as this is seen to be fundamental for the formation of regular patterns of behaviour among people. It is through communication that people tell each other what they approve, disapprove, accept or reject in each other's behaviour. Thus, it is through communication that we gain knowledge of ourselves in relation to others. We gain an image of who we are, or a 'self-identity'. It is also communication which gives an individual consciousness of the organization in which he finds himself. The discussion of communication is followed by consideration of change and conflict. Some form of communication is necessary before social change occurs, and communications problems are not infrequently identified as one of the reasons for conflict in organizations.

7.2 The nature of communication

Communication is the process by which people convey and receive information, meanings and emotions. It is a process which involves two or more people. Dance (1970) examined 95 definitions of communication and studied their content in order to establish the main themes on which they were based. He found that the definitions varied according to the level of observation. Some focused on all behaviour, while others focused on 'purposive behaviour of human beings in conscious interaction'. Definitions also varied in their emphasis on the 'intention' of the person to communicate. For example, one's style of handwriting may communicate something about oneself to a cartographer, when it was not one's intention to reveal anything about oneself. It is, in fact, very difficult to know whether an initiator intends to communicate that which a recipient experiences in communication. The third feature identified by Dance was the inclusion of 'successful interaction' in some definitions – i.e. some writers regard communication to have occurred where 'the intent of the sender is achieved as a result of the communication event'.

Other writers distinguish between information and communication. Farace and MacDonald (1974) see information as referring 'to the movement of matter energy which on occasion exhibits patterning that is perceived by some member of the system'. Earlier Miller (1955) described how some energy moving in a system would be perceived by some people to be forming a pattern, while the remainder of the energy would be patternless 'noise'. Thus, it depends on the perception of an individual, and his ability to perceive a pattern, whether information is received or not. Communiction can only take place when people know and agree the patterns which they use to interpret the energy flows, which they perceive.

7.3 One-way and two-way communication

A dyad (group of two) is the smallest number of people possible for communication. The stages of the communication process are illustrated in *Figure 7. 1*. Let us suppose that a person A suddenly remembered the time, and that he and a person B had planned to go to the theatre

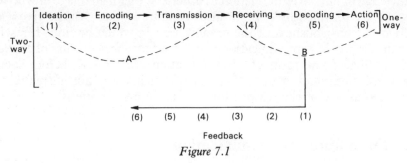

Figure 7.1

together that night. Having conceived his ideas (ideation) (1), A then (2) selects suitable symbols to convey his idea to B. In this case, he selects appropriate words, but he could decide to draw a picture or to ring a bell to convey his idea. When he says 'Goodness, it's 6.45 p.m.!' transmission (3) takes place. B listens and receives the message (4). Then B translates the symbols he receives into a meaning (decoding (5)) and decides what action to take (6). B could simply store the information in his memory, but in this instance he answers (going through stages 1–3) by saying 'We'd better hurry'. When A has received (4), decoded (5) and decided on action (6) in response to B's message, 'feedback' can be said to have occurred. It is worth noticing that the actual symbols used, 'Goodness, it's 6.45 p.m.!', have a particular meaning and significance for B, because of his previous arrangement with A. If B had not replied 'We'd better hurry', A would not have known whether B had appreciated the full significance and meaning of his message. The 'feedback' which B gave to A established that they both attached the same meaning to the information. Thus, A received positive feedback. If B had responded by saying 'So what?' A would have received negative feedback and he would have found it necessary to remind B of their plans to go to the theatre.

People need feedback as a means of establishing views about themselves. One may receive the approval or disapproval of others for one's behaviour. This may result in one modifying one's behaviour, or in deciding that other people's opinions of one are satisfactory, inaccurate or too difficult to alter. For example, an employee may feel that he can never change his boss's view of himself no matter how much he changes his own behaviour. Feedback can also help us to realize how other people see us, but if it is to be of value, we sometimes have to be able to accept what other people say without becoming defensive. The ability to accept feedback must depend on a person's feelings of self-security, the credibility and status of the person giving the feedback, and the degree of trust which exists between the initiator and the receiver of feedback. Feedback is particularly important during times of uncertainty or insecurity. For instance, when undertaking a new job, it may be a relief to know that one is liked and that one's work is regarded as satisfactory. In learning a new skill or activity the giving of feedback, or 'knowledge of results', helps to improve performance. Managers may use two-way communications as one means of encouraging people to feel involved in work. However, if employees find that their views are, for no apparent reason, ignored in decisions taken, they may be annoyed and frustrated.

In work organizations feedback is essential, as it provides the information necessary for effective decision-taking. Communications have been likened to the nervous system of organizations. Feedback on activities within and outside the organization is vital for effective planning and control in organizations, and the planning of good information systems is itself a complex process in large organizations. Managers have to decide what information is required for decision-taking and ensure that it is available when required.

It would be wrong to assume that two-way communication is always better than one-way communication, for there are occasions when the time-consuming process of feedback is unnecessary. For example, only in special circumstances does a pharmacist require two-way communication before making up a prescription, and the daily lives of most people are made up of numerous instances where one-way communication is adequate (e.g. the route number of a bus, the prices on goods). Certainly, in times of emergency, such as when a fire bell rings, discussion could be dangerous. Exercise 7.13 at the end of this chapter provides a useful way of comparing the relative advantages and disadvantages of one-way and two-way communications.

7.4 Barriers to communication

7.4.1 The individual

In the communication process individuals have to think of ideas, encode, transmit, receive, decode and act on information. The quality of the process is therefore dependent on the capacity of human perception, and the latter is partly dependent on previous experience and personality. People often use stereotypes or simplified pictures to help them encode information. Thus, one may interpret what a particular production manager, or salesman, says in the light of a stereotype that one has established previously about production managers and salesmen in general. People also tend to interpret communications by means of their existing values. Psychologists have used the term 'cognitive dissonance' to describe what happens when people hold conflicting beliefs which they cannot reconcile. A person may believe that the wearing of car safety belts saves lives in accidents, while continually neglecting to use one when he drives his car. He is thus experiencing cognitive dissonance, and may try to overcome the incongruity of his values by denying that safety belts are useful or by suggesting that under some circumstances they will not save lives. When further evidence is published on the value of wearing car safety belts, he may respond by considering the particular safety advantages of his car or the busyness of his life, rather than admit that he should stop being lazy and discipline himself into wearing his safety belt. It has also been suggested that people differ in their ability to receive new information, for many people tend to categorize information into black and white, rather than tolerate cognitive ambiguity. This tendency to be closed-minded is regarded as a general personality trait by Milton Rokeach, and he has devised a scale to measure it.

Individuals may also make errors when they receive and decode information, because the channels of communication which operate are overloaded. They may misinterpret a communication because they are receiving so many different messages at the same time. Individuals may also transmit the communications that they think people want to hear, as they tend to be influenced by group pressures. This was demonstrated in a famous experiment (Asch, 1952), which involved altering the length of two lines displayed on a screen in a darkened room. With the presence of group pressure most subjects reported perceiving the lines to be more nearly equal in length than they really were; and they altered their individual reports on the relative difference in the length of the lines so that they were more similar to those of the rest of the group. Campbell (1958) quotes evidence of experiments that demonstrate other tendencies of human communicators. When asked to repeat information which has been communicated to them, people tend to give shorter, simpler and less detailed accounts than those which they receive. In addition, subjects tend to remember the beginning and end of a communication more easily than they remember the middle.

7.4.2 Status

There is considerable evidence that status affects communication patterns. In their study of information flows in a research and development laboratory Allen and Cohen (1969) showed that people with Ph.D.s tended to socialize and discuss technical problems with one another more than with non-Ph.D.s. There was also a tendency for lower status non-Ph.D.s to direct most of their socializing and technical discussion to Ph.D.s. Earlier Kelley (1951) experimentally designed high and low status groups and investigated their behaviour in the laboratory. Among other things, he found that, when compared with high status groups, low status groups had more communication that was irrelevant to the task which they were doing; and high status groups seldom showed confusion about their work, and made few criticisms of their job to low status people. A study of small groups undertaken by Heinicke and Bales (1953) suggested that when status hierarchies were stable, groups were more efficient in terms of 'the quality and the speed of solutions' (Kretch, Crutchfield and Ballachey, 1962). 'The research workers also suggest that the early solution by the group of the problem of establishing a stable hierarchy frees time and energy for work on the task in hand.'

Formal status refers to the position or rank of a person, which is established by the authority system of an organization.

Informal status is acquired as people evaluate one another in terms of the esteem they have for one another. Status varies according to the criteria being assessed – e.g. a boy may be highly esteemed as a footballer while being regarded as a hopeless mathematician. Communications may be formal, or they may emerge spontaneously from relationships between individuals and groups. Until the work of Elton Mayo in the late 1920s there had been a tendency for writers on organizations to focus on formal relationships, and to neglect the informal relations and communications which develop among people in working situations. One of the important findings of Mayo's Bank-Wire Room Experiment was that two distinct sub-groups or cliques emerged within a total group of 14 men. The two sub-groups roughly corresponded to those in the front and the back of the room. Informal communications and the establishing of their own standards or 'norms' helped groups to develop their own sense of identity or 'in-group' feeling. This work highlighted the satisfaction that informal communication brings people in work organizations.

Informal communications networks are often referred to as the 'grapevine'. Sutton and Porter (1968) confirmed some of the earlier findings of Davis (1953), in showing that people who were higher up the organization hierarchy tended to have more grapevine information than those lower down. They also found that relatively few people were active in 'liaison' roles, spreading information. Grapevines can, but do not necessarily, operate in a discriminatory manner. For example, a surprise party may be arranged for people leaving an office, and the grapevine will neatly exclude those leaving until the last moment.

The physical environment and the nature of the technology used in an organization also affect the informal channels of communications. Obviously, noisy machinery makes communication more difficult, although lip-reading is not uncommon in such situations. One can easily conduct a simple examination of how physical factors affect communication by observing people communicating in different coffee bars or canteens. It is worth noticing how communication is affected by the positioning of chairs and tables, the height of chairs, the presence or absence of background noise, etc.

Formal hierarchies are a particular type of status system, and communication may be blocked or distorted, both intentionally and unintentionally, as it passes through them. Information may be distorted when people relay selected parts of it and omit others. The upward flow of communications in hierarchies is also affected by the degree of trust which people have in their superiors, and by the degree of influence which superiors are perceived to have by subordinates (Read, 1962). There is also evidence that information is likely to be blocked if it is unfavourable to the sender, even if it is important. However, information that is favourable to the sender is likely to move upwards (O'Reilly and Roberts, 1974).

7.4.3 Size

While the size of groups is not necessarily a barrier to communications, size does affect the pattern which communication is likely to take. Normally, as the size of a group increases, so an individual has less chance of participating. The work of Bales et al. (1951) suggests that, as the size of groups increases, there is a tendency for the most frequent contributor to take a more important and central role. In addition, as Handy (1976) points out, there is a tendency for larger groups to contain a greater 'diversity of talent, skills and knowledge'. The degree of homogeneity (similarity) or heterogeneity (dissimilarity) of members is likely to affect the communication which develops in groups; but communication is also affected by the nature of the task which a group undertakes and the style of leadership which is adopted.

7.4.4 Channels of communication

Bavelas (1950) and Leavitt (1951) have conducted some now famous laboratory experiments on different channels of communications in small groups. Leavitt controlled communications by sitting participants (groups containing five people) around a partitioned table. Information was passed through slots in the partitions, and members could only communicate in the directions shown in *Figure 7.2*. Problems were

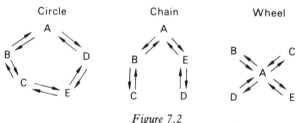

Figure 7.2

solved most slowly in the circle and most quickly in the wheel. In the circle no leader emerged; but as one moved to the chain and then to the wheel, the role of A became more important. However, in the wheel the correctness of solutions offered to problems depended very heavily on A. The enjoyment and satisfaction of group members appeared to be related to how central or peripheral they were to the group. Thus, A enjoyed the wheel, while others were less satisfied. The circle was generally inaccurate, but members enjoyed themselves.

It is only too easy to generalize from laboratory experiments to behaviour in organizations, but care must be exercised. As Handy (1976) indicates, the importance of the tasks which people undertake may well alter their motivation to engage in group problem-solving. Equally, the incentive or reward systems of an organization may affect behaviour (Burgess, 1969), and Cohen *et al.* (1969) stress how group behaviour is likely to alter when 'embedded' in larger organizations. For example, when people who feel relatively isolated on the periphery of a 'wheel' group are 'embedded' in a larger organization, they have the possibility of talking to members of other groups. While they demonstrate important principles, laboratory experiments restrict some behaviour possibilities.

7.4.5 Language

There seems little doubt about the importance of the written and the spoken word as a major means of communication in work organizations.

Observations in one study (Klemmer and Snyder, 1972) of technical, professional and administrative personnel in a research and development laboratory concluded that 69 per cent of the working day was spent in some form of communicating. Earlier studies (which did not include measurement of time spent on data analysis and computations under writing) suggested that about 61–62 per cent of the working day was spent communicating. Rosemary Stewart's study of 160 managers (Stewart, 1967) used a diary method and concluded that 78 per cent of the managers' total working time was spent in communication. The studies suggest that many of us spend a very large part of our working time on written and verbal communication. However, communication also takes place by facial expression and other forms of body language. People also attach meanings to their experiences of the reward and punishment systems in organizations, and there is a sense in which they are a means of communicating management attitudes and policies to employees.

Communication problems often arise because words have more than one meaning. In addition, different organizations develop their own vocabularies which are a mystery to the uninitiated. Often 'jargon' forms a type of verbal shorthand, which saves time when people are clear what the jargon means. Words may have denotative meanings which make explicit the definition of a word, but they may also give rise to many different connotations, or ideas and feelings in the minds of people. 'Freedom' and 'profitability' are examples of words which have wide connotations. Osgood (1957) developed a technique for measuring the meaning of words which is known as a semantic differential. His work enabled him to define three dimensions of meaning. The *evaluative* dimension is measured by determining whether a word has good or bad, pleasant or unpleasant connotations. The *potency* of a word depends on whether it is perceived to be weak or strong, big or small, heavy or light. The *activity* dimension is determined by measuring how active or passive, fast or slow a word is. This work demonstrates something of the complexity of language, and provides a way of building up profiles of different words.

7.5 Written communications

Written communications in work organizations take the form of memoranda, internal and external letters, instructions and manuals, formal and informal reports, minutes and notices. Written documents form a permanent record which can always be verified at a later date. Written communications are particularly useful if a large number of people have to be contacted together, and as a means of providing detailed information which could not be remembered as a result of oral communication. The style and choice of words used in written communications should be appropriate to the climate of the organization and to the level of understanding of the reader. Attention may be drawn to important parts of written material by underlining, using print of different colour or marking items as urgent. Documents which provide general information are often circulated from one person to another. This system depends on each person immediately reading the information and passing it on. People sometimes complain that they receive too much written communication. Rapid reading techniques help solve such problems, particularly if used as a means of categorizing communications into different priorities. This involves separating communications which require immediate action from those which can be left until the next day.

7.6 Oral communication

The advantages and disadvantages of one-way and two-way communications were discussed earlier in this chapter. Obviously, oral communication normally permits of more rapid feedback than the written word. The exceptions to this are the use of television, Tannoy systems and radios, with which the message is essentially one-way. The inclusion of detail is more easily achieved in written rather than oral communication; and in face-to-face oral communication perception of responses may prompt one to alter one's style of speech or to repeat points which have not been understood. Most students are given an opportunity to give an oral presentation of written work. This provides an opportunity to learn how to gain the attention of an audience, how to stress important issues, and how to speak slowly and clearly. There is also a skill in listening, and in perceiving and noticing the essential elements of a speech.

7.7 Change and conflict: introduction

We are now concerned with an examination of change and conflict. The study of change in organizations is located in a framework of more general theories of social change, and discussed in relation to the importance of underlying assumptions about the nature of persons in society. This serves as a foundation for an approach to the planning of change in organizations and to an introduction to 'organization development'. The study of conflict is approached through an examination of the various arguments put forward for the origins of conflict, together with relative and alternative theories of conflict. The discussion concludes with an analysis of forms of conflict and the areas in which such conceived forms are said to occur. The chapter ends with a case which can be used to focus upon a number of issues raised in the preceding discussion.

7.8 Change

One of the difficulties in approaching discussions of change arises from the fact that most people start from implicit theories of social order and/or social control which influence, and indeed structure, orientations. There are also many emotive connotations associated with change (e.g. people are often considered by definition to be resistant to change). Change, therefore, is usually debated in an 'essentially contestable' arena. Those emphasizing elements of social order might see change as involving a continual process of adaptation and adjustment towards stability and integration, while those emphasizing social control might see change as involving action aimed at controlling the strains and tensions of inherent contradictions. Change, however, in whatever view, is a central feature of social life, and any discussion of change in organizations needs to pay attention to relevant assumptions about the nature of man in society.

The approach developed in this section starts with an examination of various theories of social change and moves towards locating such theories specifically in an organizational context. This serves as the foundation for a study of the planning of change, and leads to an examination of the notion of 'change agent' in organizations, and to an introduction to 'organization development'.

7.8.1 Theories of social change

Perhaps the most fruitful starting place for a discussion of change is in the writings of the influential theorists of the nineteenth century. Such writers were particularly concerned with the problems posed by various emerging industrial societies, and while not being the first to examine questions of society and change, they have been characterized as representing the formalization of an approach to a 'science of society' (they are often referred to as the 'founding fathers').

Spencer was one such theorist in England who was concerned with the nature of developing industrial society. Stemming from the British liberal traditions (Adam Smith, J.S. Mill, etc.), he derived an evolutionary perspective of societal change. It was suggested by Spencer (indeed, it has been held by some that he had a profound influence on Darwin) that societal change took place in the form of an evolutionary differentiation which stemmed from the increasing differentiation in the division of labour, as specialization became more widespread in the very essence of advancing industrial societies.

This increasing differentiation was held by Spencer to be counter-posed by a progressive integration of individuals within more compre-hensive associations (from 'incoherent homogeneity' to 'coherent heterogeneity'). Change in society was thus seen to rest upon the evolutionary development of 'free associations of men' counterbalancing the inevitable differentiation. However, the idea of a freedom to associate masked the problem that not everyone could have that kind of freedom and that in effect such freedom tended to be merely an expression of the capitalist entrepreneur class.

One of the most influential publications concerning the subject of change was published in Germany in 1877 by Tönnies. In his view, European society at that time was changing from *Gemeinschaft* to *Gesellschaft*, terms which have usually been roughly translated as 'community' and 'association'. The concepts represent in effect a whole series of interrelated social changes, but in essence Tönnies conceived *Gemeinschaft* as a community based upon personal living together, and *Gesellschaft* as association represented by the idea of impersonal and limited contractual relations (see Worsley, 1970, pages 257–261). Although Tönnies considered that there were elements of both *Gemein-schaft* and *Gesellschaft* in social relations in all societies, he did emphasize that human history was a process of increasing *Gesellschaft* and decreas-ing *Gemeinschaft*. Thus, increasing industrialization and urbanization were part of the relentless process of social change with profound implications for human relationships.

In a similar vein to this, Durkheim also saw a process of social change which was inevitable and irreversible, although he was less inclined to attribute such change to the will of individuals than was Tönnies. In fact, Durkheim was concerned with the idea of Spencer's transition from 'incoherent homogeneity' to 'coherent heterogeneity', which he char-acterized as involving a change from 'mechanical solidarity' to 'organic solidarity'. He suggested that with 'mechanical solidarity' societies would exhibit more uniformity of beliefs, opinions and conduct, whereas in societies exhibiting 'organic solidarity' there would be a greater diversity of beliefs, opinions and conduct. He specifically identified a change from 'mechanical' solidarity to 'organic' solidarity with the idea of the increasing division of labour and greater specialization of indi-viduals (Durkheim, 1964).

In each of these views change is considered as inevitable, as societies become more complex owing to greater industrialization and urbaniza-tion. There is thus a concentration on the kinds of change involved in this inevitability, and on the problems faced by such societies. However, there are differences in the way in which this relentless process of change is conceived as originating. While in Spencer there is a suggestion that the process is an expression of the evolutionary nature of the cosmos, in Tönnies there is at least an introduction of the part played by individual will as representing something more complex than an evolutionary 'freedom' to contract in 'association'. This distinction is more apparent in Durkheim's work, in which he was concerned both with the problem of achieving social integration in an 'organic' society and with the question of anomie (whereby some members of society experienced lack of purpose and commitment to 'moral authority') but without lapsing into mere psychological explanation.

Before we turn to the more recent work on social change and specifically locate this in organizations, it will be propitious to examine two of the strands in Marx's analysis of social change. This involves making a distinction between 'explanatory theory' and 'liberation theory' (see Taylor, 1978) – a distinction which is somewhat contentious but nevertheless useful for this discussion.

Briefly, the concern of Marx was to examine the relations of production which were developing from the so-called freedom to 'associate', and to demonstrate that the implications were such that those who had the means to engage in contractual relations (the entrepreneur class) could be seen to be exploiting those who were 'selling' merely their labour. Marx highlighted a perspective which views the relations of production in the shape of the expropriation of surplus labour (i.e. that labour which is in excess of that which can be unequivocally identified with the value of the product which that labour has produced – 'excess profit'). This exploitation was specifically related, then, to the societal position of 'some' in relation to the societal position of 'others'.

Rather than representing an inevitable evolutionary feature of developing industrial society, however, Marx argued that those with the power to enter into contractual relations and 'use' the surplus labour of others for their own gain had a vested interest in ensuring that those particular relations of production were perpetuated. The entrepreneur class, therefore, were seen to be active in the process of developmental social change.

The second element to address in Marx's analysis concerns the nature of this developmental process, the essence of which some writers have indeed treated as inevitable. But is it necessary for societies to develop in this way, with a perpetuating imbalance in the relations of production?

It is often argued that since the 'liberation' elements in Marx's programme (that the proletariat would 'rise up' and change the relations of production, taking over ownership and control – indeed, that they must) have demonstrably not occurred (even in apparent communist societies), Marx was in some way 'wrong'. It does seem, nevertheless, that if such contentions can be approached a little more dispassionately,

Marx's analyses of social change can have significant import for the treatment of problems of change current in organizations (e.g. debates about increasing participation and industrial democracy may be illuminated by the idea that perhaps such theories are manifestations of 'liberation' pressures distorted by legitimization processes). This will be returned to more specifically in the chapters on industrial relations.

It is always a hazardous operation to try to identify themes in current theorists' work and attribute these to certain 'founding fathers'. However, it is evident that certain streams of thought deriving from earlier theorists do become incorporated in intellectual strands, and some of the ways in which this has occurred in analyses of social change will become apparent.

As suggested at the outset, considerations of change have been influenced by such implicit theories, and recent social theory has often been structured around a series of polarizations of these (e.g. 'consensus' views against 'conflict' views, and 'systems' perspectives against 'action' perspectives). While the substantive discussion of conflict in the next sub-section will highlight much of this aspect of change and the way in which conflict theories do trace elements back to, for instance, Marx, it will be useful here to concentrate upon some of the aspects of 'consensus' views and 'systems' perspectives which have been used to address change, and the ways in which such schemes reflect elements of earlier theorists.

There is, of course, something of a paradox in discussing 'consensus' views of the world in an examination of social change. In fact, Rex (1961) has argued that such views as they are normally represented as functionalist theories are logically debarred from being able to offer a theory of change. To the extent that consensus views do place emphasis upon how societies, organizations, etc., operate, they must be located within the strands of functionalism, although as theories of social change it may be more fruitful to describe them as limited by self-imposed parameters rather than as totally illogical, as Rex suggests.

With the concentration upon how things operate, functionalist theories do produce analyses of change which emphasize the adaptive and developmental aspects of societies and organizations, reproduced as social systems. Thus, there is little concern with the possibility of alternative structures. The systems view, of organisms seeking to redress forces which tend to produce imbalance and thereby re-establish equilibrium, masks the fact that organizations are people-directed and that choices are made especially by those people with power.

The structural functionalism of Parsons, which is probably one of the most influential strands in functionalist/systems theory, has been clearly traced by Gouldner (1970) to the earlier theorists discussed. Gouldner suggests that Parsons' work can also be related to an apparent rise of

Marxism in Russia, and must be seen in the context of an energetic attempt more systematically to develop a functionalist theory of capitalist society, building upon the work of the earlier theorists. The essential elements of Parsons' functionalism are located in the idea of society as a social system (Parsons, 1951). The part of change in this system is confined to the adjustments which are held to occur in four basic conditions ('functional imperatives') which have to be met for the system to operate. Briefly, these four conditions are:

(1) Adaptation to environment – society must make the required arrangements with its physical environment.
(2) Goal attainment – society must have agreement between its members about aims and priorities.
(3) Pattern maintenance and tension management – members of society have to be motivated and tensions in individual interactions have to be managed.
(4) Integration – internal co-ordination and control have to be arranged.

Even in this telescoping of Parsons' argument (for a more comprehensive treatment see Cuff and Payne, 1979, pages 34–35), it is not difficult to see why, with its emphasis on conservatism and maintaining the *status quo*, functionalism cannot provide an adequate theory of social change. Nevertheless, such views of the world are extremely widespread and influential, and some would argue that such views dominate the thinking of those involved in the management (and, indeed, those involved in developing theories of management) of organizations (see Nichols, 1969; Clegg, 1979; Salaman, 1979).

7.8.2 Change in organizations

Organization theory, then, has tended to be dominated by systems and functionalist views, and, consequently, the study of change in organizations has been limited to such views. There has been a concentration upon adjustments required to maintain or regain perceived equilibriums and a corresponding neglect of considerations of alternative structures. Theorists have been occupied with apparent inevitabilities such as technological 'advances' and with overcoming supposed resistances to change. The contradictions inherent in having 'active' resistance to change in a homeostatic system have seldom been explored.

Silverman (1970) has summarized the main limitations of systems and functionalist perspectives, and argues for an action approach which takes more account of the fact that organizations are not simply organisms reacting to their environments – individuals within organizations act and make decisions, and, indeed, seek to control environments (see Chapter 5). Child (1972) has also emphasized the idea that individuals make choices which determine directions of change. The fact that only some individuals are in a position (have power) to make choices has been largely masked in the history of organization theory.

It is evident that much of organizational theory does reflect some of the earlier consensus/systems/functionalist perspectives, and there is a sense in which a preoccupation with such views is quite natural and in terms of everyday values to be applauded. The idea of 'finding out how it works' in the basic idea of functionalism is a self-evidently 'good' thing to be doing for the inquisitive, imaginative human species. The question of 'Why find out?' or the even more potent question of 'What do I do if I find out?' conceals the essential asymmetry and masks the 'control needs' of the human kind. Thus, if the idea of a system seeking to maintain balance (i.e. ignoring asymmetry) is an attractive analogy, then manifestations of asymmetry can be defined as forces having the effect of disturbing the system and preventing equilibrium (that so desirable state) from being maintained. This theme will be returned to in a later chapter to illuminate some of the problems in industrial relations, but in this context it is apparent that considerations of change in organizations lose considerable impact if examinations are locked in a systems/functionalist view of the world.

In their more recent work Burrell and Morgan (1979) have suggested that approaches to organizational analysis need clearly to recognize the fundamentally different assumptions underlying the alternative views of the world. They argue that distinctions between 'consensus' and 'conflict' kinds of perspectives might usefully be reformulated in terms of 'regulation' and 'radical change'. They characterize 'regulation' as referring to 'the writings of theorists who are primarily concerned to provide explanations of society in terms which emphasise its underlying unity and cohesiveness' (Burrell and Morgan, 1979, page 17). Alternatively, 'radical change' is seen to stand in stark contrast to 'regulation', in that 'its basic concern is to find explanations for the radical change, deep-seated structural conflict, modes of domination and structural contradiction which its theorists see as characterising modern society' (ibid.).

The characteristics of the two schemes are illustrated in *Table 7.1*. The schema is later expanded by Burrell and Morgan to include subjective/objective dimensions, and the resulting model is used to locate the various traditions in social and organizational analysis. It remains clear, however, that, in relation to considerations of change, the perspectives taken are structured by the underlying assumptions about man and society.

It ought now to be apparent that any discussion of change in organizations cannot realistically be undertaken in isolation from concurrent examination of the underlying assumptions and views of the world

Table 7.1 The regulation–radical change dimension (Burrell and Morgan, 1979, page 18)

The sociology of regulation is concerned with:	The sociology of radical change is concerned with:
(a) The *status quo*	(a) Radical change
(b) Social order	(b) Structural conflict
(c) Consensus	(c) Modes of domination
(d) Social integration and cohesion	(d) Contradiction
(e) Solidarity	(e) Emancipation
(f) Need satisfaction	(f) Deprivation
(g) Actuality	(g) Potentiality

of those party to the discussion. From this point, therefore, the discussion will diverge. The 'radical change' perspective is laid aside, to be resumed in the next section under the rubric of conflict, and the remainder of this section examines some of the work done on organizations which should be seen as part of the 'regulation' perspective, even though on occasions the proponents have thought of themselves as in many ways radical.

7.8.3 The planning of change

The idea that change can be planned owes much to perceived desirability of control over uncertainty by those involved in managing organizational life. The administrative logic (see McNeil, 1978) is such that control comes to be seen as the means of achieving calculability of results (i.e. measurement of profit), but unfortunately the complexity of organizational life is at odds with this desire for calculability and, therefore, efforts so easily become efforts towards efficiency of control rather than towards efficiency of operation. The planning of change is often part of this misdirection, as those in control seek to improve calculability in any change undertaken.

An illustration of this can be seen in almost any change programme carried out. Taking manufacturing industry as an example, a common starting point will be a decision to introduce a new product line, often accompanied by some change in technology. This is likely to be defined in terms of a systems perspective, where a change in the market (the external environment) is seen to produce a 'need' for the organization to adapt. The fact that markets can be created does not fit the systems view. In addition, a change in technology is likely to be defined as necessary so as not to fall behind competitors, or, indeed, to give an advantage over competitors (the external environment again). The planning of change now becomes a problem of how to achieve a smooth changeover, conceived of as how to avoid any production problems (the internal environment). The underlying fundamental concern to protect and improve calculability is masked by this apparent concentration on action. The whole process is thus conceived of according to the 'regulation' model, and any opportunity to rethink in a radical way is lost by the pervasiveness of the administrative logic.

In order to illustrate the power of this underlying logic, the above example has, of course, grossly oversimplified the process of a product launch, but the case study at the end of this chapter gives a more detailed example and opportunity to try alternative explanations and strategies.

One of the resultants of perceived control needs of those charged with managing organizations has been a concern to construct a paradigm for utilization of social science findings. (While a great many social scientists would wish to dissociate themselves from such a paradigm, both from the view that social science is more problematic than that, and cannot so easily be devolved into 'findings', and from a wish to avoid being incorporated into the 'regulation' perspective, nevertheless a good deal of work has followed this utilization paradigm.)

Much of the work done in this area has been concerned with the idea of 'changing people'. Harman (1972), for instance, in summarizing some of the approaches to change, uses the phrase 'change people's heads'. However, there has been an increasing move to focus on 'the group' rather than 'the individual'; and training in groups has been a feature of this type of change programme. Thus, Schein (1970, page 103) argues for 'group-dynamics training by laboratory methods' as a 'more promising approach to effectiveness', and Blumberg and Golembiewski (1976, page 20) state that 'there has always been a strong element of science associated with the group movement, and its leading exponents are respected [sic] behavioural scientists'.

Inherent in programmes of individual and group change is usually a simplistic notion of improving organizational performance, but a more direct approach to the part played by social science in organizations is typified by Likert (1971, page 559) in his argument for the use of social science measurement to improve control and hence calculability:

Industry needs more adequate measure of organisational performance than it is now getting. Progress in the social sciences now makes these measurements possible. As a consequence, new resources are available to assist company presidents in their responsibility for the successful management of their companies.

Which is fine is you happen to be a company president!

Many of the 'change people' approaches to organizational change conceive of the idea of a 'change agent' as a means of bringing about change. As Lippitt (1970, page 146) has put this:

> From our studies we have come to conceive the research utilisation function of our staff as requiring them to *be linking agents* at various points in the flow of research utilisation. We have to develop new skills of retrieving and organising research-based knowledge so that it links up to the needs of the social practitioner or client population.

The notion of a social science-trained specialist in organizational change is central to the practice of organization development, which attempts to integrate utilization and research into the same practice.

7.8.4 Organization development

Although there is no general agreement on what constitutes organization development (and, indeed, this ought to be seen as a positive asset rather than a negative problem, given the problematic nature of organizational life), it is, nevertheless, possible to identify certain themes and concerns.

Organization development arose in a predominantly US tradition, from a framework of 'change people' in various versions of individual and group strategies (but for an early statement from a 'non-behavioural' perspective in the UK see Emery and Trist, 1960). There has been something of a reaction to such programmes. However, many of these reactions have been restricted by the application of a systems view. Katz and Kahn (1972, page 304) give an example of this kind of reaction:

> The major error in dealing with problems of organisational change, both at the practical and theoretical level, is to disregard the systemic properties of the organisation and to confuse individual change with modifications of organisational variables.

While the critique of strategies which conflate individual change with organizational performance is sound enough (e.g. cold shower effects of individual training programmes when the individual returns 'home'), unfortunately Katz and Kahn fare no better (see also Argyris, 1973, for the idea of the 'client system' – a further popular 'systems view' simplification). Nevertheless, the systems-based work in organization development does represent a significant widening of perspectives (see Emery, 1969) from some of the earlier work, which amounted to not much more than a strong humanist value stance. Such value statements, while laudable enough in themselves, inevitably appear naïve when set against the realities of organizational life. The strong 'Theory Y' (McGregor, 1960) position of much early organization development is typified by the work of Beckhard (1969) – 'Man should be striving to meet higher-order needs for self worth and for realising his own potential'; Tannenbaum and Davis (1972) – '. . . away from a view of man as essentially bad toward a view of him as basically good . . .'; and French and Bell (1973) – '. . . most individuals have drives toward personal growth and development . . .'. The neglect of the way in which hierarchical organizations represent a structure of domination (a command structure) in such positions is a detraction from the fact that we live in a 'Theory X' (McGregor, 1960) world (see Chapter 5).

Although some of the 'process-centred' work in organization development has been a little more aware of structure (e.g. Schein, 1969), it has still been from a systems-dominated position (Schein, 1969, page 11): 'In order to survive as organisations they must conserve stability in the face of recurring disintegrative pressures from the environment.' The confusions between the terms 'structure' and 'system' (see Boudon, 1971) have compounded this problem. Structure is implicitly defined (Schein, 1969, page 10) as relating to static elements: 'Early studies of organisation were dominated by the "scientific management" school of thought leading to an almost exclusive preoccupation with the "structural" or static elements of organisation.' This view of structural perspectives (representing a particularly gross version of structural functionalism) has diverted attention to a systems perspective which is supposed to be more concerned with action (Schein, 1969, page 11): 'I believe that the consultant must also examine the *processes* which occur between people as a way of understanding the informal relationships, the traditions, and the culture which surrounds the structure.' The irony is that this apparent move to a concern with action masks the essentially asymmetrical nature of 'ability to act'. Action is lost to the individual, in a mass of reification: '. . . we believe that a highly adaptive organisation is most likely to search out and use the most effective methods for conducting its business' (Fordyce and Weil, 1971, page 8). Change in this view is thus confirmed as an adaptive and inevitable process of seeking to restore a presumed equilibrium, and a 'system' is seen to be concerned with 'dynamics', whereas 'structure' is defined as the 'static' elements of organization. The perspective which views 'structure' as socially constructed is not considered.

The following section will include an examination of such alternative treatments of 'structure' and the extent to which such alternatives can illuminate theories of conflict in organizations. An examination will be made of the 'radical structuralist' position developed by Burrell and Morgan (1979) from their initial distinction between 'regulation' and 'radical change' already considered.

7.9 Conflict

As with change, the study of conflict not only involves an examination of a particular concept, but also inherently encompasses a certain view of man and society. The way in which inherent views influence approaches to conflict has been illustrated by Kelly (1974). In evaluating his comparison Kelly suggests that one might, in fact, see one approach as 'the old view' and the other as 'the new look' (see *Table 7.2*: Kelly, 1974, page 555). This section will examine some of the views of conflict and

Table 7.2

Old view	New look
Conflict is by definition avoidable.	Conflict is inevitable.
Conflict is caused by troublemakers, boat rockers and prima donnas.	Conflict is determined by structural factors such as the physical shape of a building, the design of a career structure or the nature of a class system.
Legalistic forms of authority such as 'going through channels' or 'sticking to the book' are emphasized.	Conflict is integral to the nature of change.
Scapegoats are accepted as inevitable.	A minimal level of conflict is optimal.

highlight the underlying assumptions which are in large part the foundation of such views. The examination will take the form of a discussion of the origins and the theories of conflict, and a consideration of the relevant areas of conflict in organizational life.

7.9.1 Origins of conflict

Numerous ideas have been put forward to explain the origins of conflict and it will be useful at the outset to summarize some of these.

Personality factors
One obvious source of conflict that has been offered as an explanation concerns the clashes which are said to occur when individuals with

differing personalities and temperaments are brought together in interaction. There is a natural attraction to this explanation in that it is straightforward and simple, and accords with most people's common-sense view of the world. There is, indeed, a sense in which individual differences are bound to be aired in naturally occurring interaction. The schema does, however, in placing such emphasis upon individual factors, forget that interaction takes place in a structure which has elements of continuity.

Communications
Another explanation at the level of the individual suggests that conflict arises whenever there are poor communications. The assumption here is that better communications between individuals would alleviate the manifestations of differences. Again there is a neglect of structural factors and a taking for granted of settings in which interactions occur.

Conflicting interests
A further explanation starts with an individual level framework, in which differences between individuals are identified, but links this to procedural factors in organizational interactions. Thus, it is argued, individual differences are in fact highlighted by the procedures which individuals undertake. The structure of organizational tasks is seen, therefore, to provide an arena for the manifestation of differences. In a refinement of this explanation the idea of inevitable structural elements in the actual origins of the manifestations of differences is identified. The very structures of interactions in organizational life are thus seen to be causes of, for instance, competition for scarce resources.

Class divisions
A much stronger 'structuralist' version of this idea is a still more deterministic explanation in which the structure of organizations is seen as a special case of the societal structure in which the organization exists. Organizations are thus seen to reflect the class structure of society and, indeed, to represent a means of perpetuating that particular class structure. Conflict is consequently seen as stemming from the nature of the societal context in which the organization operates, and is inevitable in a class-emphasized society such as the UK today (albeit not as simply structured as some commentators might argue). In emphasizing the deterministic elements of organizational life, this explanation does neglect the possibility of individually based origins of conflict.

The alienating nature of work environments
In an extension of the above view an explanation is offered that, because of the asymmetrical nature of organizational relations (the structure of

domination), the majority of jobs are inevitably alienating, because individuals do not have control and responsibility over their own sphere of operations, and, furthermore, the very structure (deriving from the degree of specialization required) means that it is difficult to see an end product and thus a sense of purpose. Again in concentrating upon the structural factors this explanation neglects the part played by individual aspects and also misses the fact that some individuals may apparently be grateful for a job in which the responsibility has largely been transferred 'upwards'.

Lack of control
The strong 'structuralist' position (in the sense of the alternative treatment referred to in the previous section) of the above two explanations may be counterposed with the 'systems'-based view which emphasizes the lack of effective controls as the origin of conflict. In this explanation the emphasis is placed upon the necessity for close control over operations, since in the kind of complex world in which organizations have to operate it would be unrealistic to expect the required degree of commitment to organizational goals of each individual employed. This explanation neglects the essential asymmetry of individuals and the power invested in some people to make decisions and change directions.

Given the diversity of explanations and the essentially ideological (i.e. deriving from entrenched views of the nature of man and society) nature of such explanations, it is not surprising that no really comprehensive theory of conflict has been put forward. Indeed, it is not difficult to see how theories which have been postulated reflect and build upon these underlying explanations of the origins of conflict.

7.9.2 Theories of conflict

There are, then, as many theories of conflict as there are explanations of origins, and some of the main ones, by no means exhaustive, are discussed below.

Agitator theory
The main thrust of this theory is located in the idea of significant individuals who go around 'stirring up discontent' and agitating for successive showdowns. It is held that some shop-stewards, among others, have no other goals than to ensure that trouble is regularly surfaced. The theory neglects the fact that most shop-stewards spend a large part of their time preventing the outbreak of trouble and stopping the escalation of disputes. The concentration upon the individual level of

explanation, moreover, masks the fact that it is not possible for an individual to agitate and harness discontent unless the seeds of discontent are already sown in the situations.

Communications theory

This theory conceptualizes conflict as a manifestation of the results of 'poor communications' and suggests that there is perhaps something inherent in the human condition which inevitably leads to imperfect communications; therefore, there are bound to be differences which become institutionalized. Improving communications is therefore seen to be a fundamental need. The theory is widely subscribed to, as witness the preponderance of courses for managers and supervisors which are built around the idea of improving communication skills. The presentation of the problem as one requiring the improving of 'skills' is again locating the problem at the individual level, which masks the elements attributable to situations. It does not, for instance, sufficiently explain why some industries have vastly different levels of manifestation of conflict compared with others, given that, even within the tenets of the theory itself, the capacity for improving communication skills is limited.

There is in this theory also a strong value element deriving from the 'human relations' school of thought, giving rise to the belief that the way to avoiding conflict lies in improving the quality of working relationships. Improving communications is thus implicitly a 'good' thing to be doing. Unfortunately for this theory, the 'quality of working life' is not something which can be realistically conceived of in isolation from a conception of the structure within which it is supposed to be achieved.

Integration theory

This theory has two main strands. In the first version it is suggested that in some industries there are particularly strong associations in working relations which build up a sense of integration and solidarity which forms the foundation of concerted actions. This kind of relationship forms in industries where, for instance, there is a high degree of shop floor contact such as in engineering manufacturing industries, whereas in contrast, for example, postmen do not have much contact with their fellow workers. This forms a basis for the explanation of why the engineering manufacturing industry is more prone to manifestations of conflict than is the postal delivery service. In a further version of the theory an extension is made from working relations to community relations, and it is suggested that industries which have tight-knit communities (e.g. as are to be found in the coal mining industries, where a large amount of the population of the same village or locality all work in the same mine) also develop a strong sense of integration and solidarity which forms the foundation of what might be termed community action in the workplace. One problem with both versions of this theory is that variations which occur in different parts of the country, or, indeed, in different countries, are not explained.

Technological determinism

As an alternative to the community- and workplace-derived idea of integration and solidarity providing a base for the development of conflict, a theory which suggests the importance of common technology has been suggested. It holds that the mode of production has features which determine certain aspects of the structure of relationships and thereby determine the propensity for concerted action. Again, however, such a theory does not account for the wide differences across different countries (e.g. the difference often pointed to between British and Japanese motor industries in cases where there are similar technologies).

Socio-technical theory

In this theory it is argued that, rather than simply technology, it is the relationship between technology and the social organization which has to be considered, since the social organization has elements of its own which are independent of technology. This undoubtedly represents an improvement from technological determinism but still has the limitation of considering social organization in its interaction with technological factors as stemming simply from 'the organization'. The extent to which societal structure determines the parameters of organizational social structure, and therefore the potential for conflict, is masked.

Economic theory

There are several versions of economic theory, from the idea of conflict being seen as a manifestation of individuals perceiving differentials (of pay, status, etc.) which give rise to dissatisfaction, to the idea of workers actually being obsessed with economic rewards (conveniently ignoring the possibility that workers might be excluded from concern with anything else – decision making, for example – in the organization). Such theories might be regarded by 'societal theorists' as particularly gross versions of economic determinism.

Societal theory

Proponents of this kind of theory conceptualize conflict in organizations as merely a special case of theories of conflict in society. Thus, industrial conflict is seen as being a part of conflict inherent in, for instance, UK capitalist society and as related to derivation and imbalance in the ownership of the means of production, the asymmetrical distribution of power and wealth and the endemic class divisions in society. The argument is that all these things are inevitably reproduced in organizations and that therefore conflict is equally inevitable while such asymmetrical relations exist. Perhaps the main criticism of this kind of theory is that it has failed to develop an alternative conception of the structure of society and organizations outside of the somewhat vague notions of equalization.

Up to this point not much has been said about the form conflict takes in organizations, and while it is not practicable, or even perhaps very useful, to provide all-embracing definitions, the discussion now turns to an examination of the manifestations of conflict.

7.9.3 Arenas of conflict

The term 'conflict' is usually associated with strikes, although often the more euphemistic 'industrial action' will be used, stemming from the media treatment of industrial relations. There are, however, even by the most conservative standards, several forms of industrial conflict which are identifiable quite independently of strikes.

At the outset a distinction might be made between individual and organized group conflict, but both are undoubtedly manifestations of the kinds already identified above. An example of individual manifestations of conflict might be highlighted in the incidence of absenteeism, and indeed the more organized kinds of group conflict which are as prevalent as strikes might be identified in restrictions of output, working to rule and subtle attempts to sabotage production. Thus, the idea that conflict is synonymous with strikes is a confusion in addition to being an oversimplification. Indeed, Hyman (1977) has argued that it is possible to view strikes in a somewhat different light from the usual one by reconceiving of them as an *extension* of collective bargaining rather than as a *breakdown* of collective bargaining.

Most of these issues will be examined in more detail in the chapters on industrial relations, but there are other conceptions of conflict which have been approached quite independently of the confusing arena that has come to be called 'industrial relations'. The idea that there is an arena, or a concept, or a subject area which can be called industrial relations is, in fact closely bound up with the 'regulation' perspective of Burrell and Morgan (1979). The development of a specific subject area of industrial relations can thus be seen as an expression of the control-needs (the desire for calculability, etc., identified in the previous section) of *some* organizational members.

A further manner in which conflict is approached is to be found in the attention given by social psychologists to group competition in organizations. Schein (1970), Hinton and Reitz (1971) and Thomas and Bennis (1972) have all addressed the problems of intragroup and intergroup conflict. Schein, particularly, has conceived of these problems as representing manifestations of conflict stemming from the naturally occurring competition (for scarce resources, etc.) in organizational life.

Schein has developed a schedule of the effects within groups and between groups which has formed a basis for a great deal of work on the idea of the management of conflict. The basis has even been used in an industrial relations setting wherein the 'management' and the 'unions' are defined as the two groups (see Blake, Mouton and Sloma, 1970). The elements of Schein's schema (1970, page 97) are as follows:

(A) What happens *within* each competing group?
(1) Each group becomes more closely knit and elicits greater loyalty from its members; members close ranks and bury some of their internal differences.
(2) Group climate changes from informal, casual, playful to work- and task-oriented; concern for members' psychological needs declines, while concern for task accomplishment increases.
(3) Leadership patterns tend to change from more democratic towards more autocratic; the group becomes more willing to tolerate autocratic leadership.
(4) Each group becomes more highly structured and organized.
(5) Each group demands more loyalty and conformity from its members in order to be able to present a 'solid front'.

(B) What happens *between* the competing groups?
(1) Each group begins to see the other groups as the enemy, rather than merely a neutral object.
(2) Each group begins to experience distortion of perceptions – it tends to perceive only the best parts of itself, denying its weaknesses, and tends to perceive only the worst parts of the other groups, denying their strengths; each group is likely to develop a negative stereotype of the other ('they don't play fair like we do').
(3) Hostility towards the other group increases, while interaction and communication with the other group decrease; thus, it becomes easier to maintain negative stereotypes and more difficult to correct perceptual distortions.
(4) If the groups are forced into interaction (for example, if they are forced to listen to representatives plead their own and the others' cause in reference to some task), each group is likely to listen more closely to their own representative and not to listen to the representative of the other group, except to find fault with his presentation; in other words, group members tend to listen only for that which supports their own position and stereotype.

The concentration in Schein's work upon the processes within and between groups is a further demonstration of the tendency to emphasize the dynamics of organizational life as group issues and this is clearly to reinforce the 'regulation' perspective. Before concluding this chapter, therefore, it will be useful to return to the analysis of Burrell and Morgan (1979) and close with some directions for future thought and theory on conceptions of change and conflict.

In developing a 'radical change' perspective Burrell and Morgan suggest the idea of a 'radical structural' approach to organization theory. They define the elements of such a position as stemming from a commitment to *radical change, emancipation* and *potentiality*. They argue that the emphasis of such an approach should be upon *structural conflict, modes of domination, contradiction* and *deprivation* (1979, page 4). Although there are some problems with Burrell and Morgan's typologies, they do represent an alternative way to proceed, to escape the somewhat ossified perspectives which have dominated organization studies in the past. Indeed, as Burrell and Morgan themselves have suggested (1979, page 389), such an approach is more likely to offer *new* insights into our understanding of organizations in society.

Questions

1. Describe the advantages and disadvantages of one-way and two-way communication. Give examples of when it would be appropriate to use each method.
2. Consider one lecture/talk you received this week, and describe the barriers to communication that were evident.
3. Describe the reasons why 'feedback' is important to
   (a) the workforce, (b) managers in work organizations.
4. Write brief notes comparing the uses and relative merits of written and oral communications.
5. How do theories of social change in society relate to problems of change in organizations?
6. What is the relationship between change and 'maintaining stability' in organizations?
7. Can change be planned?
8. What part can 'organization development' play in the problems of change in organizations?
9. Is conflict inevitable in organizations?
10. In what way do underlying assumptions influence views of conflict in organizations?
11. How is organizational conflict manifested?
12. Can conflict in organizations be resolved?
13. A communication exercise to compare one-way and two-way communications. This type of experiment was originally conducted by Leavitt and Mueller (1951). This simple adaptation can be conducted in the classroom.

Stage 1: Two volunteers A and B are asked to draw a pattern composed of three squares, four rectangles and two triangles (the number and type of shapes can be varied). The diagram should not be shown to others. An example is provided in *Figure Q7.1*, but it is best to develop your own.

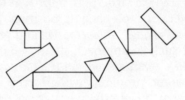

Figure Q7.1

Stage 2: About eight students are selected out of the class and divided into two groups, A and B.

Stage 3: Volunteer A is asked to describe his pattern to group A, who have to follow instructions to try to reproduce the pattern. Group members must not compare attempts. Volunteer A must not face his group, and must not use gestures to describe his pattern. Group A must not ask any questions of volunteer A.

Stage 4: Volunteer B is then asked to describe his pattern to group B, who have to follow instructions to try to reproduce the pattern. (Ideally, volunteer B and group B should not observe stage 3, as they may learn from their observations.) Group B may ask questions of volunteer B. The latter may face his group but may not use gestures to describe his pattern.

Stage 5: (1) Compare the diagrams produced by groups A and B. Consider the accuracy and common errors in the diagrams.

(2) Compare the time taken by groups A and B (one way is likely to be faster).

References

Allen, T.J. and Cohen, S.I. (1969). 'Information flow in research and development laboratories', *Administrative Science Quarterly*, **14**, 12–20

Argyris, C. (1973). *Intervention Theory and Method – A Behavioural Science View*, Addison-Wesley, Reading, Mass.

Asch, S.E. (1952). *Social Psychology*, Prentice-Hall, Englewood Cliffs, N.J.

Bales, R.F., Strodtbeck, F.L., Mills, T.M. and Roseborough, M. (1951) 'Channels of communication in small groups', *American Sociological Review*, **16**, 461–468

Bavelas, A. (1950). 'Communication patterns in task-orientated groups', *Journal of Acoustical Society of America*, **22**

Beckhard, R. (1969). *Organisation Development: Strategies and Models*, Addison-Wesley, Reading, Mass.

Bennis, W.G., Benne, K.D. and Chin, R. (Eds) (1970). *The Planning of Change*, Holt, Rinehart and Winston, London

Blake, R.R., Mouton, J.G. and Sloma, R.L. (1970). 'The union-management intergroup laboratory: strategy for resolving intergroup conflict', in Bennis, Benne and Chin (1970)

Blumberg, A. and Golembiewski, R.T. (1976). *Learning and Change in Groups*, Penguin, Harmondsworth

Boudon, R. (1971). *The Uses of Structuralism*, Heinemann, London

Burgess, R.L. (1969). 'Communication networks and behavioural consequences', *Human Relations*, **22**, 137–160

Burrell, G. and Morgan, G. (1979). *Sociological Paradigms and Organisational Analysis*, Heinemann, London

Campbell, D.T. (1959). 'Systematic error on the part of human links in communication', *Systems Information and Control*, **1**, 334–369

Child, J. (1972). 'Organisation structure, environment and performance: the role of strategic choice', *Sociology*, **6**, 1–22

Clegg, S. (1979). *The Theory of Power and Organisation*, Routledge and Kegan Paul, London

Cohen, A.M., Robinson, E.L. and Edwards, S.L. (1969). 'Experiments in organisational embeddedness', *Administrative Science Quarterly*, **14**, 208–221

Cuff, E.C. and Payne, G.C.F. (Eds) (1979). *Perspectives in Sociology*, Allen and Unwin, London

Dance, F.E.X. (1970). 'The concept of communication', *Journal of Communication*, **2**, 261–310

Davis, K. (1953). 'Management communication and the grapevine', *Harvard Business Review*, **31**, 43–49

Durkheim, E. (1964). *The Division of Labour in Society*. Free Press, New York (first published in French in 1893)

Emery, F.E. (Ed.) (1969). *Systems Thinking*, Penguin, Harmondsworth

Emery, F.E. and Trist, E.L. (1960). 'Socio-technical systems', in Churchman, C.W. and Verhulst, M. (Eds), *Management Science, Models and Techniques*, Vol. 2, Pergamon, London

Farace, R.V. and MacDonald, D. (1974). 'New directions in the study of organisational communication', *Personnel Psychology*, Spring, 1–19

Fordyce, J.F. and Weil, R. (1971). *Managing With People*, Addison-Wesley, Reading, Mass.

French, W.L. and Bell, C.H.Jr. (1973). *Organisation Development – Behavioural Science Interventions for Organisation Improvement*, Prentice-Hall, Englewood Cliffs, N.J.

Gouldner, A.W. (1970). *The Coming Crisis of Western Sociology*, Heinemann, London

Handy, C.B. (1976). *Understanding Organisations*, Penguin, Harmondsworth

Harman, W. (1972). 'The nature of our changing society', in Thomas and Bennis (1972)

Heinicke, C. and Bales, R.F. (1953). 'Developmental trends in the structure of small groups', *Sociometry*, **16**, 7–38

Hinton, B.L. and Reitz, H.J. (Eds) (1971). *Groups and Organisations*, Wadsworth, Belmont, Cal.

Hyman, R. (1977). *Strikes*, Fontana, London

Katz, D. and Kahn, R.L. (1972). 'Organisational change', in Thomas and Bennis (1972)

Kelley, H.H. (1951). 'Communication in experimentally created hierarchies', *Human Relations*, **4**, 39–36

Kelly, J. (1974). *Organisational Behaviour – An Existential-systems Approach*, Irwin, Homewood, Ill.

Klemmer, E.T. and Snyder, F.W. (1972). 'Measurement of time spent communicating', *Journal of Communication*, **22**, 142–158

Kretch, D., Crutchfield, R.S. and Ballachey, E.L. (1962). *The Individual in Society*, McGraw-Hill, New York, pp. 467, 468

Leavitt, H.J. (1951). *Journal of Abnormal and Social Psychology*, January

Leavitt, H. and Mueller, R.A.H. (1951) 'Some effects of feedback on communications', *Human Relations*, **4**, 401–410

Likert, R. (1971). 'Measuring organisational performance', in Hinton and Reitz (1971)

Lippitt, R. (1970). 'The process of utilisation of social research to improve social practice', in Bennis, Benne and Chin (1970)

McGregor, D. (1960). *The Human Side of Enterprise*, McGraw-Hill

McNeil, K. (1978). 'Understanding organisational power: building on the Weberian legacy', in *Administrative Science Quarterly*, **23**, March, 65–90

Mayo, E. (1976). Cited in Handy (1976)

Miller, J.G. (1955). 'Toward a general theory for the behavioural sciences', *American Psychologist*, **10**, 513–531

Nichols, T. (1969). *Ownership, Control and Ideology*, Allen and Unwin, London

O'Reilly, C.A. III and Roberts, K.H. (1974). 'Information filtration in organisations: three experiments', *Organisational Behaviour and Human Performance*, **II**, 253–265

Osgood, E.E., Suci, G.J. and Tannenbaum, P.H. (1957). *The Measurement of Meaning*, University of Illinois Press, Urbana, Ill.

Parsons, T. (1951). *The Social System*, Routledge and Kegan Paul, London

Read, W. (1962). 'Upward communication in industrial hierarchies', *Human Relations*, **15**, 3–16

Rex, J. (1961). *Key Problems in Sociological Theory*, Routledge and Kegan Paul, London

Salaman, G. (1979). *Work Organisations Resistance and Control*, Longmans, London

Schein, E.H. (1969). *Process Consultation: Its Role in Organisation Development*, Addison-Wesley, Reading, Mass.

Schein, E.H. (1970). *Organisational Psychology*, Prentice-Hall, Englewood Cliffs, N.J.

Silverman, D. (1970). *The Theory of Organisations*, Heinemann, London

Stewart, R. (1967). 'How managers spend their time', *Management Today*, June, 2–160

Sutton, H. and Porter, L.W. (1968). 'A study of the grapevine in a government organisation', *Personal Psychology*, **21**, 223–230

Tannenbaum, R. and Davis, S. (1972). 'Values, man and organisations', in Margulies, N. and Raia, A.P. (Eds), *OD-Values, Process and Technology*, McGraw-Hill, London

Taylor, C. (1978). 'Marxist philosophy', in Magee, B. (Ed.), *Men of Ideas*, BBC, London

Thomas, J.M. and Bennis, W.G. (Eds) (1972). *The Management of Change and Conflict*, Penguin, Harmondsworth

Worsley, P. (Ed.) (1970). *Introducing Sociology*, Penguin, Harmondsworth

Further reading

Batstone, E.V., Boraston, I. and Frenkel, S. (1977). *Shop Stewards in Action: The Organisation of Workplace Conflict and Accommodation*, Blackwell, Oxford

Fox, A. (1971). *A Sociology of Work in Industry*, Collier Macmillan, London

Rex, J. (1973). *Discovering Sociology – Studies in Sociological Theory and Method*, Routledge and Kegan Paul, London

Appendix 7.1: Case study

This case study is presented for the assistance of teachers, who may be able to use it to illuminate several issues raised during this chapter.

Background

Frost and Co. is a medium-sized engineering manufacturing concern in the north of England. The company makes high quality engineering tools both for the engineering industry and for individual tradesmen (fitters, mechanics, etc.). Of the two markets, the latter has been the most stable, and the maintenance of high quality in the products has in the past been regarded as the key to maintaining the stability of this market and to the sustaining of high profitability in the company.

Profitability

The company is indeed a profitable operation and is a public company with UK shareholders widely distributed:

Annual turnover	£10 000 000
Trading surplus (pre-tax)	£1 300 000
Net assets	£4 000 000
Return on net assets	approximately 30 per cent

The future

More recently the company has launched into the chain store market with a cheaper range of tools aimed at the do-it-yourself car maintenance customer.

Production

Production on the shop floor has traditionally been in small batches, with a few individual 'hand-made' items in addition, although the introduction of the cheaper range of tools has involved the setting up of larger batch runs, with corresponding alterations in quality control, packing, etc. The priority to be given to individual and small batch production as against the larger batch runs is a continual source of trouble between the production and sales departments.

The labour force

Total	850
Manual	
skilled production	300
semi-skilled production	250
unskilled production	50
maintenance and tradesmen	25
Non-manual	
managerial	20
supervisory	35
administrative	100
technical	70

The labour force has been stable for a number of years, although more recently labour turnover has been increasing. However, no figures are kept to substantiate this.

Trade union membership

AUEW	500
TGWU	50
EEPTU	15
ASTMS	25

The company is not a member of the Engineering Employers' Federation.

Industrial relations

The company does not have a personnel department, mainly because the managing director does not believe that 'service departments' can contribute to profitability. Dick Franks, however, the works manager, believes that the company should have a personnel department and feels that his own time and that of his assistants and foremen is becoming more and more occupied with 'personnel matters'.

The increased labour turnover is one example; on the one hand, his staff seem to be perpetually interviewing for replacement production workers, and yet no-one has time to collate figures which could be used to convince the managing director of the need for a personnel department.

Negotiations with trade unions are normally carried out by Dick Franks and John Jenkins, the wages manager, on behalf of the company, and the four senior shop-stewards on behalf of the trade unions. Dick Franks feels that his time is increasingly wasted on matters which should be settled at departmental level and that a procedural agreement should be introduced to achieve this. Again, however, no-one seems to have time to devote to this.

Action

On Monday, 19 February 1979 Dick Franks is making his way to the traditional Monday morning meeting he has with the managing director. He is considering how best to raise once again the question of a personnel department, when he is intercepted by Tom Drake, one of his departmental foremen.

'T'men have just gone out, Dick,'

'Out . . .?' Dick Franks stopped in his tracks.

'Aye, summat about being sick and tired o' t'dominating attitude o' t'management.'

'What . . .?'

'It seems 't'drilling foreman sent home one o' t'operators this mornin' for not wearin' t'safety protection.'

'Sent home . . .?'

'Well, he'd told him three times afore . . . but t'men said it wer' typical o' t'rigid attitude o' t'management. . . .'

Dick Franks lowered his head and rubbed the back of his neck vigorously . . .

Chapter 8

Discrimination in employment

8.1 Introduction

This chapter discusses the legislation relating to discrimination in employment, which is a matter of crucial importance for people and their employing organizations. It traces how women, particularly through their participation in two world wars, began to achieve political and social equality which much later (especially after 1970, through the Equal Pay and Sex Discrimination Act) began to come little nearer to economic equality. The other problem of discrimination with which it deals is that towards people who are racially different from the majority of the inhabitants of Great Britain. The chapter is concerned with some of the legal aspects of the Race Relations Act 1976 and its enforcement. Because the law on equal pay, sex and race discrimination is complicated and every word in the Acts has a specific meaning, it has been felt that actual quotations of the Acts are preferable to a rendering in more colloquial language which could be misleading as to its actual meaning and legal interpretation.

8.2 Women

8.2.1 Development of female employment

The Industrial Revolution (a period in English history which, according to most historians, took place between 1780 and 1850) transformed England from a predominantly agricultural country into an industrial one, which with some justice was called the workshop of the world. In this period the English peasantry was transformed into the English working class. An appreciation of the development of female employment, in particular, is necessary for an understanding of much of the legislation which has been enacted.

The role of women at work in this period saw a dramatic change from unpaid domestic work. Women in increasing numbers entered industry and thus took on a dual role of breadwinner and housewife without relinquishing domestic unpaid work in a male-dominated society.

The 1844 census lists 457 industries and professions. Of these, 76 are given as having around a total of 2 million women in them, some in very small numbers. Of 1075 women in professions other than teaching and nursing (which had 32 192 and 13 188, respectively), 448 were actresses. Almost a million women were engaged in some form of domestic work, including boarding house keepers, with 908 471 domestic servants among them. There were 305 081 women in all branches of the textile industry, nearly 170 000 in the cotton industry. Almost 300 000 were in all branches of the clothing industry. Among other working women, 13 182 are given as factory workers, 14 614 as labourers and 76 174 as agricultural labourers.

Later in the nineteenth century and up to the 1911 census the female labour force grew from 3 887 000 in 1881 to 5 424 000 in 1911; in the same period the female population over 10 years of age grew from 11½ to 18½ million. Over the same period the male labour force grew from 8 851 000 to 13 656 000 and the male population over the age of 10 grew from around 10½ million to 16½ million.

The first returns on married women in industry were made in 1907. These showed that 24.1 per cent of the female labour force in textiles were married, 16.3 per cent in non-textiles and 28 per cent in laundries.

The pattern of employment for women changed a great deal during World War I but especially after the introduction of conscription in 1916. In July 1914 there were 212 000 women employed in the engineering/munitions industries; by July 1915 it had risen to 256 000; by July 1916 to 520 000; by July 1917 to 819 000; and by the end of the war to almost one million.

In industry as a whole the total employment of women and girls over 10 years of age between 1914 and 1918 increased by about 800 000 from 2 179 000 to 2 971 000. The most dramatic increase, of 100 000 women, occurred in transport, from 18 000 in 1914 to 117 000 by 1918. Domestic service is the industry which shows a substantial decline of female employees, from 1 658 000 in 1914 to 1 258 000 in 1918 – a decline of 400 000 during the war. It still remained a substantial employment area for women in the 1920s. Since then domestic service in private households has dramatically declined.

After transport the biggest proportional increases in the employment of women were in clerical, administration and educational activities. Banking and finance female employees increased from 9500 in 1914 to 63 700 in 1917. During the war years the number of women employed in commerce and allied occupations rose from 505 000 to 934 000. In national and local government employment, which included teaching, the numbers rose from 262 000 to 460 000 during the war years.

During these war years the pattern of women's employment in the twentieth century were set. While during the inter-war years fluctuations in specific industries and occupations occurred, World War II and the post-1945 period saw further development of the established trend, so that now there are approximately 9 million women employed; about 42 per cent of the total available female labour force between the ages of 16 and 60.

Changing technology has been responsible for making women compete for jobs which in the past were the preserves of males. While at an earlier period muscular strength was a prerequisite in many industrial occupations, physical strength has become less important. Therefore, as technology advances, women tend to be able to compete with men on more equal terms. Where manual dexterity is required, women seem to have an advantage over men, and as far as mental abilities are concerned, few dare to suggest to-day that women are not equal to men.

8.2.2 Concentration of women in certain industries

Although about 42 per cent of employed workers are women, a closer analysis reveals that more than half of all employed women are concentrated in three sectors of industry: miscellaneous services (including catering, hairdressing and cleaning); professional and scientific services (including education, social work and banking); and distributive trades.

Within the manufacturing sector, women are similarly concentrated into particular sections – i.e. food, textiles and clothing. There is no comparable concentration of male workers in any industry or sector. Over the whole period in which the number of employed women has increased, their concentration into specific areas of work has remained a constant feature. (Between 1951 and 1971 the labour force grew by 2.5 million people, of whom 2.3 million were women. By 1971 they constituted 38.7 per cent of the workforce. The figure is now 40 per cent.)

The trends seem to indicate that certain sectors mainly employing women have expanded and not that women have moved in any significant numbers into 'men's' jobs. There seems to be no evidence that the demarcation lines between 'men's' and 'women's' work have begun seriously to shift.

8.2.3 The legal position of women in employment

The legal position of women in our society has undergone a radical change in the last 120 years. The most radical changes took place after 1918, when women obtained the right to vote and to be elected if over 30 years of age. In 1929 the age limit was dropped to 21 years of age and in 1971 youths of both sexes obtained the franchise at 18.

In the 1970s several pieces of legislation were adopted which have changed the legal position of women at work considerably. They are the Equal Pay Act of 1970; The Sex Discrimination Act 1975 and the maternity provision of the Employment Protection Act 1975; the Employment Protection Consolidation Act of 1978; and one provision of the Employment Act 1980.

8.2.4 The Equal Pay Act 1970

The Equal Pay Act was adopted by Parliament in 1970 after about 100 years of agitation to achieve equal pay for women. It stipulated that it should become operative at the beginning of 1976, allowing 5 years of grace in which women's pay was to be raised to the level of men's.

While the trade union movement talked of 'equal pay for equal work', the International Labour Office (ILO) (an international organization in which employers, trade unions and governments of the majority of countries are represented) formulated the demand for pay equality differently. The formula of the ILO is 'equal pay for work of equal value', which has a very specific meaning. In terms of the analysis presented in Chapter 3, this can be interpreted to mean that, in given employments, if a woman has (or would have) the same marginal revenue product as a man, she should receive the same wage. This would be the case if 'equal value' was taken to mean output of equal value. The formula of the Equal Pay Act 1970 is different and the difference is important from the point of view of eventually achieving pay equality for women.

The conditions for pay equality are spelled out in the Equal Pay Act 1970, Section 1 (4):

A woman is to be regarded as employed on like work with men if, but only if, her work and theirs is of the same or a broadly similar nature, and the differences (if any) between the things she does and the things they do are not of practical importance in relation to terms and conditions of employment; and accordingly in comparing her work with theirs regard shall be had to the frequency or otherwise with which any such differences occur in practice as well as to the nature and extent of the differences.

In Section 1(5) the Act further defines the grounds for equal pay:

A woman is to be regarded as employed on work rated as equivalent with that of any men if, but only if, her job and their job have been given an equal value, in terms of the demand made on a worker under various headings (for instance effort, skill, decision), on a study undertaken with a view to evaluating in those terms the jobs to be done by all or any of the employees in an undertaking or group of undertakings, or would have been given an equal value but for the evaluation being made on a system setting different values for men and women on the same demand under any heading.

It is important to note that the equality provisions as well as pay only apply when the comparison between men's and women's work is made in the same firm or by associated employers – i.e. according to Section 1 (2) of the Equal Pay Act 1970:

at the same establishment or at establishments in Great Britain which include that one and at which common terms and conditions of employment are observed either generally or for employees of the relevant classes.

The effect of the legislation after 1970 has been to raise women's pay on average to about two-thirds of the average pay of men, but since 1977/78 the average pay of women has begun to decline again in relation to male average earnings (see *Figure 8.1*). The reasons for this are

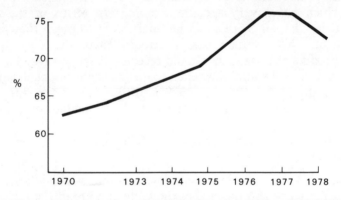

Figure 8.1 Women's earnings as a proportion of men's earnings, 1970–1978. Average gross hourly earnings, including the effect of overtime pay and overtime hours, of employees aged 18 and over. Source: Department of Employment *New Earnings Survey*

complex, but one is that the meaning of the British phrasing of 'broadly similar work' is difficult to interpret and comparisons between male and female occupations are difficult to make. Neither is an employer compelled to establish values of work by job evaluation schemes. In any case, comparisons can only be made within a firm or establishment under the same management. If the ILO formula of 'equal pay for work of equal value' had been adopted and job evaluation made compulsory across the board and between industries (for example, comparing the value of work done by a tool-maker and a clothing machinist), earnings of women would by now be more equal to those of men, especially if occupational barriers had also been removed.

Another possible explanation why average hourly gross earnings of women have declined since 1977/78 is the way wage increases have been negotiated since the £6 across the board increase under the Social Contract arrangements. Since then wage and salary increases have been based on percentages which tend to increase differentials between the higher male rates and the lower women's rates. An absolute amount increase for all wage or salary earners tends to narrow differentials, especially if, as under the Social Contract of 1975/76, an upper limit is put on wage increase entitlement.

Since 1978 there have been few cases concerning equal pay issues which have come before industrial tribunals. It seems that the limitations of the legislation to secure a genuine equality of pay for work of equal value is now well understood by employers, employees and their trade union representatives.

8.2.5 The Sex Discrimination Act 1975

This Act came into force on 29 December 1975. It marked the culmination of a long and sometimes bitter campaign to make discrimination against women unlawful. While the Act covers the wider aspects of discrimination against women, in the present context we wish primarily to deal with discrimination in the working environment.

The preamble of the Act states its intention in the following terms:

An Act to render unlawful certain kinds of sex discrimination and discrimination on the ground of marriage, and establish a commission with the function of working towards the elimination of such discrimination and promoting equality of opportunity between men and women generally; and for related purposes.

It then defines discrimination:

Part 1 (1)

A person discriminates against a woman in any circumstances relevant for the purposes of any provision of this Act if
(a) on the ground of her sex he treats her less favourably than he treats or would treat a man but –
   (i)   which is such that the proportion of women who can comply with it is considerably smaller than the proportion of men who can comply with it, and
   (ii) which he cannot show to be justifiable irrespective of the sex of the person to whom it is applied, and
   (iii) which is to her detriment because she cannot comply with it.

As far as marital status is concerned the Act stipulates:

Part I

(2) If a person treats or would treat a man differently according to the man's marital status, his treatment of a woman is for the purposes of subsection (1)(a) to be compared to his treatment of a man having the like marital status.

Discrimination in the employment field:

Section 3 (1)

A person discriminates against a married person of either sex in any circumstances relevant for the purposes of any provision of Part II (in employment) if –

(a) on the ground of his or her marital status he treats that person less favourably than he treats or would treat an unmarried person of the same sex, or

(b) he applies to that person a requirement or condition which he applies or would apply equally to an unmarried person but –
  (i)   which is such that the proportion of married persons who can comply with it is considerably smaller than the proportion of unmarried persons of the same sex who can comply with it, and
  (ii) which he cannot show to be justifiable irrespective of the marital status of the person to whom it is applied, and
  (iii) which is to that person's detriment because he cannot comply with it.

It is important to note that the discrimination applies equally to men, and the Act expresses it thus:

(2) For the purposes of subsection (1), a provision of Part II [i.e. employment] framed with reference to discrimination against women shall be treated as applying equally to the treatment of men, and for that purpose shall have the effect with such modifications as are requisite.

Part II of the Act deals with 'discrimination against applicants and employees'. In Section 6 (1) it states:

it is unlawful for a person, in relation to employment by him at an establishment in Great Britain, to discriminate against a person –
  (a) in the arrangement he makes for the purpose of determining who should be offered that employment, or
  (b) in the terms on which he offers her that employment, or
  (c) by refusing or deliberately omitting to offer her that employment.

(2) It is unlawful for a person, in the case of a woman employed by him at an establishment in Great Britain, to discriminate against her –

    (a) in the way he affords her access to opportunities for promotion, transfer training, or to any other benefits, facilities or services, or by refusing or deliberately omitting to afford her access to them, or

    (b) by dismissing her or subjecting her to any other detriment.

However, there are certain exceptions applying to *private households* and *small firms*. In the guide to the Sex Discrimination Act these exceptions are stated to be, according to Section 6 (3),

Sex discrimination and discrimination against married persons (but not victimisation) by an employer are not unlawful in relation to his existing employees or potential employees where:

    (a) the employment in question is for the purposes of a private household, or

    (b) the employer, together with any asociated employers of his, does not employ a total of more than five persons (including part-time employees but excluding persons employed for the purposes of a private household); if the employer has more than one establishment, it is the total of all his employees which determines whether the exception applies.

There are exceptions when sex is a genuine occupational qualification and these exceptions apply to opportunities for promotion or transfer to, or training for, such employment. The exceptions occur where the nature of the job calls for a man or woman 'for reason of physiology (excluding physical strength or stamina) or, in dramatic performances . . . for reasons of authenticity'; or for reasons to preserve decency or privacy. Other exceptions include location of an establishment, sleeping arrangements, etc.; or when

the holder of the job provides individuals with personal services promoting their welfare or education . | . or the job needs to be held by a man because of restrictions imposed by the laws regulating the employment of women| or the job needs to be held by a man because it is likely to involve the performance of duties outside the UK in a country whose laws or customs are such that the duties could not, or could not effectively, be performed by a woman| or the job is one of two to be held by a married couple.

The Sex Discrimination Act allows women governors to be in charge of male prisons, and vice versa; it allows women on special assignments to go down into a coal mine; and it permits males to take on the office of a midwife.

Other unlawful acts include:

to publish or cause to be published an advertisement which indicates, or might reasonably be understood as indicating, an intention by a person to do any act which is or might be unlawful by virtue of any of the above stipulations. For this purpose the use of a job description with a sexual connotation (such as 'waiter', 'salesgirl', 'postman', or 'stewardess') shall be taken to indicate an intention to discriminate, unless the advertisement contains an indication to the contrary.

When it comes to enforcement of the Act, the following stipulation is worth a great deal of attention. Section 66 (4) says:

For the avoidance of doubt it is hereby declared that damages in respect of an unlawful act of discrimination *may include compensation for injury of feeling*, whether or not they include compensation under any other head.

To supervise the operation of the Act an Equal Opportunities Commission was established, appointed by the Secretary of State:

(a) to work towards the elimination of discrimination,
(b) to promote equality of opportunity between men and women generally, and
(c) to keep under review the working of this Act and the Equal Pay Act 1970 and, when they are so required by the Secretary of State or otherwise think it necessary, draw up and submit to the Secretary of State proposals for amending them.

The enforcement of the Act in the employment field shall take place through a complaint to an industrial tribunal.

The Commission is empowered to render assistance to a claimant if they think fit to do so on the ground that –

(a) the case raises a question of principle, or
(b) it is unreasonable, having regard to the complexity of the case or the applicant's position in relation to the respondent or another person involved or any other matter, to expect the applicant to deal with the case unaided, or by reason of any other special consideration.

The assistance as laid down in the Act is comprehensive and may be costly.

8.2.6 Maternity provisions

The Employment Protection Act 1975, and later the Employment Protection (Consolidation) Act 1978, for the first time in English legislation make provision to protect the pregnant woman from unfair dismissal and grant specific maternity rights to women, depending on the length of service with a particular firm.

The Employment Protection Consolidation Act 1978 puts the question of unfair dismissal on the grounds of pregnancy as follows:

Section 60

(1) An employee shall be treated for the purposes of this Part unfairly dismissed if the reason or principal reason for the dismissal is that she is pregnant or is any other reason connected with her pregnancy, except one of the following reasons –

(a) that at the effective date of termination she is or will have become, because of her pregnancy, incapable of adequately doing the work which she is employed to do;

(b) that, because of her pregnancy, she cannot or will not be able to continue after that date to do that work without contravention (either by her or her employer) of a duty or restriction imposed by or under any enactment.

Paragraph (b) above applies to such radiation or chemical hazards as well as lifting of loads which might be deleterious to women's health or injurious to the fetus.

Further the Act stipulates that:

(2) An employee shall be treated . . . as unfairly dismissed if her employer dismisses her for a reason mentioned in subsection (1) (a) or (b) above, but neither he nor any successor of his, where there is a suitable available vacancy makes her an offer before or on the effective date of termination to engage her under a new contract of employment complying with subsection (3).

In subsection (3) (b) the Act stipulates:

The new contract of employment must

(b) be such that the work to be done under the contract is of a kind which is both suitable in relation to the employee and appropriate for her to do in the circumstances, and

(c) be such that the provisions of the new contract as to the capacity and place in which she is to be employed and as to the other terms and conditions of her employment are not substantially less favourable to her than the corresponding provisions of the previous contract.

Maternity provisions are covered by section 33 of the Employment Protection (Consolidation) Act 1978 and these provisions are concerned with certain payments during the period of maternity leave and an entitlement to return to work. Section 33 (1) states:

An employee who is absent from work wholly or partly because of pregnancy or confinement shall, subject to the following provisions of this Act, –
(a) be entitled to be paid by her employer a sum to be known as maternity pay; and
(b) be entitled to return to work.

These entitlements are conditional on her having worked for the same employer for 2 years at least prior to 11 weeks before the expected confinement. However, she must inform her employer (in writing if he so requests) at least 21 days before her absence begins that she will be absent from work because of pregnancy and that she intends to return to work with her employer.

The maternity pay a woman is entitled to if she complies with the above conditions of at least 2 years' service is nine-tenths of a week's pay reduced by the amount of maternity allowance payable for the week under Part I of schedule 4 of the Social Security Act 1975, whether or not the employee in question is entitled to the whole or any part of the allowance.

8.2.7 Right to return to work

Section 45 of the Employment Protection (Consolidation) Act 1978, deals with the

right to return to work with her original employer . . . at any time before the end of the period of twenty-nine weeks beginning with the week in which the date of confinement falls, in the job in which she was employed under the original contract of employment and on terms and conditions not less favourable than those which would have been applicable to her if she had not been absent.

The above terms mean, as regards seniority, pension rights and other similar rights, that the period or periods of employment prior to the employee's absence shall be regarded as continuous with her employment following her absence. The period in which a woman is entitled to resume her previous employment can be extended for 4 weeks on medical grounds.

The above legislation giving women certain rights is by no means generous by European standards; in fact, the provisions are the worst in the EEC according to a report by the Low Pay Unit. Even then, only a tiny fraction of working women get maternity leave and return to their jobs. There is no onus on employers to inform women of their rights and, of course, the employer may be ignorant of the maternity provision.

Government-commissioned research in 1978 revealed that of a random sample of 301 firms with fewer than 50 employees only 11 per cent knew of the qualifying conditions for maternity leave.

Only 11 600 women enjoyed maternity leave between July 1978 and July 1979. That figure represents 3 out of 1000 childbearing women. However, the present government intends on the one hand to limit women's rights further, excluding those employed by small firms with fewer than six employees, and on the other to give pregnant women certain additional rights according to the Employment Act 1980.

8.2.8 Proposed changes in the Employment Act 1980

The return procedures in the Employment Act 1980 have been tightened up by requiring an additional notice in writing as well as requiring the woman who intends to return to her previous job to give notice of her intent 21 days (instead of 7 days, as under the 1978 Act) before her intended return. The pregnant woman has to have 12 months' continuous service before she has the right not to be unfairly dismissed because of pregnancy according to Statutory Instrument 1979/959, The Unfair Dismissal (Variation of Qualifying Period) Order 1979.

8.2.9 Time off for ante-natal care

In only one case was the Employment Protection (Consolidation) Act 1978 amended and improved by the Employment Act 1980. This was because of the importance of early and regular ante-natal care to combat perinatal and infant mortality. Employment Act 1980 Section 31A (1):

> An employee who is pregnant and who has, on the advice of a registered medical practitioner, registered midwife or registered health visitor, made an appointment to attend at any place for the purpose of receiving ante-natal care, shall, subject to the following provisions of this section, have the right not to be unreasonably refused time off during her working hours to enable her to keep the appointment.

and Section (4) states:

> An employee who is permitted to take time off during her working hours in accordance with subsection (1) shall be entitled to be paid remuneration by her employer for the period of absence at the appropriate hourly rate.

8.2.10 The discussion over equality and positive discrimination

Since the Coal Mining Act of 1842 there has been positive discrimination in favour of women. The Act of 1842 forbade the underground employment of women and girls and the Factories Act of 1844 brought women workers within 'the slender protection of the statute as well as young persons' (Lord Wedderburn, 1971). The hours of women as well as young persons were restricted to ten hours per day by 1848.

Today Part VI of the Factories Act 1961 protects women and young persons at work through the operation of Section 84–94. The main features of this legislation are:

(1) The total hours worked by women, excluding intervals for meals and rest, must not exceed 9 in any day or 48 in any week.
(2) The period of employment must not start before 7.00 a.m. nor end after 8.00 p.m. (1.00 p.m. on Saturdays).
(3) The working spell must not last longer than 4½ hours without a break of at least 30 minutes; or 5 hours if there has been at least a 10 minute break.
(4) Overtime – can be done provided that total hours worked do not exceed 10 in any day and work does not start before 7.00 a.m. nor finish after 9.00 p.m. (1.00 p.m. on Saturdays). Overtime must not be worked at a factory for more than 6 hours in any week.
(5) Nightwork is specifically prohibited, and most shift systems are also prevented by the regulations. There are, however, specific exceptions to the restrictions; and there is provision for exemption from the requirements.

8.2.11 The Equal Opportunities Commission (EOC)

The Sex Discrimination Act 1978 established the Equal Opportunities Commission, consisting of at least 8 but not more than 15 individuals, each appointed by the Secretary of State on a full-time or part-time basis, which shall have the following duties:

(1) to work towards the elimination of discrimination;
(2) to promote equality of opportunity between men and women generally; and
(3) to keep under review the working of this Act and the Equal Pay Act 1970, and when they are so required by the Secretary of State or otherwise think it necessary, draw up and submit to the Secretary of State proposals for amending them.

The Commission is also charged to review discriminatory provisions in health and safety regulations, and to draw up proposals and submit them to the Secretary of State for amending the relevant legislation.

8.2.12 The Equal Opportunities Commission's report on women's working hours

In March 1980 the EOC, after 3 years of deliberation, presented a report to the Employment Secretary entitled 'Health and Safety Legislation. Should We Distinguish between Men and Women?' The report is concerned about the way women are treated differently from men on the factory floor, particularly over hours of work. The EOC says that the hours of work laws are out of date, form a barrier to equal pay and job opportunity and should therefore be abolished. This would mean an end to the regulations which limit nightwork, double day shifts and the number of weekly hours a woman may work.

This report of the EOC has stirred up a hornet's nest of opposition, especially from the trade union movement, whose demand for a reduction in working hours to 35 is featuring in all pay negotiations and whose approach to the problem is to bring men's conditions up to the level of women's conditions both in regard to working hours and, especially, in regard to lowering the retirement age of men to 60.

The EOC argued that 'if the law is changed there appear to be numbers of women willing to take up night-work if it is available', but the Commission's own survey said:

> For the least socially acceptable working times, such as weekends, the size of the minority who said they are willing to work shifts was less than 20% of working and non-working women alike. On nightwork 80% of the sample said they would never consider it and only 11% said they would definitely consider it.

However, the most important finding was that full-time workers in manufacturing industry were least in favour of the repeal of protective legislation.

8.2.13 The TUC and the EOC

The TUC at its Congress in 1979 passed the following motion unanimously:

> Congress notes with regret the Report of the Equal Opportunities Commission on health and safety legislation and their recommendations that, with few exceptions, the hours of work provision in the Factories Act should be abolished. Congress considers that the first principle concerning the working life of all must be their health, safety and welfare and reiterates its long-standing opposition to the wholesale abolition of Part VI of the 1961 Factories Act. Furthermore, Congress recommends that discussions be initiated with the Health and Safety Commission with a view to extending the protection at present afforded to women on nightwork and shift work to men and to those categories of women at present without such protective legislation.

As a postscript to the debate on sex discrimination, we may quote a Cabinet Minister, Patrick Jenkins, who stated on television as reported in the *Guardian* on 6 November 1979:

> Quite frankly, I don't think mothers have the same right to work as fathers. If the Good Lord had intended us to have equal rights to go out to work, he wouldn't have created men and women. These are biological facts, young children do depend on their mothers.

8.3 Equal opportunities and race relations

Having discussed the question of equal opportunities for women, we must now focus our attention on another group of people whose presence has compelled Parliament to put legislation on the statute book to provide a civilized environment for people who are ethnically or racially different from the majority of the population. There are about one-and-three-quarters million black people in Britain today, and about 40 per cent were born here and know no other country. Therefore, Britain is and will remain a multiracial society.

8.3.1 The Race Relations Act 1976

The preamble to the Act states:

> An Act to make fresh provisions with respect to discrimination on racial grounds and relations between people of different racial groups; and to make in the Sex Discrimination Act 1975 amendments for bringing provisions in that Act relating to its administration and enforcement into conformity with the corresponding provisions in this Act.

Then, in Section (1) of the Act, Parliament has spelled out *what racial discrimination is in law*.

(1) A person discriminates against another in any circumstances relevant for the purposes of any provision of this Act if –
    (a) on racial grounds he treats that other less favourably than he treats or would treat other persons; or
    (b) he applies to that other a requirement or condition which he applies or would apply equally to persons not of the same racial group as that other but –
        (i) which is such that the proportion of persons of the same racial group as that other who can comply with it is considerably smaller than the proportion of persons not of that racial group who can comply with it; and
        (ii) which he cannot show to be justifiable, irrespective of the colour, race, nationality or ethnic or national origins of the person to whom it is applied; and

(iii) which is to the detriment of that other because he cannot comply with it.

(2) It is hereby declared that, for the purposes of this Act, segregating a person from other persons on racial grounds is treating him less favourably than they are treated.

This Act means that discrimination on racial grounds in employment, education, and the provision of goods, facilities and services is illegal. Discrimination on racial grounds means discrimination on grounds of a person's colour, race, nationality (which includes citizenship) or ethnic or national origins.

As with the law on sex discrimination, the Race Relations Act contains provisions relating to: (a) genuine occupational qualifications and (b) positive action.

8.3.2 Genuine occupational qualifications

This means that if authenticity requires it, then jobs can be reserved for a particular race (e.g. someone Chinese to be a waiter in a Chinese restaurant; a white to play Richard III, or a black to play Othello).

8.3.3 Positive action

This means that where there have been no or comparatively few workers of a particular racial group in certain jobs over the past 12 months, an employer can lawfully provide special training for this group to equip them to do this work. The law does not, however, allow employers to discriminate by reserving certain jobs for workers from a particular racial group following this training.

8.3.4 Advertising

As with acts of discrimination against women, 'it is unlawful to publish or cause to be published an advertisement which indicates, or might reasonably be understood as indicating, an intention by a person to do an act of discrimination'.

8.3.5 Commission for Racial Equality

The Act also established the Commission for Racial Equality (CRE), which works together with local community relations councils. The Commission has broad powers to undertake investigations for any purpose connected with its duties. Where it finds discrimination, it may issue a non-discrimination notice requiring this to cease. It may bring proceedings against persistent discriminators. It undertakes advisory and education work, and assists community relations councils, ethnic minority organizations and other organizations in the promotion of equality of opportunity and good race relations. It has a responsibility to draw up a code of practice in employment. Although the Commission is not obliged to investigate individual complaints, it has a discretion to advise and assist complainants where there are special reasons for so doing.

The work of the CRE at local level is mainly channelled through community relations councils, to which local authorities, churches, tenant organizations, trade unions, etc., may be affiliated.

8.3.6 Legal procedures and remedies

If a grievance over racial discrimination cannot be solved through normal procedures, the case can go to an industrial tribunal, within 3 months of the date of the act complained of. A tribunal can make a declaration of rights, award compensation or recommend a particular course of action to remedy the discrimination.

It is true to say that the law so far has mainly an educational impact and is designed to make it suitable for a multiracial society to function in the UK. Very few cases that go to a tribunal are won by workers, because by its very nature discrimination is frequently very difficult to prove. It is even more difficult in cases concerning job applications, since the Appeal Court ruled that employers cannot be asked to disclose confidential documents relating to other candidates being considered for jobs. The case which made this clear is Vyas versus Leyland Cars.

8.3.7 Incitement to racial hatred

The Race Relations Act 1976 created a new criminal offence by its amendment of the Public Order Act 1936. Section 5A states:

(1) A person commits an offence if –
   (a) he publishes or distributes written matter which is threatening, abusive or insulting; or
   (b) he uses, in any public place or at any public meeting, words which are threatening, abusive or insulting, in a case where, having regard to all the circumstances, hatred is likely to be stirred up against any racial group in Great Britain by the matter or words in question.

However, the Race Relations Act does not apply to Northern Ireland, and, furthermore, no prosecution for an offence of racial hatred shall be instituted in England and Wales except by or with the consent of the Attorney General.

8.4 Concluding observations

It will be evident from the foregoing that the legislation which has been enacted in respect of discrimination is of considerable importance for organizations and the people who are employed by them. As already indicated, however, there is no evidence to suggest that some of the former and probably many of the latter have more than only a limited knowledge of their obligations and rights. While this chapter has attempted to outline some of the more important aspects of the legislation, space has inevitably imposed its limitation. Moreover, the reader should be aware that new and amending acts are frequently passed which change, modify or extend the law, and those with particular interests in this area should keep themselves informed of such developments.

We have seen in this chapter that the law has been used as a method of (at least partly) dealing with the problem of discrimination in employment. However, this constitutes only one aspect of its use in the employment field, and in the following chapter more general aspects of legislation are considered along with the role of some related organizations.

Questions

1. Enumerate and analyse the causes which made Parliament pass legislation to deal with discrimination against women at work.
2. Under what circumstances can a woman claim equal pay?
3. Under what circumstances can a woman be fairly dismissed because she is pregnant?
4. Under what circumstances is a woman entitled to resume her previous occupation after giving birth to a child?
5. Under what circumstances is a woman entitled to maternity pay?
6. What are the changes proposed in the Employment Act 1980 in regard to women's rights?
7. What do you understand the term 'positive discrimination' to mean, and what are the items of positive discrimination in the Factories Act 1961.
8. The Public Order Act 1936 was amended in 1976. Discuss.
9. Discuss the following cases and work out whether the action described is lawful or unlawful according to the Race Relations Act 1976.

    (a) An employer situated in the centre of Liverpool does not engage people who live in the Liverpool 8 district, because experience has shown that such workers usually bring trouble with them in the shape of their unemployed friends hanging around the shop during working hours.

(b) A Bradford textile manufacturer operates his mill on a three shift system. He has found in the past that his Pakistani and Indian employees do not work well when they are together. He therefore arranges for one shift to be comprised of Pakistanis, another of Indians and the other of indigenous workers, allocating new recruits accordingly. He says he is not discriminating unlawfully as the terms and conditions are the same on each shift.

(c) An employer wishes to increase the employment opportunities he offers to members of racial minority groups. He notices that there are very few coloured typists in the pool and asks his personnel manager to give preference to coloured applicants for future vacancies.

(d) A civil engineering company refuses to employ a Sikh surveyor as the company rules forbid any employee to work on a site without wearing a safety helmet.

(e) A West Indian applies for promotion to supervisor. The employers say that although he is qualified for the job, and he personally would be prepared to give him a try, he cannot accept him as the men he would be in charge of have told him they could not work for a black man.

(f) A firm makes 15 West Indians and 5 white men redundant. When their union protests that only 10 per cent of the workforce are West Indian, he says that he is not discriminating as he is simply abiding by the jointly agreed 'last in–first out' rule.

(g) A lady seeking a daily help refuses to accept a woman of Hungarian origin who has been referred to her by a local employment agency.

(h) The Manager of an 'Olde Englande' banqueting hall refuses to recruit a Spanish chef because he says that he has to recruit English staff only, to maintain the special atmosphere sought by his clients.

(i) A craft trade union requires all members to have been employed in their trade in this country for 10 years before becoming eligible to stand for election for official posts.

(j) An industrial training board in the electronics industry specifies that all its trainees must have passed 'O'-level mathematics and English language, or their equivalent for work, on the assembly line.

(k) A theatrical agency is asked to supply actors for audition as Richard II in a television broadcast for schools. They send three white actors and one black actor who they consider would be suitable. Without conducting an audition, the casting direcctor rejects the black actor, as he says he is unsuitable for the part.

(l)   Over lunch, the works manager remarks to one of his supervisors how much he agreed with Enoch Powell's speech on race relations which was reported in the paper. Remembering this conversation 2 weeks later, the supervisor does not submit the names of any of his workers from racial minority groups for a promotion panel.

(m) A white employer on the point of offering a job to a white female applicant discovers during the conversation that she is married to a black West Indian. He changes his mind as a result and does not offer her the job.

(n)   An employer running a TV repair business decides against offering a job to a black TV engineer on the grounds that the job is mainly repairing sets in people's homes and the employer fears that some of his customers would not like a black man in their home.

(o)   The foundry in a heavy engineering firm is manned entirely by West Indians. The rest of the workforce elsewhere in the firm is mainly white, and to produce what he thinks is a healthier balance the employer transfers some black foundry workers into the factory and replaces them with white workers from the factory.

(p)   A trade union is worried that only a small proportion of the Asian workers eligible for membership have actually joined the union. They decide to appoint a coloured liaison officer of Indian national origin to encourage a higher recruitment rate.

References

Ramelson, Marian (1976). *The Petticoat Rebellion*, Lawrence and Wishart, London
Report of the War Cabinet Committee on Women in Industry, Cmd. 135/1919, HMSO, London
Webb, Mrs Sydney (1919). *Men's and Women's Wages: Should they be Equal?*, Fabian Society, London
Lord Wedderburn (1971). *The Worker and the Law*, Penguin, Harmondsworth, p. 239.

Further reading

Miscellaneous TUC *Annual Reports* on the Employment of Women, TUC Publications, London

Chapter 9

Legal relationships between people and organizations

9.1 Introduction

In the post-war period we have seen a great increase in legislation dealing with the employment relationship between people and organizations. The area which this chapter will cover includes trade union legislation, health and safety, the Employment Protection (Consolidation) Act 1978 and minimum wages legislation.

9.2 Development of legislation

Over the centuries the law has played a significant part in the relationship between people and organizations. For example, the Ordinance of Labourers in 1349 made magistrates in Quarter Sessions responsible for fixing wage rates and the Statute of Labourers of 1351 subjected workmen who failed to fulfil their duties to the masters employing them to criminal penalties, including imprisonment. Several hundred pieces of legislation regulating the relationship between people and organizations have been put on the statute book since the Statute of Labourers. The nineteenth century started by outlawing all trade unions (or 'combinations', as they were called) because their activities were considered to be 'criminal conspiracies in restraint of trade'. Trade was supposed to proceed uninhibited by monopolies of labour, or manufacturing or trading organizations. By 1825 Parliament repealed the Combination Acts of 1799 and 1800 and the long history of a legal trade union movement entered the stage of history in Britain.

The device which made trade unions legal was to grant trade unions immunities for activities which according to common law concepts were otherwise unlawful. The entire history of trade union legislation since 1825 is concerned with the extension of immunities at one period and in another reducing these immunities again. Thus, again, in 1980 we witnessed Parliament in the process of reducing the immunities of trade unions and trade unionists which had been established by the passage of the Trade Union and Labour Relations Act of 1974 and its Amendment Act of 1976.

Apart from the legislation dealing with the activities of trade unionists and trade unions, Parliament enacted a considerable amount of legislation dealing with employer–employee relationships. Much of it is designed to protect the employee from unscrupulous employers, to protect fair employers from being undercut by unfair employers, to protect the employee's health and to protect the environment.

Other legislation which has an impact on employer–employee relationships and which has been the subject of campaigning by trade unions is the social responsibility of both the State and the individual employer towards the individual employee. It deals with those events and periods in an employee's life when the employee is unable to earn a living and is either prevented from working or unable to work, when old age, sickness or unemployment severs the employer–employee relationship. This type of legislation, while it does not deal directly with the relationship of people in organizations, nevertheless has a profound influence on the behaviour of people in organizations.

The modern legislation dealing with trade unions commenced in the 1870s. Between 1901 and 1906 there was a marked change in attitudes towards trade unions, and the Trade Union Act of 1906 laid the basis for the present legislation. In 1971 the Industrial Relations Act reversed the process of extending immunities after a long debate on trade union rights in which the Royal Commission on Trade Unions and Employers' Associations under Lord Donovan played a prominent part.

In 1974 under a Labour administration the Trade Union and Labour Relations Act (TULRA) was passed and in 1976 slightly amended. While certain of its provisions are likely to be again amended, this Act forms the basis of the present legal position of trade unions and the activities of trade unionists.

9.3 The Trade Union and Labour Relations Act 1974 (TULRA)

9.3.1 Trade unions and immunities

The Trade Union and Labour Relations Act of 1974 established the legal meaning of a trade union. The definition is important because of its wide scope in providing immunities for individuals and organizations engaged in trade union activities.

TULRA describes a trade union in the following terms in Section 28 (as elsewhere in this volume, we prefer to quote from the appropriate documents so that misinterpretations are avoided which may occur with paraphrasing):

In this Act, except, so far as the context otherwise requires, 'trade union' means an organisation (whether permanent or temporary) which either –

(a) consists wholly or mainly of workers of one or more descriptions and is an organisation whose principal purposes include the regulation of relations between workers of that description or those descriptions and employers' associations; or

(b) consists wholly or mainly of –

    (i) constituent or affiliated organisations which fulfil the conditions specified in paragraph (a) above (or themselves consist wholly or mainly of constituent or affiliated organisations which fulfill those conditions), or

    (ii) representatives of such constituent or affiliated organisations; and in either case is an organisation whose principal purposes include the regulation of relations between workers and employers or between workers and employers' associations, or include the regulation of relations between its constituent or affiliated organisations.

It is evident from this definition that any type of organization, whether permanent or temporary, whose principal purposes include the regulation of relations between workers and employers is a trade union in law and therefore protected in law.

The next question that follows from the above definition is: what is protected? What activities attract immunities from actions in tort[1] for a breach of contract? What is the meaning of a trade dispute which can be conducted with immunity? The meaning of a trade dispute is defined in TULRA (Section 29) as follows:

(1) In this Act 'trade dispute' means a dispute between employers and workers, or between workers and workers, which is connected with one of the following, that is to say –

    (a) terms and conditions of employment, or the physical conditions in which any workers are required to work;

    (b) engagement or non-engagement, or termination or suspension of employment or the duties of employment, of one or more workers;

    (c) allocation of work or the duties of employment as between workers or groups of workers;

    (d) matters of discipline;

    (e) the membership or non-membership of a trade union on the part of a worker;

    (f) facilities for officials of trade unions; and

    (g) machinery for negotiation or consultation; and other procedures, relating to any of the foregoing matters, including the recognition by employers or employers' associations of the right of a trade union to represent workers in any such negotiation or consultation or in the carrying out of such procedures.

Disputes between workers employed by the Crown are defined in Section 29 (2) of TULRA. Equally covered are disputes which relate to matters occurring outside Great Britain in Section 29 (3) of TULRA.

Having dealt with the question of what is a trade union and what constitutes a trade dispute, we now have to ask what constitutes restrictions on legal liability and legal proceedings, which are the so-called immunities, in relationship to acts in contemplation or further-ance of a trade dispute. This is dealt with in Section 13 of TULRA as amended in 1976. It reads as follows:

An act done by a person in contemplation or furtherance of a trade dispute shall not be actionable[2] in tort on the ground only –
(a) that it induces another person to break a contract or interferes or induces any other person to interfere with its performance; or
(b) that it consists in his threatening that a contract (whether one to which he is a party or not) will be broken or its performance interfered with, or that he will induce another person to break a contract or to interfere with its performance.

TULRA further reinforces the immunity enjoyed by trade unions under the Act by stating in Section 13, paragraph 2:

For the avoidance of doubt it is hereby declared that an act done by a person in contemplation or furtherance of a trade dispute is not actionable in tort on the ground only that it is an interference with the trade, business or employment of another person, or with the right of another person to dispose of his capital or his labour as he wills.

However, the above immunities are severely limited by the Employ-ment Act 1980 where 'secondary action' is involved. Section 17 (1) of the Employment Act 1980 states:

Nothing in Section 13 of the 1974 Act shall prevent an act from being actionable in tort on a ground specified in subsection 1(a) or (b) of that section in any case where –
(a) the contract concerned is not a contract of employment, and
(b) one of the facts relied upon for the purpose of establishing liability is that there has been secondary action which is not action . . . which gives specific immunities.

Section 16 (2) of the Employment Act 1980 defines secondary action thus:

For the purposes of this section there is secondary action in relation to a trade dispute when, and only when, a person –

(a) induces another to break a contract of employment or interferes or induces another to interfere with its performance, or

(b) threatens that a contract of employment under which he or another is employed will be broken or its performance interfered with, or that he will induce another to break a contract of employment or to interfere with its performance,

if the employer under the contract of employment is not a party to the trade dispute.

The concept of secondary industrial action has been developed, the validity of which the unions have refused to recognize, since it seems to be primarily directed at acts of trade union solidarity or against 'blacking' during industrial disputes.

A further significant curtailment of immunities established by TULRA in the Employment Act 1980 is the repeal of Subsection (3) of Section 13 of the 1974 Act, which reads as follows:

(3) For the avoidance of doubt it is hereby declared that –

(a) an act which is by reason of subsection (1) or (2) above is itself not actionable[2];

(b) a breach of contract in contemplation or furtherance of a trade dispute;

shall not be regarded as the doing of an unlawful act or as the use of unlawful means for the purpose of establishing liability in tort.

Repealing the words 'unlawful means' is seen by some lawyers as undermining the concept of any immunity in the pursuit of industrial disputes.

9.3.2 No compulsion to work

An important provision of TULRA Section 16 states:

No court shall, whether by way of –

(a) an order for specific performance or specific implement of a contract of employment, or

(b) an injunction or interdict restraining a breach or threatened breach of such a contract,

compel an employee to do any work or attend at any place for the doing of any work.

But a court can compel a person to maintain himself and, if the person has no means other than by working, a person can also be compelled to maintain dependents. At the same time, a court cannot compel an employer to re-employ a person even if a tribunal has decided that a person has been unfairly dismissed and advocates re-employment.

9.3.3 Peaceful picketing

In the relationship between people and organizations conflicts, highlighted by the media, find expression which, in demonstrations, picketing (in strike situations) and factory occupations, sometime result in violent confrontations both between workers and between striking workers or demonstrators and the police.

The law has tried to deal with these aspects of violent conflict. TULRA 1974 in Section 15 tackled this problem and the Employment Act 1980 has considerably extended Section 15 of TULRA and tightened it up.

TULRA 1974 defines picketing in Section 15 as follows:

It shall be lawful for one or more persons in contemplation or furtherance of a trade dispute to attend at or near –
(a) a place where another person works or carries on business; or
(b) any other place where another person happens to be, not being a place where he resides,
for the purpose only of peacefully obtaining or communicating information, or peacefully persuading any person to work or abstain from working.

This has been the law, with the exception of picketing a place of residence, since 1871. The Employment Act 1980 substantially restricts the right to picket and confines it, according to Section 15 of the Employment Act 1980,

(a) at or near his own place of work, or
(b) if he is an official of a trade union, at or near the place of work of a member of that union whom he is accompanying and whom he represents.

and an act of picketing is actionable in tort unless it is done in the course of attendance declared lawful by Section 15 of the above Act.

9.4 The closed shop

The 'closed shop', which is an arrangement between employers and trade unions where membership of a particular union and a specific branch is a condition in the contract of employment, has long been a controversial issue. The Industrial Relations Act of 1971 made the closed shop unlawful by stipulating that a person had 'the right to belong or not belong to a trade union'.

TULRA repealed the 1971 Act and the 'closed shop' became lawful again, although in spite of the Act of 1971 closed shop arrangements made previously remained in force and the law remained a dead letter; it was unenforceable because trade unions defied the law, some employers found the closed shop convenient and the courts were helpless in the face of sustained opposition which included industrial action. The only reason for a person to opt out of a closed shop arrangement was on the basis of religious conviction. For example, the Plymouth Brethren are a sect to whom this exception applies.

In the Employment Act 1980 the grounds on which a person can object to be a member of a union where a closed shop arrangement applies have been considerably extended to include 'genuine objections on grounds of conscience or other deeply held personal conviction to being a member of any trade union whatsoever or of a particular trade union'. Furthermore, the Bill provides for a strict procedure to be followed to reach a closed shop agreement. For example, at least 80 per cent of the people involved in the contemplated closed shop agreement have to vote in favour of it in a secret ballot.

9.5 A code of practice to promote good industrial relations

An important innovation already in the Industrial Relations Act 1971 was the provision which enabled the Secretary of State to publish a Code of Practice 'containing such guidance as would be helpful for the purpose of promoting good industrial relations'.

The first Code of Practice came into effect in February 1972 and it is still in force after more than ten impressions. The Code of Practice gives practical guidance for promoting good industrial relations. It stresses 'the importance of freely conducted collective bargaining, orderly procedures for settling disputes, free association of workers and employers and freedom and security for workers'.

The Employment Act 1980, using very much the same language as previous Acts, explains the impact of a Code of Practice thus:

A failure on the part of any person to observe any provision of a Code of Practice issued under this section shall not of itself render him liable to any proceedings; but in any proceedings before a court or industrial tribunal or the Central Arbitration Committee –

(a) any such Code shall be admissible in evidence, and

(b) any provision of the Code which appears to the court, tribunal or Committee to be relevant to any question arising in the proceedings shall be taken into account in determining that question.

9.6 Health and safety

9.6.1 Health and Safety at Work Act 1974

The Health and Safety at Work Act has a profound influence on the legal relationship between people and organizations. The Act was a result of the 'Robens Report on Safety and Health at Work' (1972), which was commissioned because of the rise in serious accidents at work in the post-war period, the increase in environmental pollution and the profusion of legal enactments on health and safety which tended to be confusing.

The preamble of the 1974 Act admirably sums up the purpose of the legislation:

> An Act to make further provision for securing the health, safety and welfare of persons at work, for protecting others against risks to health and safety in connection with the activities of persons at work, for controlling the keeping and use and preventing the unlawful acquisition, possession and use of dangerous substances, and for controlling certain emissions into the atmosphere; to make further provision with respect to the employment medical service; to amend the law relating to building regulations, and the Building (Scotland) Act 159; and for connected purposes.

Acts of Parliament dealing with health and safety at work have been on the statute book for 180 years. What is new in the 1974 Act is the coverage the law gives to all places of work. It gives legal recognition to trade union representatives, who take on a watch-dog function in their place of work on behalf of their union, the protection of the environment from industrial pollution. It creates for the first time a separate new office of State: a Health and Safety Commission and Executive to deal with all matters of health and safety connected with work.

9.6.2 General duties of employers and their employees

Section 2 of the Act spells out the duties of employers in regard to health and safety; the most important section is:

> 2.(1) It shall be the duty of every employer to ensure, so far as is reasonably practicable, the health, safety and welfare at work of all his employees.

It then lists these duties in some detail:

Section 2
(a) the provision and maintainance of plant and systems of work that are safe and without risks to health;

(b) arrangements for ensuring safety and absence of risks to health in connection with the use, handling, storage and transport of articles and substances;

(c) the provision, instruction, training and supervision as is necessary to ensure the health and safety at work of his employees;

(d) the maintainance of any place of work in a condition that is safe and without risks to health and the provision and maintenance of means of access to and egress from it that is safe and without such risks;

(e) the provision and maintenance of a working environment for his employees that is safe, and without risks to health, and adequate as regards facilities and arrangements for their welfare at work.

The phrase 'reasonably practicable' occurs at every stage in the health and safety legislation. The explanation of its meaning is found in the interpretation of the courts, mainly in cases connected with the application of the Factory Acts.

In the reference work *Redgraves Health and Safety in Factories* page 36 gives the following explanation:

'Reasonably practicable' . . . is a narrower term than 'physically possible', and implies that a computation must be made in which the quantum of risk is placed in one scale and the sacrifice involved in the measures necessary for averting the risk (whether in money, time or trouble) is placed in the other, and that, if it be shown that there is a gross disproportion between them – the risk being insignificant in relation to the sacrifice – the defendants discharge the onus upon them. Moreover, this computation falls to be made by the owner at a point of time anterior to the accident.

We all accept risks in the pursuit of work and pleasure which we find acceptable. We travel in motor cars where the risk of death according to Lord Rothschild is 1 in 7000 per annum. We fly in aeroplanes, climb mountains and ride motor cycles and find the risk weighed against the sacrifice of not doing these things socially and individually acceptable.

The word 'practicable', if it stands alone, imposes a stricter standard than when preceded by 'reasonably'. In the case Wallhead versus Ruston and Hornsby Ltd (1973) 14 K.I.R.287, 'practicable' was held to imply a consideration of what is possible in the light of current knowledge and invention.

9.6.3 General duties of employers towards outsiders and the outside world

Section 3 of the Act states:

It shall be the duty of every employer to conduct his undertaking in such a way as to ensure, so far as reasonably practicable, that persons not in his employment who may be affected thereby are not thereby exposed to risks to their health and safety.

A similar duty applies to self-employed persons. Persons who have control of non-domestic premises have specific duties in relationship to health and safety for persons not employed by them who make use of these premises.

9.6.4 Protection of the environment

Section 5 of the Health and Safety Act 1974 states:

It shall be the duty of the person having control of any premises . . . to use the best practicable means for preventing the emission into the atmosphere from the premises of noxious or offensive substances and for rendering harmless and inoffensive such substances as may be emitted.

9.6.5 General duties of manufacturers as regards articles and substances for use at work

In line with the now universally accepted concepts of consumer protection, the industrial originator has an enhanced responsibility to both his own workers and the public at large in regard to articles he imports, manufactures and sells.

Section 6 of the Act stipulates:

(1) It shall be the duty of any person who designs, manufactures, imports or supplies any article for use at work –
   (a) to ensure, as far as reasonably practicable, that the article is so designed and constructed as to be safe and without risk to health when properly used;
   (b) to test the article;
   (c) to give information on its safe use.

9.6.6 Obligation for research

(2) It shall be the duty of any person who undertakes the design or manufacture of any article for use at work to carry out or arrange for the carrying out of any necessary research with a view to the discovery and, so far as is reasonably practicable, the elimination

or minimisation of any risk to health or safety to which the design or article may give rise.

The duties and responsibilities of employers are clear and decisive but the individual responsibility of employees is equally spelt out. Section 7 of the Health and Safety Act states:

It shall be the duty of every employee while at work – to take reasonable care for the health and safety of himself and of other persons who may be affected by his acts or omissions at work.

From the individual responsibility of the employer and worker we now proceed to the supervision of the law by the organizations of the mass of the workers: the trade union movement.

9.6.7 Trade union health and safety representation

A most important innovation affecting legal relationship between people and organizations is the provision contained in Section 2, paragraph 4, of the Health and Safety Act, which allows the Secretary of State to make regulations which 'may provide for the appointment in prescribed cases by recognised trade unions of safety representatives from among the employees'.

In Statutory Instrument No. 1977/500, which may be cited as the Safety Representatives and Safety Committees Regulations 1977 and which came into operation in October 1978, it is stated that 'a recognised trade union may appoint safety representatives from among the employees in all cases where one or more employees are employed by an employer by whom it is recognised'. The qualification of the trade union representative is that he shall 'so far as is reasonably practicable either have been employed by his employer throughout the preceding two years or have had at least two years' experience in similar employment'.

9.6.8 Functions of the safety representatives

More than 200 000 representatives had been appointed by 1980 in the UK. Under Section 2 (6) of the Act, every employer is required

to consult safety representatives with a view to the making and maintainance of arrangements which will enable him and his employees to cooperate effectively in promoting and developing measures to ensure the health and safety at work of the employees and in checking the effectiveness of such measures.

9.6.9 The specific functions of a safety representative

(1) To investigate potential hazards and dangerous occurrences at the workplace (whether or not they are drawn to his attention by the employees he represents) and to examine the causes of accidents at the workplace;
(2) to investigate complaints by any employee he represents;
(3) to make representation to the employer;
(4) to carry out inspections;
(5) to represent the employees he was appointed to represent in consultations at the workplace with inspectors of the Health and Safety Executive and of any other enforcing authority; and to receive information from inspectors in accordance with Section 28 (8) of the 1974 Act – (the employer is entitled to receive the same information);
(6) to attend meetings of safety committees when he attends in his capacity as a safety representative in connection with any of the above functions.

It is important to note that 'no function given to a safety representative by this paragraph shall be construed as imposing any duty on him'.

In certain cases safety representatives need not be employees, where this is not practicable – for instance, in the entertainment industry.

9.6.10 Enforcing the law on health and safety – powers and penalties

The Health and Safety at Work Act 1974 provides for three main systems of compulsion on employers to provide and maintain a safe and healthy place of work.

The Health and Safety inspectors, some of whom are employed by the Health and Safety Executive and others by local authorities, suitably qualified for the task, may issue improvement notices or prohibition notices or may proceed through the courts, which can levy increased fines or may imprison law breakers. When the inspector serves an improvement notice, the employer is required to put things right within a specified time. If the necessary action is not taken within the specified time, a prohibition notice may be issued stopping the particular operation which gives rise to the hazard. An inspector also has power to issue an immediate prohibition notice stopping an operation if there is a risk of immediate danger to workers or the general public. Appeals against these notices must be made to an industrial tribunal. An appeal can lead to a stay of execution of an improvement notice, but there can be no delay in the implementation of a prohibition notice if the inspector is of the opinion that there is an immediate risk of serious personal injury. In cases where the inspector thinks that there is no immediate risk, he may give some time for remedial action to be taken. This would constitute a deferred prohibition notice.

Non-compliance with these notices would constitute an offence and could lead to a maximum fine of £1000 on conviction at a magistrates' court, or an unlimited fine or up to 2 years' imprisonment in the case of trial by indictment. In addition to these penalties, there could be a continuing fine of £50 per day for non-compliance with the notices.

9.6.11 The Health and Safety Commission (HSC) and the Health and Safety Executive (HSE) and their respective functions

With the passing of the Health and Safety at Work Act 1974 a new administration was established to organize, develop and control all the activities connected with health and safety in the area of work.

The Health and Safety Commission was established in October 1974 and is made up of a full-time, independent chairman and nine part-time commissioners. The commissioners are made up of three TUC members, three CBI members, two from local authority and an independent member. This body has taken over responsibility formerly held by various government departments for the control of most occupational safety and health matters. The Commission is responsible for the new reorganized and unified inspectorate.

> The Health and Safety Executive shall consist of three persons of whom one shall be appointed by the Commission with the approval of the Secretary of State to be director of the Executive and the others shall be appointed by the Commission with the like approval after consultation with the said director (Health and Safety Act Section 10 (5).

The former government inspectorate, i.e. the Factory Inspectorate, Mines and Quarries Inspectorate and Explosives Inspectorate, have since 1 January 1975 been merged into one body now called the Health and Safety Executive Inspectorate. *Chart 9.1* illustrates the organization of Health and Safety supervision.

9.6.12 New legislation

The provisions of the Health and Safety at Work Act give comprehensive powers to the Commission to make new regulations and to draw up proposals for the extension, revision or replacement of existing legislation concerning the protection of the safety and health of workpeople.

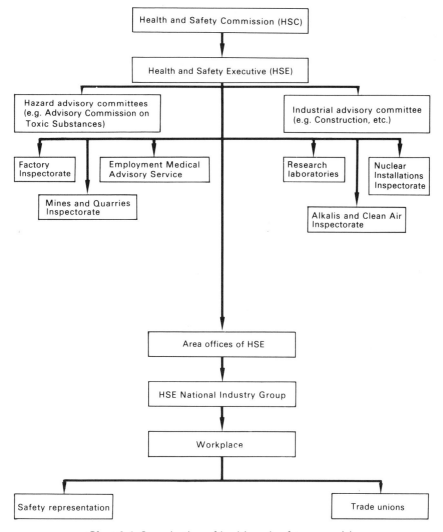

Chart 9.1 Organization of health and safety supervision

However, the Act states that there will be no change in existing statutory protection until adequate measures are available to replace them. The meaning of the last sentence is that the Factories Act 1961, the Offices, Shops and Railway Premises Act 1963 and a long list of other Acts dealing with health and safety in particular circumstances and industries, including fire protection, remain in force for the time being. The Health and Safety at Work Act 1974 is a piece of enabling legislation. It is likely that a Consolidation Act taking in most of the protective legislation will be considered by Parliament in the foreseeable future.

9.7 Employment protection legislation

In this chapter we have so far dealt with the legal relationship between people and organizations where 'people' constitute an organized group. We shall now proceed to deal with the legal relationshp between people and organizations where people are individuals and organizations are either employers or the State.

9.7.1 The contract of employment

Under common law a contract is a bargain to which there are two parties or sides. Each side does something or promises to do something in exchange for an act or promise from the other side. For the worker the contract of employment means that the employer agrees to pay wages for his labour. The agreement does not have to be in writing or be formal.

There is a difference between the legal and the trade union approach to rights at work and the contract of employment. Lawyers would focus attention on the individual contract written or implied, while the trade union approach would regard the collective agreement as the basic document that tells workers what they can expect from their employer and what their employer expects from them.

Since in the UK the density of trade union organization is high (as shown in *Table 1.1*, it is 53 per cent overall, but it is much higher in the public service and manufacturing industry), the collective agreement arrived at through a process of collective bargaining is the key element in contractual arrangements between employers and workers.

In the last 20 years there has been a great deal of standard-setting legislation, but because of space constraints it is only possible in this book to deal with some of the more important aspects of the legislation affecting people in organizations which are to be found in the two Acts, the Employment Protection Act 1975 and the Employment Protection (Consolidation) Act 1978. The Employment Protection (Consolidation) Act 1978 consolidated a number of individual rights scattered throughout several Acts of Parliament, including the Redundancy Act 1965, the Contracts of Employment Act 1972, parts of the Trade Union and Labour Relations Act 1974 and TULRA 1976 and parts of the Employment Protection Act 1975. The Consolidation Act 1978 contains some of the *individual rights* – e.g. written particulars of terms of employment, guaranteed payments, trade union membership and activities, time off, maternity rights, notice periods, unfair dismissal and redundancy payments. *Collective rights* established under the Employment Protection Act 1975 – e.g. disclosure of information for collective bargaining, redundancy consultation, recognition procedures, wages councils – are found in this Act. However, it was the intention eventually to bring these together with the collective provisions of TULRA in a TULRA Consolidation Act.

9.7.2 Rights to a written statement

Wherever a worker has specific rights under an Act of Parliament, the employer has specific obligations in law towards his employee. All employees should by law (Employment Protection (Consolidation) Act 1978, Section 1) receive a written statement setting out their main terms and conditions of employment within 13 weeks of starting work. The written statement must contain particulars of the following terms, or must refer to documents where these terms are set out:

(1) identification of the position;
(2) date employment began;
(3) continuity details where there is a change of employer;
(4) job title;
(5) rate of pay and interval of payments;
(6) hours of work (including normal and overtime hours);
(7) holiday, sick pay and pensions entitlement (if any);
(8) notice periods.

An additional note must also give information on disciplinary rules and procedures and grievance procedures.

9.7.3 Itemized pay statements

The Payment of Wages Act 1960 already established that where a manual worker asks to be paid otherwise than in cash, the worker is entitled to an itemized pay statement from the employer. The Employment Protection Act 1975 extended this principle further to all groups of workers whether they are paid in cash or by cheque.

The provisions on itemized pay statements are now found in the Employment Protection (Consolidation) Act 1978, Sections 8–10. Every pay statement must include the following:

(1) the gross amount of the wages or salary;
(2) the amount of any fixed deductions and the purposes for which they are made (e.g. union contributions, social clubs, etc.);
(3) the amount of any variable deductions and the purposes for which they are made (e.g. national insurance contributions, PAYE, pension fund contributions, etc.);

(4) the net amount of wages and salary payable;
(5) where different amounts of the net amount are paid in different ways, the amount and method of each part payment.

9.7.4 Guaranteed pay – payment during suspension on medical grounds

Some jobs are covered by special health and safety regulations under which an employee may be suspended from his normal work on medical grounds, etc., under regulations on lead and radiation. The EMP (Consolidation) Act, Sections 19–22 provides that after 4 weeks' service suspended workers are entitled to a normal week's pay for every week of suspension, up to a maximum of 26 weeks.

9.7.5 Guaranteed pay during lay-offs

The Employment Protection (Consolidation) Act 1978, Sections 12–18 provides for guaranteed earnings under the following conditions. An employee must have at least 4 weeks' continuous service and work 16 hours or more a week. An employee must be laid off for the whole of his normal working hours on a day that he normally works. The employee must be laid off because of: a diminution in the requirements of the employer's business for work of the kind which the employee is employed to do or any other occurrences affecting the normal working of the employer's business (apart from a strike within the company).

9.7.6 How is the pay collected?

The guaranteed hourly rate is calculated by dividing 1 week's basic pay, including any bonuses (excluding overtime), by the number of normal working hours; this sum is then multiplied by the number of normal working hours on the day in question. But there is a 'ceiling' set down in law. In February 1979 this ceiling was £7.25. But this payment may be made for up to 5 days in any 3 month period – according to the Employment Act 1980.

9.7.7 Time off work

Over a long period of time through the device of custom and practice a right had been built up to have time off either with or without pay to participate in various public duties, such as serving on local authorities or as Justices of the Peace or attending to trade union duties as delegates to conferences or committees.

In the EMP (Consolidation) Act 1978, Sections 27–32, the right to time off has been firmly established in law. Broadly, time off, for duties or training directly concerned with industrial relations in one's place of work as laid down in the Code of Practice issued by ACAS[3], is with pay, and where the public duty is recompensed out of public funds the employer has no responsibility for making up for the loss of earnings.

The time off which an employee is to be permitted to take has to be reasonable in all the circumstances, having regard to the Code of Practice in the case of trade union duties, and in the case of public duties having regard to a reasonable discharge of those duties, taking into consideration the effect on the employer's business.

9.7.8 Time off to look for work or make arrangements for training – Employment Protection (Consolidation) Act, Section 31

An employee who is given notice of dismissal by reason of redundancy shall be entitled before the expiration of his notice to be allowed by his employer reasonable time off during the employee's working hours in order to look for new employment or make arrangements for training for future employment, and be entitled to paid remuneration by his employer for the period of absence at the appropriate hourly rate.

9.7.9 Termination of employment

With the rising tide of unemployment in our society, the procedures in connection with the termination of employment are of increasing social importance.

The rights of employer and employee of a minimum period of notice
These rights are laid down in Section 49 of the Employment Protection (Consolidation) Act 1978. The notice required to be given by an employer to terminate the contract of employment of a person who has been continuously employed for 4 weeks or more shall not be less than 1 week's notice, and 1 week's notice for each year of continuous employment and no less than 12 weeks' notice after 12 years of continuous employment. The notice required to be given by an employee who has been continuously employed for 4 weeks or more to terminate his contract of employment shall be not less than 1 week.

Written statement of reasons for dismissal – Employment Protection (Consolidation) Act 1978, Section 53

An employee shall be entitled to be provided by his employer, on request, within 14 days of that request, with a written statement giving particulars of the reasons for his dismissal. However, there is a qualifying period of 26 weeks of continuous employment. A written statement provided under this section of the Act shall be admissible in evidence in any proceedings.

Unfair dismissal

The termination of employment by dismissal has always been a most powerful instrument of enforcing discipline at the disposal of the employer. In the past employers had the power to hire and fire at will, backed up by laws that made it a criminal offence for a worker to break his contract of employment. More recently, in many firms foremen and managers have had the power to give workers their cards on the spot. The common law developed by judges has always held that an employer can dismiss someone without notice for 'gross misconduct'. In more recent times these managerial prerogatives have been challenged. Trade unions have aimed to restrict the scope of management to hire and fire at will and to extend the rights of workers to a secure job. Also, the International Labour Office in its recommendation 119 gave a lead by laying down the general principle that 'termination of employment should not take place unless there is a valid reason . . . connected with the capacity or conduct of the worker or based on the operational requirements of the undertaking, establishment or service'.

The legal concept of unfair dismissal was first introduced in the Industrial Relations Act 1971 and is now covered by Sections 54–76 in the Employment Protection (Consolidation) Act 1978. The right not to be unfairly dismissed is contained in Section 54 and is as follows: 'In every employment to which this section applies every employee shall have the right not to be unfairly dismissed by his employer.' While the redress for unfair dismissal is through an industrial tribunal, the industrial tribunal, even if it has established that a dismissal was unfair and recommends reinstatement or re-engagement, cannot compel an employer to re-engage an unfairly dismissed worker; it can only force the employer to pay an amount in compensation which can be quite substantial, the maximum compensatory award in 1980 being £6250, but together with an additional award the highest compensation possible is £14 778.

Qualifying period and upper age limit

The right not to be unfairly dismissed is subject to a qualifying period, and since 1 October 1979 an employee has had to be continuously employed for not less than 52 weeks ending with the effective date of termination. Also, the right not to be unfairly dismissed does not apply beyond the normal retiring age in a particular occupation, or if a man has attained the age of 65 or a woman the age of 60. The Employment Act 1980 further reduces the qualifying period to 2 years for firms with fewer than 20 employees.

The Employment Act 1980, Section 5, when amending the Employment Protection (Consolidation) Act 1978 in regard to determining the fairness of dismissal by industrial tribunal, allows the tribunal to take into consideration the 'size and administrative resources of the employer's undertaking' whether the employer acted reasonably or unreasonably in treating it as a sufficient reason for dismissing the employee.

9.7.10 Redundancy

In a situation of rising mass unemployment redundancy assumes considerable importance. However, the question of whether and how job loss should be handled and compensated has engaged the attention of the public and legislators for the past 20 years.

The main legislation in the UK is based on the Redundancy Payment Act 1965. This was modelled on the Cotton Industry Act 1958, which first established the principle of a legal right to a lump sum compensation for workers dismissed for redundancy.

The provisions on redundancy compensation are now found in the Employment Protection (Consolidation) Act 1978, Sections 81–102. The legal definition of redundancy is contained in the Employment Protection (Consolidation) Act 1978, Section 2 (a), and (b), as follows:

> . . . an employee who is dismissed shall be taken to be dismissed by reason of redundancy if the dismissal is attributable wholly or mainly to –
> (a) the fact that his employer has ceased, or intends to cease, to carry on the business for the purposes of which the employee was employed by him, or has ceased, or intends to cease, to carry on that business in the place where the employee was so employed, or,
> (b) the fact that the requirements of that business for employees to carry out work of a particular kind, or for employees to carry out work of a particular kind in the place where he was so employed, have ceased or diminished or are expected to cease or diminish.

The major qualifications in relation to those who can claim redundancy pay are: the worker must have had at least 2 years' continuous service since the age of 18 and must have worked at least 16 hours per week (or at least 8 hours per week for 5 years or more) and must have been dismissed for redundancy or volunteered for redundancy which counts as dismissal. On the other hand, the following are excluded: part-time workers who work less than 16 hours per week or who have not worked at least 8 hours per week for 5 years or more, the self-employed, registered dock workers, crown servants, NHS workers and most merchant seamen, shore fishermen, employees of a foreign government, domestic servants employed by a close relative and employees married to their employers.

The calculation of redundancy payment is based on three factors: (1) the amount of weekly pay; (2) the employee's age; (3) the number of full years continuous service since the age of 18. (See *Table 9.1*.) The maximum number of years service which can be taken into account is 20.

Table 9.1

Years' service/age	No. of weeks' pay
for each year's service between the ages of 18 and 22	½
for each year's service between the ages of 22 and 41	1
for each year's service between the ages of 41 and 65	1½

The maximum redundancy entitlement is £3300 (May 1979). It is important to remember that the Redundancy Payments Act was introduced to encourage the mobility of labour.

Ray Gunter, the Minister of Labour introducing the Redundancy Payments Bill in 1965, said:

> We see this bill as an important step in the government's general programme to push forward the modernisation of British Industry as fast as possible, and to enlist the cooperation of workers as well as managers in this process . . . one object is to encourage mobility of labour by reducing resistance to change.

This measure was linked to the Selective Employment Tax described elsewhere and both have failed in their objective. Redundancy payments have certainly undermined the resistance of workers and their unions to the 'shaking out' process of labour.

9.8 The Wages Councils

The legal relationship between people and organizations which affects several million workers in determining their minimum wages and conditions is found in wages council legislation. Fixing wages by Justices was already known in the fourteenth century, but it was the upper limits of wages for labourers that the law mostly dealt with. At the turn of the century, public concern about unorganized and highly exploited groups of workers (many of them Jewish refugees from the pogroms in Tsarist Russia) in the 'sweated trades' (especially in the garment-making factories) resulted in the setting up of Trades Boards, now called Wages Councils, to fix minimum wages and other conditions for these workers. Wages Councils date back to the Trades Boards first established in 1909, and exist to give some statutory protection to workers in industries where trade unions are weak.

The Wages Council Act 1959 describes the function of the Minister in regard to the establishment of Wages Councils thus:

Section 2 Wages Council Act 1959

An order establishing a wages council may be made by the Minister either –

(a) if he is of the opinion that no adequate machinery exists for the effective regulation of the remuneration of the workers described in the order and that, having regard to the remuneration existing among those workers, or any of them, it is expedient that such a council should be established; or

(b) if he thinks fit, to give a recommendation of a commission of enquiry made on the reference to them. . . .

Wages Councils establish a legal minimum 'rate for the job' where workers do not have the power to establish this through collective bargaining. Minimum arrangements also include holidays, bonus pay, working hours and in some cases rest periods for workers working on conveyor belts.

The industries include retailing, clothing manufacture, hotels, catering and agriculture. There are 48 Wages Councils altogether covering 3.6 million workers.

Wages Councils are appointed by the Employment Secretary. They consist of an equal number of trade union and employers' representatives, with one or more independent members. The wages council regulations are enforced by an inspectorate attached to the Department of Employment. Every year the courts deal with many breaches of the regulations compelling employers to observe the law and pay 'back pay', and in some cases impose heavy finds for persistent breaches of the law.

It is evident from this and preceding chapters that legislation has played an increasingly important role in the development of employment relationships between people and organizations, not least where trade unions have been involved. Inevitably, therefore, the law is again an important element in the following chapter, which is specifically concerned with collective bargaining.

Questions

1. What are immunities? Why did Parliament find it necessary to legislate and provide immunities?
2. What is the legal definition of a trade union?
3. In what way has the Employment Act 1980 amended TULRA 1974 and 1976.
4. What are the implications of 'no compulsion to work'?
5. What is a closed shop? What are the legal provisions for establishing a closed shop?
6. What are the obligations of the employer towards his employees to safeguard their safety and health?
7. How is the Health and Safety at Work Act 1974 enforced?
8. What rights have trade unions in supervising health and safety at work?
9. What are individual rights and what are collective rights in the Employment Protection Act 1975 and the Employment Protection (Consolidation) Act 1978?
10. When is a dismissal fair and when is it unfair?
11. What is the legal meaning of 'redundancy' and how is the employee compensated in a redundancy situation?
12. How has Parliament dealt with the problem of the sweated industries?

Notes

[1] Tort is a legal term and means a private or civil wrong.
[2] Actionable means affording ground for an action at law.
[3] ACAS stands for Advisory Conciliation and Arbitration Service, established in its present form according to Section 1 of the Employment Protection Act 1975.

References

McMullen, J. (1978). *Rights at Work*, Pluto Press
Pelling, H. (1972). *A History of British Trade Unionism*, Penguin, Harmondsworth
Royal Commission on Trade Unions and Employers' Associations (1968). (Chairman: Lord Donovan), HMSO, London
Safety and Health at Work (1978). TUC, London
Lord Wedderburn (1971). *The Worker and the Law*, Penguin, Harmondsworth

Chapter 10

Organizations and collective bargaining

10.1 What is a bargain?

The *Oxford Dictionary* defines a bargain as an 'agreement on terms of give and take' and bargaining as 'haggle over terms of give and take'. There are two types of bargains: an individual bargain and a collective bargain. Sydney and Beatrice Webb in their work *Industrial Democracy* (page 173) describe an individual bargain in the following way:

> In unorganized trades the individual workman, applying for a job, accepts or refuses the terms offered by the employer, without communicating with this fellow workman, and without any other consideration than the exigencies of his own position. For the sale of his labour he makes, with the employer, a strictly individual bargain.

Contrasting this process with a collective bargain, the Webbs define it thus:

> But if a group of workmen concert together and send representatives to conduct the bargaining on behalf of the whole body, the position is at once changed. Instead of the employer making a series of separate contracts with isolated individuals he meets with a collective will, and settles, in a single agreement, the principle upon which, for the time being, all workmen of a particular group, or class, or grade, will be engaged.

There is no issue or matter affecting the relationship between employers and workers that could not be the subject of bargaining and negotiation between the two sides. In fact, this concept of bargaining can be extended to include the running of an enterprise, future planning including investment embracing the concepts of participation in management, or, as the Germans call it, 'co-determination' – i.e. restricting managerial prerogatives. It is worth noting that until 1871 combination for any other objects or purpose than the improvement in wages or hours was a criminal offence.

10.2 Organizations with which bargains are made

Negotiation and bargaining is carried out at all levels of employment from the individual workman with his employer to the shop-steward with the manager and by the TUC and its General Secretary with the Cabinet and the Prime Minister.

There is a long list of organizations with which bargains are made and negotiations conducted. They include trade union organizations at all levels, professional organizations, the various ministries and the Government itself, local authorities, the Police Federation and the Army Pay Review Board. Also, there are special bodies set up such as the Burnham Committee to deal with teachers' pay and conditions.

While there is some form of bargaining between the Government, represented by the Home Office, and the Police Federation, the police are specifically forbidden, since Parliament passed the Police Act in 1919, to belong to a trade union. The position of the armed forces is somewhat different. While no trade union has the right to bargain or negotiate on behalf of members of the armed forces, individual members of the armed forces may belong to and may join trade unions, and a growing number, including officers, do so, especially towards the end of their service.

The right of members of the police and of the armed forces in many West European countries to belong to trade unions catering for the various services is different, particularly in Holland, Sweden, West Germany and France, where only the police are unionized. However, civilian employees of both the police and the armed forces are allowed to be members of trade unions, and a high proportion are.

10.3 Who is included in the bargaining structure?

To get an idea of the numbers of people subjected to some form of collective bargaining, we must have a look at the numbers of the UK working population, which in 1979 were as shown in *Table 10.1*. The self-employed, the unemployed, the armed forces and the police have to be subtracted from the collective bargaining process, which leaves about

Table 10.1

Population of working age (i.e. males between 16 and 65 and women between 16 and 60	33 million (including 1½ million over 16 in full-time education)
Total working population in UK	26½ million
full-time employment	18½ million (including ¼ million armed forces)
part-time (mostly women)	4½ million
self-employed	2 million
unemployed	1½ million

Table 10.2 Trade union density in the UK, 1974, by industry (%)

Agriculture and forestry	22.2
Fishing	60.5
Coal mining	96.2
Other mining	51.8
Food and drink	51.2
Chemicals	51.2
Metals and engineering	69.4
Cotton/man-made fibres } Other textiles }	40.9
Leather	46.6
Clothing	60.0
Footwear	79.0
Bricks and building materials	40.4
Pottery	93.8
Glass	78.5
Wood and furniture	35.2
Paper, printing and publishing	71.6
Rubber	55.9
Construction	27.2
Gas, electricity and water	92.0
Railways	96.9
Road transport	95.1
Sea transport	99.6
Ports and inland water transport	94.7
Air transport	93.6
Post office and telecommunications	87.9
Distribution	11.4
Insurance, banking and finance	44.8
Entertainment and media services	64.9
Health	60.9
Hotels and catering	5.2
Other professional services	3.7
Education and local government	85.6
National government	90.5

Source: Price and Bain – reprinted in the *Bullock Report*, pp. 12 and 13.
The following industries are not included in this table: miscellaneous transport services, other manufacturing (less rubber), business services (property owning, advertising and market research, other business services, central offices not allocated elsewhere), other miscellaneous services (betting and gambling, hairdressing and manicure, laundries, dry cleaning, motor repairs, distributors, garages and filling stations, repair of boots and shoes and other services). Union density in this heterogeneous group of industries was less than 3 per cent in 1974; total employment was 2.4 million.

22½ million in 1979 who could be included in the process. Of this labour force, over 12 million are organized in TUC-affiliated unions – i.e. well over 50 per cent of the entire eligible workforce. Since 1974 union membership and density has increased as the employed working population has somewhat declined.

All industries mentioned in *Table 10.2*, with one or two exceptions, have a method of determining wages and conditions by collective bargaining. It is either direct bargaining by trade unions with the employers' organization or through the medium of Wages Councils or Joint Industrial Councils. This means that the great majority of wage-earning and salaried workers, whether they are members of trade unions or not, have their remuneration and conditions determined by collective bargains.

In those industries where trade unions are traditionally powerful, as in the engineering industry, direct bargaining prevails; in the public sector Joint Industrial Councils are the most common arrangement; and in industries where unions are weak, as in the retail trade, hotels and catering and clothing (an industry where 'sweating' prevailed), Wages Councils have been set up to determine minimum pay and conditions and establish enforcement agencies.

10.4 The law of contract and bargaining

The legal relationship between worker and employer is governed by the ordinary law of contract based on principles of common law developed by judges. Because there is a contract of employment recognized by common law, the worker can take the employer to court if he fails to pay the wages due to him, and the employer can sue the worker if he fails to fulfil his obligation under the contract.

However, the agreement that is arrived at after a process of collective bargaining, whatever area of the relationship between the employer and worker is covered by such an agreement, is binding in honour only unless both parties agree that it should be legally enforcible.

Of course, where there is statute law (e.g. of the Wages Councils type or the Factories Act or the Employment Protection Act or the Health and Safety at Work Act), such statutes are legally binding and any agreement to circumvent statute law would be *ultra vires* – i.e. void. It must, however, be understood that the legislation contained in the above-mentioned Acts is the absolute minimum legal requirement in regard to wages, working conditions or rights at work. There is no reason why these should not be exceeded and, in fact, trade unions continually build on the minimum requirements of the law, and seek through bargaining to achieve conditions that enhance or are better than the law prescribes.

That applies especially to Wages Council pay scale legislation. Very few workers – for instance, in the garment-making industry – ever work for the minimum rates laid down in Wages Regulation Orders provided for by the Wages Council Act.

The gentleman's agreement. By and large, agreements between employees and trade unions are binding in honour only. This has been accepted in practice for over 100 years. The concept 'binding in honour only' was challenged by the wording contained in the Industrial Relations Act 1971, where Parliament attempted to make agreements binding in law unless the parties to the agreement specifically stated otherwise. In practice this met with resistance by the trade unions and proved, like the rest of the Act, to be unenforcible. It should be noted that agreements between trade unions and employers in many other countries are enforcible in law.

10.5 The place of bargaining in law

It should be noted that there are legal obligations on the part of the employer to consult with recognized trade unions (recognized by the employer). These are laid down in certain Acts of Parliament – i.e. the Social Security Pensions Act of 1975, the Industry Act of 1975, the Wages Council Act 1959, the Employment Protection Act 1975, the Employment Protection (Consolidation) Act 1978 and the Health and Safety at Work Act 1974 and its Statutory Instrument 1977/500.

According to the Social Security Pensions Act 1975, companies are required to consult with recognized trade unions over occupational pension schemes and there has been widespread bargaining over these schemes. Failure to arrive at a satisfactory agreed pension scheme has led recently to a prolonged strike at Hopkinson's in Huddersfield. The terms of the final agreement have to comply with the provisions of the Act and the resultant schemes are both collective agreements and statutory rules.

According to the Industry Act 1975, there is a provision for planning agreements and companies are required to furnish information to recognized trade unions. However, there are very few planning agreements in existence. The outstanding example is the one arrived at between Chrysler and the unions.

The Wages Councils Act 1959 provides the framework for compelling employers' organizations and unions to set up bargaining machinery for industries employing millions of workers. According to the Employment Protection Act 1975 Section 17 (1),

(a) the employer is required to disclose 'information without which the trade union representatives would be to a material extent impeded in carrying out with him such collective bargaining, and

(b) information which it would be in accordance with good industrial relations practice that he should disclose to them for the purpose of collective bargaining.

10.6 The procedure for handling redundancies

The Employment Protection Act compels an employer both to notify the Secretary of State of certain redundancies and to 'consult representatives of that trade union' (recognized by the employer) about dismissals in accordance with regulations, giving the reasons and the method of dismissal and the number involved. In the course of consultation . . . the employer shall

(a) consider a representation made by the trade union representatives; and
(b) reply to those representations and, if he rejects any of those representations, state his reasons.

10.7 Time off work

The Employment Protection (Consolidation) Act 1978 provides for time off for public duties, trade union activities and training. The ACAS Code of Practice No. 3 dealing with this problem lays down the following procedure and advises:

Employers and unions, at the appropriate level, will need to review *jointly* their current time off provisions. . . . In some situations time off arrangements will have to be revised and it may be helpful to set out any such revised arrangements in formal agreements.

10.8 The Health and Safety at Work Act 1974

This Act provides for trade union representatives to act as watch-dogs over the application of the legislation to places of work and entitles trade unions to call for the establishment at places of work of health and safety committees and for trade union representatives to sit on these committees to ensure that the Act is applied. In every case the actual application of the various rights is subject to negotiation with management.

It is trade practice to expand the safety policy of a particular establishment into a 'Health and Safety Agreement', treating the Statute as the basis and building upon it.

10.9 Steps followed in the collective bargaining process

The beginning of a bargaining process is recognition by the employer of a specific organization or individuals entitled to bargain on behalf of a group of people usually employed in a particular firm or by a particular organization. The recognition process is usually established by a document entitled the recognition agreement. The recognition of a bargaining unit by an employer is by no means a foregone conclusion. Many strikes and other forms of industrial action have taken place over many decades to secure recognition by employers. The Grunwick dispute provided a good example of how difficult it can be to bring a recognition agreement about.

The Employment Protection Act 1975 provided a procedure through the intervention of ACAS to bring about recognition. But the Grunwick dispute proved that the procedure was inadequate and the Employment Act 1980 repeals Sections 11–16 of the 1975 Act.

The recognition of trade unions by employers is an issue which in the past has led to many disputes. An analysis of conciliation cases dealt with by ACAS shows that pay and terms of conditions of employment account for slightly more than half the cases and that recognition disputes constitute almost half of the remainder; then come dismissals, redundancy and 'other trade union matters'. The recognition agreement between a trade union and an employer is of great importance in regard to inter-union relationships. Once a particular union has established its rights to organize and negotiate in a particular sector of industry, of a department or of an organization, no other union may poach members or recruit non-members who are included in a particular recognition agreement. A breach of this practice, which goes under the name of the 'Bridlington' procedure, would result in the dispute being dealt with by the Dispute Committee of the TUC, which has been able to enforce its recommendations to unions.

The latest version of the disputes procedure was decided at the 1979 Congress of the TUC and is laid down in a document containing eight Principles, a set of Regulations and Rules 11, 12 and 13 of the TUC Rules and Standing Orders. The Employment Act 1980 abolishes Section 11 of the Employment Protection Act 1975, dealing with recognition. It will compel trade unions to achieve recognition by the use of 'industrial muscle'; the law will be of no help. The conclusion the TUC came to after the Grunwick dispute was summed up by its General Secretary, Len Murray, thus:

The dispute revealed that exploitation, particularly of immigrants, continues to exist where workers are not organised within trade unions, and if exploitation is to be brought to an end in any work place the first move must be to establish a base of trade union organisation there.

The issue has shown that present procedures of enquiry enable a devious and defiant employer to delay and obstruct the independent Advisory, Conciliation and Arbitration Service in carrying out the duties laid on it by law. The procedures need revision so that the intentions of Parliament are not frustrated.

With the Employment Act 1980 on the statute book and in a sense the action of the Grunwick management vindicated by the abolition of a legal recognition procedure, the final sentence of Len Murray's statement is not without significance for the future.

Even so, the events of Grunwick have shown that, despite high local unemployment and other particularly difficult circumstances, workers will spontaneously take a stand on principle and will be brave and determined in the struggle that follows. It is a lesson that other employers are clearly not finding it easy to ignore.

10.10 The procedure agreement

When a recognition agreement has been signed, the next stage is to deal with procedures and sign a procedure agreement which embodies a set of rules whose purpose is to influence the behaviour of management, employees and trade union representatives in a defined situation.

A procedure agreement should lay down how negotiations on various issues should be conducted and at what level. Some of the questions it should deal with are:

(1) a *status quo* clause, which means that management undertakes not to alter conditions of service unless negotiations have taken place and an agreement arrived at;
(2) a method of negotiating wages and payments systems;
(3) working hours, including conditions under which overtime is permissible;
(4) a grievance procedure which is open to both individuals and trade union organizations;
(5) a discipline procedure under which management can take action against an individual employee according to specified criteria;
(6) a recruiting procedure which involves union representatives in deciding manning levels;
(7) a redundancy procedure under which the problem of diminishing work requirements can be discussed in a reasonable way and rates of compensation laid down;
(8) the introduction of new technology should be subject to an agreed procedure, agreed to by both sides;
(9) Health and Safety arrangements, including the specific procedures of raising health and safety questions and the method by which a 'Health and Safety Agreement' can be negotiated supplementing the health and safety policy of the firm;

(10) a procedure should be worked out when there is a 'failure to agree' or a deadlock is reached in negotiations.

It should include a procedure to involve conciliation or arbitration to resolve the deadlock.

10.11 The Advisory, Conciliation and Arbitration Service (ACAS)

10.11.1 The role of ACAS

The Advisory, Conciliation and Arbitration Service established by the Employment Protection Act 1975 plays a very important role in the process of collective bargaining. While the process of collective conciliation is not new in British industrial relations, and has been developing for at least 85 years, it was only in the Employment Protection Act 1975 that it was established as an independent Service. Section 1 (2) of the Act outlines the purpose of ACAS thus:

The Service shall be charged with the general duty of improvement of industrial relations, and in particular of encouraging the extension of collective bargaining and the development and, where necessary, reform of collective bargaining machinery.

10.11.2 How does ACAS function?

ACAS is a national organization with a full-time staff of over 800, with offices in all English regions and in Scotlnd and Wales. The Service does not regard itself as the interpreter, monitor or enforcement agent of government policies. It seeks to improve industrial relations and to resolve disputes.

10.11.3 Advice

To deal with the problems of industrial relations, it gives advice, 'if it thinks fit', without charge, to employees, employers' associations, workers and trade unions on any matter concerned with industrial relations or employment policies, including the following: organization of workers and employers for the purpose of collective bargaining; recognition of trade union machinery for negotiations and consultation; procedures for avoiding and settling disputes and grievances; questions of communication; facilities for trade union officials; dismissal procedures; disciplinary matters; manpower planning; labour turnover and absenteeism; recruitment; retention; promotion and vocational training of workers; payment systems; and job evaluation.

10.11.4 Conciliation

Where a dispute exists between management and workers, the Service seeks to bring the parties together to settle the dispute. The Service also tries to solve disputes which are submitted to a tribunal or court to settle them by mutual agreement 'out of court'.

10.11.5 Arbitration

Section 3 of the Act states:

> . . . where a trade dispute exists or is apprehended the Service may, at the request of one or more parties to the dispute and with the consent of all parties to the dispute, refer all or any of the matters to which the dispute relates for settlement to the arbitration of –
> (a) one or more persons appointed by the Service for that purpose (not being an officer or servant of the Service); or
> (b) the Central Arbitration Committee. . . .

The Service has dealt with thousands of cases since 1975.

10.11.6 Collective bargaining in Britain

Collective bargaining is the central feature of the British industrial relations scene. Engaged in the day-by-day process are a great number of people: over half a million shop-floor representatives, lay officials and about 4000 full-time officials of some 116 trade unions affiliated to the TUC. On the other side there are hundreds of employers' organizations, with one national organization (the CBI) and with thousands at all levels engaged in bargaining on behalf of employers. Among them the Engineering Employers' Federation is the best-organized and most closely resembles in its structure a trade union (see Appendix 10.2).

However, while trade union membership in the larger enterprises in the UK is close to 100 per cent, a considerable number of the big employers are non-federated (e.g. Ford UK), which means that they are outside the employers' federation and conduct their own bargaining with the trade unions represented in their plants and not through the machinery of, in this case, the Engineering Employers' Federation.

The objective of the bargainers engaged in the process of bargaining over the price of labour power and over the conditions in which it operates is to establish a price for labour power and conditions under which labour operates at a level where the opposing sides balance each other until such times as the balance is again upset by either inflationary pressures or changes in conditions, etc., and the bargaining process has to start again to establish the new equilibrium.

10.12 Trade union objectives

Trade unions did not begin to develop until the advent of industrialization, as indicated in Chapter 1. Industrial systems have considerable complexities; similarly, union objectives can also be complex and cover economic, social and political matters. The latter two subjects have already received attention and will be returned to in Chapter 11. In this section we shall concentrate on the economic aspects of trade union objectives and, in particular, on their role in determining wages and the level of employment at organization level.

Because unions may have a multiplicity of goals, it is difficult to develop a single model based on some kind of maximizing behaviour. Although employing organizations are often analysed in this way (see Appendix 1.2, pages 28–32), the task is more difficult where unions are concerned. Union leaders must take the results of negotiation back to their members for ratification and are more vulnerable here than managers in relation to shareholders. The difficulties of union leaders are also increased when differences occur between their aims and those of rank and file members. For example, a union leader may be interested in expanding membership to increase his own influence and importance in a wider context, while the membership is mainly concerned with job security and higher real wages. Again, benefits obtained by union leaders in negotiations with employers do not, as in the case of those secured by management, accrue initially to the organization but rather to individual members.

Despite these problems, attempts have been made to develop formal models of trade union behaviour, and one such approach is to represent a union as behaving like a product market monopolist. This is illustrated in *Figure 10.1*, where D is the demand curve and MR its associated marginal revenue curve. In the case of a firm, its marginal cost curve (for simplicity, not shown in *Figure 10.1*) might slope upwards through point m so that profits would be maximized at a price w_0 and output n_0. However, if the diagram is used to represent the position of a union, it may be that not all firms in this product market are unionized. This is not an uncommon situation, and then an increase in wages obtained by unions in the firms which are organized will allow non-unionized firms to increase their share in total sales. In expanding their labour force, non-organized firms will bring about an indirect substitution of non-union labour for union labour. This will make the demand curve for union labour more elastic than if all employees belong to the union.

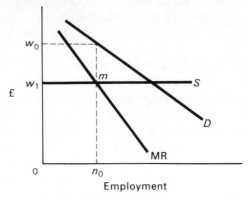

Figure 10.1

The labour supply curve to an individual employer can be represented as perfectly elastic, as indicated by that labelled S, with the MR curve showing the addition to the total wage bill which results when the wage is reduced just sufficiently to allow of the employment of one extra worker. As a monopolist, the union would seek to obtain a wage of w_0, at which level the supply price of labour is equal to marginal revenue, so that it is in an analogous position to a firm maximizing its profits. But the analogy breaks down because this equality, while relevant to a firm, has no meaning for a union. The latter is a representative of individual supplies of labour services rather than a seller of labour, and, while a firm's supply of a product is related to its production costs, a union does not have comparable costs for the members on whose behalf it negotiates. Moreover, w_0 is greater than the supply price of labour (w_1) and wages above the supply price cannot be regarded as something to be maximized, because gains and losses are involved which affect different people. Unions will come under pressure from unemployed members to obtain wage levels which will secure them jobs and from employed members to obtain higher wages. If, for example, wages were raised slightly above w_0, so that the employment level fell below n_0 by one person, the employment loss and the wage gain would accrue to different workers. Thus, union officials, in attempting to balance various interests and pressures, are not likely to act in a maximizing way.

It is possible that trade union leaders do not see wage and employment objectives as substitutes for each other. Wages are only one element in the determination of employment levels, and any effect which a union has may be lost among such other influences as technical change, shifts in product demand and changes in other input prices. It is, therefore, difficult for a union to predict the effect of a wage increase on the employment level of its members. This is not to say that unions are unconcerned with employment objectives, since in particular circumstances they are likely to assume relatively great importance. In a depression, for example, the protection of jobs may take precedence over wage objectives which are then pressed with less vigour. On the other hand, Rees (1979) argues that the weight given by unions to employment is less for cuts in wages than for wage increases. A union will, in general, insist on maintaining current wage levels even at the cost of substantial falls in employment, whereas it will not seek to raise money wages if adverse employment consequences are likely to follow.

Relative wages are also important to trade unions and especially where 'comparable occupations' are concerned, in which case wage rankings and 'established (or historic) relativities' may influence bargaining. Brown and Sisson (1975), for instance, investigated the use of comparisons in workplace wage determination in the newspaper industry in Fleet Street and the engineering industry at Coventry. They found that the use of comparisons, reinforced by the collective strength of unions, appeared to have been more important over the 1961–1973 period than supply and demand forces. Such findings are not necessarily at variance with a market forces interpretation, since many analysts would agree with the view expressed by McCormick (1970, page 98) that supply and demand forces, while determining long-run equilibrium positions in the labour market, may in the short run

> . . . be slow moving and difficult to discern. This gives rise to a zone of indeterminacy within which the wage can be fixed. The size of this zone will be fixed by that wage which will force a firm to close down and will not cause a union to collapse. . . . Short run decisions dictate the path to long run equilibrium.

It is, therefore, possible to adopt a view which allows of a short-run range of wage indeterminacy with market forces operating with varying intensities but becoming generally more important as time periods lengthen.

Questions

1. What is the meaning of the term 'collective bargaining'?
2. What is a recognition agreement? How does it restrict trade union membership?

3. What is a procedure agreement? Elaborate some of the most important features of such an agreement.
4. How far is an agreement between a trade union and an employer enforcible in law?
5. How were the workers in 'sweated industries' protected by Parliament?
6. What are the legal requirements an employer has to comply with when faced with the necessity of shedding labour?
7. What rights has a worker in taking time off work?
    (a) with pay?
    (b) unpaid?
8. What is the role of ACAS in collective bargaining?
9. Discuss the implications which may result from differences in objectives between trade union leaders and their members.

References

Brown, W. and Sisson, K. (1975) 'The use of comparisons in workplace wage determination', *British Journal of Industrial Relations*, March
The Donovan Report (1968). HMSO, London
McCormick, B.J. (1970). *Wages*, Penguin, Harmondsworth
Pelling, H. (1972). *A History of British Trade Unionism*, Penguin, Harmondsworth
Webb, S. and Webb, Beatrice (1913). *Industrial Democracy*, Longman Green, London

Further reading

Lord Bullock (1977). *Report of the Committee of Inquiry on Industrial Democracy*, HMSO, London
Rees, A. (1979). *The Economics of Work and Pay*, Harper and Row, New York
TUC (1979). *Annual Report*, TUC, London
Lord Wedderburn (1971). *The Worker and the Law*, Penguin, Harmondsworth

Appendix 10.1: Structure of the TUC in the English regions

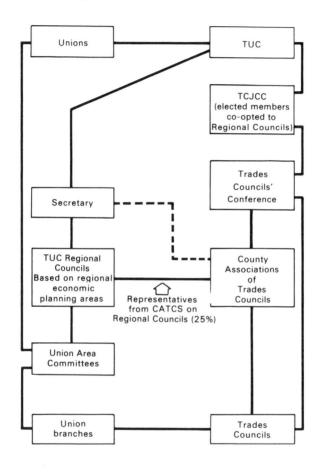

Appendix 10.2: Structure of a typical employers' organization – the Engineering Employers' Federation

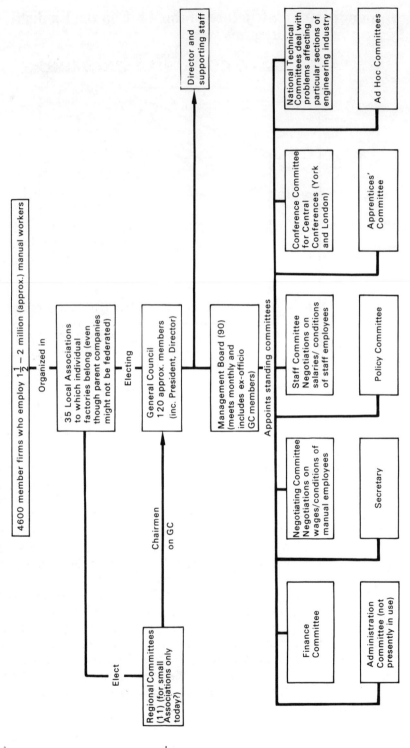

Chapter 11

The outcome of collective bargaining

11.1 Introduction

To describe the outcome of collective bargaining in the UK is an immense task, since it covers the pay and working conditions of the majority of the wage earners and a considerable proportion of the salary earners in the UK.

The first thing to consider is the various pay systems and methods used by management to arrive at pay structures and then to discuss and analyse the impact of collective bargaining on these structures as well as the impact on working hours and conditions. The examples in this chapter of the outcome of collective bargaining will only include a few agreements arrived at in 1979–1980. The estimated effects of trade unions on relative wages will then be considered.

11.2 The Truck Acts – payments in the coin of the realm

In 1831 Parliament passed the Truck Act to enforce payment of wages to workmen in cash and not in kind. The wages of any 'artificer', said the 1831 Act, 'shall be made payable in the current coin of this Realm only and not otherwise'. Any contract to the contrary is 'illegal, null and void' and the employer commits a crime. The employer must not impose any restrictions as to where or how the wages shall be spent; nor can he recover the price of any goods supplied on credit to the worker, or even set off sums allegedly owing for the goods supplied.

After the Truck Amendment Act 1887, the Truck Acts applied to all 'workmen' as defined in the Employers and Workmen Act 1875. However, the Act of 1831 allowed the employer to make certain deductions (e.g. for medical attendance, food on the premises if agreed by special contract, rent for a dwelling); later statutes have added many more (e.g. income tax, insurance, superannuation, etc.) and in 1958 deductions for maintenance of a wife where the earnings are attached by the courts.

234 The outcome of collective bargaining

Payments of trade union contributions by the 'check-off' method are legal, provided that the employee agrees. The payment of wages by cheque is legal since 1960, provided that the workman has first agreed in writing for the new method to be used.

A workman can be forced to accept either a postal order or a money order when he is absent, either on duty or sick, entitled to wages, unless he has given notice that he does not wish to receive his wages in one of the new ways.

11.3 Wages payment systems

11.3.1 Time rate

The most common method of calculating wage and salary payments is strictly according to the time for which a worker sells his labour power to an employer. Depending on the type of labour power involved, it can be by the hour, by the day, week, month, year, etc. The most common measurement is by the hour. The contract under which the worker is employed stipulates so many pounds and pence per hours. It further lays down the normal hours per week during which work should be performed. The contract would further stipulate an overtime rate of pay.

11.3.2 Piece work

In manufacturing industry piecework systems are common. Piecework payments are based on a specific piece of work done to which a price is attached. The accepted idea is that piecework price should yield a higher wage than time wage for the same work input. It is generally argued that a piecework system speeds work up and thus reduces the unit cost in manufacture. There are as many arguments against a piecework system as for it, and trade unions have always been divided in opposition to and support of piecework.

11.3.3 Measured day work

A combination of both time work and piecework is called 'measured day work'. The principle is that in a given time a certain quantity of work has to be done for a fixed wage. This method of remuneration has been widely adopted in the car industry instead of piecework.

11.3.4 Bonus payments

In addition to the various ways of paying wages, there are supplement payments to both normal wages and salaries in the form of bonuses. Bonuses are found in an infinite variety (e.g. for time-keeping, extra output, quality, share in profits, etc.). There are bonuses in kind or perks and gratuities in money or kind; some laid down in contracts, others handed out on an ad hoc basis; some taxable and some not.

11.4 The social wage

A considerable proportion of the income of an individual worker and his family consists of the social wage he and his family receive in the form of subsidies and services for which he does not pay directly but which form a large part of the income, especially of the manual worker. These services consist of the maintenance of the infrastructure, the health service, education, housing subsidies, food subsidies and a host of other items, including pensions and benefits which are 'transfer payments'. In a period of 'spending cuts' by the government it tends to be the *social wage* that is reduced, which produces a severe impact on living standards both on the individual worker and on his family.

A great deal of trade union effort is involved in defending and possibly extending the social wage. In the bargaining process the social wage is an important consideration certainly in the minds of trade union bargainers.

11.5 The constraints on collective bargaining

Marx followed Ricardo in thinking that the market price of labour power could not for long depart from the value of the subsistence which the maintenance of that labour power required, taking into consideration the influence of habit and custom. Labour power is a commodity bought and sold like any other commodity but it is different in the sense that it is attached to human beings. Marx said that the supply of labour was governed in a unique sense by the 'historical or social element', which determined what human labourers required for a livelihood. He said:

The value of labour is formed by two elements the one merely physical, the other historical or social. Its *ultimate limit* is determined by the *physical* element: that is to say, to maintain and produce itself, to perpetuate its physical existence, the working class must receive the necessaries absolutely indispensable for living and multiplying. . . . Besides this mere physical element, the value of labour is in every country determined by a *traditional standard of life*.

Therefore when trade unions sought by combined action to advance the level of wages, their action was part of the 'social element' and any gains won helped to mould the 'traditional standard of life' for the future.

The factor that limited the ability of trade union pressure to advance the level of wages was the recurrence of cyclical crises in the economic system which produced 'the industrial reserve army', the unemployed, as well as technological advance which substituted mechanical and new electronic devices for human labour power. The resulting unemployment and the tendency to export capital abroad to tap cheap reserves of labour brought heavy pressure to bear on wage levels and severely limited the power of trade unions in the long run.

11.6 Management techniques to establish wage rates

11.6.1 Work and time study

Work measurement is a common management technique and the term covers a variety of methods used to establish the time required by a qualified worker to carry out a specified job at a defined level of performance. Along with method study it is the main element of what is understood by *work study*.

There are two main types of work measurement: (1) time study using a stop watch or other means of measuring the time required to complete a particular job and (2) an indirect method of timing by using the synthesis of job times from previously collected data. Other methods are *predetermined motion time systems* (PMTS) and estimating from experience and by comparison with other jobs.

A work measurement exercise, therefore, involves the establishment of a *basic time* for job elements by time study and *performance rating* or by indirect time study or calculating standard times for jobs by adding *allowances* to basic times. Work measurement, and particularly performance rating and the determination of allowances, is the most subjective aspect of work study.

Shop-stewards often criticize and challenge work measurement methods, and especially rating and allowances, as inaccurate, inconsistent and inappropriate, and a great deal of time is spent on the shop floor and at various levels of the bargaining set-up in agreeing on the results of work measurement and its impact on the pay-packet.

11.6.2 Job evaluation

Job evaluation consists of the comparison of jobs by the use of formal and systematic procedures in order to determine the position of one job relative to another in a wage or salary hierarchy.

The Equal Pay Act 1970 makes equal pay for men and women in Section 3 (5) dependent 'on a study undertaken with a view to evaluating in those terms the jobs to be done by all or any of the employees in an undertaking or group of undertakings . . .'. It is difficult in many instances to claim equal pay for the sexes in a work situation. The increased popularity of job evaluation schemes is that wage earners have strong feelings about the *'fairness'* or *'equity'* of relative wages, this being judged normally on the basis of comparative job contents.

Job evaluation means that the job is evaluated, not the job's current occupant. However, it is true that job evaluation methods depend to some extent on a series of subjective judgements such as logic, justice and equity which could provide a field day for the determined bargainer. Therefore, a job evaluation scheme and method of application which are not supported by both sides are likely to be useless in arriving at any pay structure.

11.7 Local and national bargaining

There are primarily two levels in the collective bargaining process. There is the day-by-day bargaining, communication and discussion on the shop floor between the shop-stewards or even individual workers and individuals in the management structure – i.e. the supervisor, foreman, floor-manager, etc. This bargaining process, however, takes place within the wider framework of national agreements between very big employers – e.g. Fords, BL, or the managements of the nationalized industries – and national trade union leaderships, or between employers' organizations such as the Engineering Employers Association and national trade union leaderships – in this case the Confederation of Shipbuilding and Engineering Unions (CSEU).

The shop floor bargaining serves the purpose of applying the national agreement to the specific circumstances of the firm, the department or even the individual. The agreement that is arrived at on the shop floor not only has to comply with the framework of the national agreement, but must also be consistent with *local custom* and *practice* and local or branch rules as well as guidelines laid down by the TUC.

11.8 The outcome of collective bargaining in public and private industry

Table 11.1 shows that in 1974 the trade union density was about 72 per cent in the private sector. The density is now somewhat bigger, because white collar trade union membership in the private sector has increased,

Table 11.1 Unionization by industrial sector and by establishment* size in the UK, 1974

		Labour force (000's)		Union membership (000's)		Density* (%)
	Total	23 339		11 755		50.4
less Public sector		6 113		5 079		
			17 226		6 676	38.8
less Agriculture, fishing and forestry		428		100		
			16 798		6 576	39.1
less Distribution		2 810		322		
			13 988		6 254	44.7
less Construction		1 429		388		
			12 559		5 866	46.7
less Miscellaneous services†		1 622		§		
			10 937		5 866	53.6
less Other private sector services‡		1 294		§		
			9 643		5 866	60.8
less Manufacturing establishments with less than 100 workers		1 487		297		
			8 156		5 569	68.3
less Manufacturing establishments with less than 200 workers		870		348		
			7 286		5 221	71.7

* As defined in the Standard Industrial Classification.
† Comprises property owning and managing; advertising and market research; other business services; hairdressing, laundries; dry cleaning; motor repairs, boot and shoe repair; other miscellaneous services.
‡ Comprises law; accountancy; religion; hotels and catering.
§ Union membership negligible.

Source: Price and Bain, *Bullock Report*, p. 16, HMSO, London.

especially the membership of ASTMS and TASS. In the larger establishments, of 2000 or more workers, the trade union density is over 90 per cent.

Tens of thousands of bargains have been struck at all levels of industry, and a selection of some since 1978 are described to indicate what is involved. One of the most important is the settlement of the engineering dispute of November 1979. In order to understand the settlement, it is worth while looking at the policy decisions of the TUC in 1979 after the change of government, as it can be assumed that guidelines laid down by the TUC now, just as during the previous Government's term of office, indicate the trend of bargaining with employers and influence the conduct of industrial relations in every sphere.

11.8.1 Key TUC decisions 1979

Industrial relations legislation
Congress carried unanimously a motion opposing the Government's proposals on trade union employment rights. It rejected

> . . . any undermining of the existing statutory protection of trade unionists in relation to the closed shop, effective picketing, redundancy, unfair dismissal and allied issues and any attempts by the government to interfere in the internal democratic procedures of individual trade unions.

This resolution is particularly important because it has to be seen as connected with TUC advice to include in bargaining and then agreements with individual firms clauses which maintain rights which are contained in the Employment Protection Act 1975 and the Consolidation Act 1978 and amended or repealed in the Employment Act 1980 and other legislation. Further, it should be noted that the TUC is campaigning for and the Labour Party is pledged to repeal the Employment Act 1980 and other legislation in total.

Economic policy
In a series of resolutions the Government's economic policy was condemned. The General Council moved a resolution which called for a 'positive alternative strategy'. This included:

> . . . measures to strengthen the economic base including the strategic use of North Sea oil and gas revenues and effective policies against increasing import penetration; . . . major advances in industrial democracy and a strengthening of the effectiveness of the industrial strategy, . . . taxation policies whch promote the achievement of stable prices; . . . a recognition of the indispensable part which pensions, child benefits and the education, health and other public services play in the 'social wage' . . . recognition of the increasingly vital role of public enterprise and public investment. . . .

Public spending was dealt with in a resolution which condemned the use of cash limits and rejected the policy of offsetting wage increases by cutting services.

Wages policy. In a key resolution for bargainers Congress reaffirmed 'its total opposition to wage restraint in any form'.

Unemployment. In a resolution on unemployment and the shorter working week Congress agreed to 'give top priority to reductions in the working week without loss of pay with a reduction in overtime and other measures of work sharing'. In particular, this motion called for a national campaign by the General Council to assist unions to negotiate a 35 hour working week.

New technology

On the introduction of new technology Congress advised unions that the priority in negotiations should be 'to control and take advantage of the introduction of new technologies in order to ensure that the benefits obtained by their application are used in the interests of the community as a whole'.

Health and safety

Congress referred to the inadequate level of government spending on implementing health and safety legislation, and the hazards of deafness, stress and fire involving upholstered furniture.

On the *health service* itself, apart from opposing any spending cuts, Congress opposed the growth of private medicine, and called on affiliated unions not to negotiate any agreements providing private health care for their members as a fringe benefit.

11.8.2 Examples of settlements

National

The engineering industry settlement. The Confederation of Shipbuilding and Engineering Unions (CSEU) (the federation of trade unions organized in the engineering industry, with over 3 million members) began to bargain in 1979 for a £80 minimum for skilled workers and £60 for unskilled workers, a rise of £20 and £15, respectively, as well as a progressive reduction in hours to 35 by 1982 without loss of earnings and 2 days' extra holidays and a common anniversary date throughout the industry.

The bargainers got nowhere; the result was industrial action, including an overtime ban followed by a series of 1 day strikes. In September the final offer by the employers was £70 and £50, respectively, but a total rejection of extra holidays or a shorter working week or a common anniversary date for pay advances. After further industrial action the bargainers agreed to a settlement on 4 October which resulted in a 21.7 per cent rise in the minimum skilled rate of £73 per week and £52.50 for unskilled and an increase of 17.5 per cent for semi-skilled workers. Five days' extra holidays to be phased in over the next 4 years with 2 extra days from November 1980 and a 1 hour cut in hours from 1981. The agreement also improved the percentage differential for apprentices with rates as follows: age 16 = 45 per cent; age 17 = 60 per cent; age 18 = 75 per cent; and age 19 = 90 per cent. It further eliminated the qualifying conditions on statutory holidays. With the majority of the 2 million engineering workers earning more than the nationally agreed rates, the main effect of the new agreed rates was to improve shift, overtime and other premiums based on the minimum rates. At national level, pay negotiations until 1983 will now be restricted to minimum rates.

It is interesting to note that the pressure the negotiators applied in individual firms resulted in 60 firms (members of the Engineering Employers' Federation) and 600 non-federated firms meeting the CSEU claim in full prior to the national agreement of 4 October.

Ford settlement. Manual workers at Ford accepted a pay offer of 21.5 per cent across the board as from 24 November 1979, which gave a new weekly rate of from £81.88 to £104.12. The company also agreed to negotiate on ways of reducing the working week over the next year. Any changes were to be implemented in the 1980 settlement. Other features of the agreement were a rise in the attendance allowances from £3.48 to £5. It should be noted that Ford is a non-federated firm.

In line with the TUC 1979 resolution on the 35 hour week it should be noted that nearly all negotiators include in their demands a shorter working week and there is a trend in settlements to include a clause reducing working hours slightly without loss of pay.

Thirty-eight hour week agreed in plumbing. A long-term pay agreement, not renewable until 1982, has been concluded by the joint industry board for 30 000 plumbing workers. The agreement includes pay rises in three instalments, a *retail price index link*, and a 2 hour cut in the working week.

The dates for increases in hourly rates were 6 August 1979, 4 February 1980 and 2 February 1981. The cut in hours from 40 to 38 was effective from 4 February 1981 – but after that, overtime rates were only payable from 42 hours.

The wage increases agreed included, e.g., for an advanced plumber from £1.60 to £2.00 and £2.24 to £2.48. The agreement's *complex price index link* was to be used to adjust the wage increases due in February 1981. 'Indexations' were to be based on the amount by which prices went up between September 1979 and September 1980. The February 1981 increases were to be raised 1 penny for every ¾ per cent the RPT exceeded 9 per cent in that period. The agreement also included increases in the form of special supplements, for top welding and abnormal conditions, of about 20 per cent.

Furniture workers, 39 hour week. A 1 hour cut in the working week from January 1980 was agreed by the British furniture trade JIC. This agreement covered about 70 000 workers in the industry. Hourly rates were increased by about 18 per cent. The minimum weekly rate for journeymen/women (timeworkers) was raised from £63.33 to £75.00. The JIC set up a permanent joint committee on new technology.

The following settlements were made in January 1980:

Farmworkers received rises of from 19.6 per cent to 24.4 per cent, raising the weekly minimum pay to £58 per week for the lowest grade and £78.30 for the highest. Overtime rates were raised from £2.07 to £2.50 per hour. Entitlement to sick pay was raised to up to 26 weeks after 15 years' service. In 1982 farmworkers will receive an extra week's holiday.

Merchant seamen gained an increase of 24 per cent, which would raise the average earnings of able seamen from £113.34 to £141.02 per week.

There were many more settlements reached in that month yielding similar increases after hard bargaining without the unions having to resort to industrial action.

ICI concedes shorter hours to 37½. ICI agreed to staged cuts to 37½ hours per week for manual workers by 1985; 1 hour in 1981, 1 hour in 1983 and ½ hour in 1985.

On pay ICI offered 51 000 production workers 16 per cent across the board in addition to the 3 per cent received in January as compensation for price rises. The offer includes improved shift allowances as well as call out payments, which the unions accepted in July 1980.

British Rail agree to 20 per cent and 39 hours. British Rail agreed to a shorter working week from November 1981 for manual workers and white collar workers (38 hours reduced to 37 hours). The agreement lifted the minimum earnings level from £55.50 to £66.60 per week and gave a rise in the London allowance from £382 to £459 per annum. From January 1981 employees with 2 years' service receive 4 weeks' holiday.

The Clegg Awards. A new approach to deal with pay awards was introduced in 1978 by the Labour Government by establishing 'The Standing Commission on Pay Comparability'. It represented a way to avoid a return to 'free collective bargaining' proposed by the TUC in 1977. The Conservative Government initially allowed the work of the Commission chaired by Professor Clegg to continue its work, but later discontinued it.

The underlying idea was to arrive at a national pay structure by comparing one industry and service with another, using the technique familiar in *job evaluation*, unions and employers submitting to the Commission their rival claims and the Commission in the end making a recommendation to the employers. A considerable number of industries and services were being considered and some important recommendations were made (with regard to, e.g., teachers, nurses). These recommendations were then considered by the negotiators. In the case of the teachers an agreement was reached on the basis of the recommendation. The Government was not prepared to accept the Clegg award for nurses of 19.6 per cent, but a settlement was reached after lengthy negotiations on the basis of a 14 per cent rise. The Comparability Commission was a new approach in the attempt to achieve an equitable pay structure throughout the economy.

Agreements with particular firms

The examples of settlements dealt with above are national agreements. There are many areas where agreements have been reached with specific firms which are better and enhance both national agreements and minimum legal requirements. They cover such areas as holiday entitlements, occupational pensions, time off work for various public and trade union duties and activities, shorter working week and maternity and paternity leave.

Maternity/paternity. The minimum legal requirements of pregnancy and maternity were discussed in Chapter 8. An examination of 20 top employers in the UK (employing 4.8 million workers, with a substantial proportion of females) shows that the minimum requirement was exceeded in line with TUC policy, which has always stipulated that legal requirements are an absolute minimum. While the concessions gained are by no means generous, they are a start in the right direction – e.g. 6 out of the 20 employers have negotiated agreements which entitle women to maternity leave and pay after 1 year's service, all of these being in the public sector. Seven employers improved on the statutory minimum and gave women maternity pay for 2 months or longer. Only one of these (Grand Metropolitan) is in the private sector.

On qualifying service, 36 employers give women paid maternity leave after 1 year's service, a further five agreements reduced the qualifying period to 21 months or less and in one organization, the National Coal Board, women are automatically entitled to paid maternity leave. A number of employers give unpaid maternity leave to women who have not accumulated enough service to qualify for paid leave.

Length of leave. While the entitlement is 40 weeks after 2 years' service, there are organizations where the leave is extended up to 90 weeks – e.g. in the Open University.

Maternity pay. A survey has revealed that a number of different methods are used to improve maternity pay. Twenty-nine agreements provide for an additional number of weeks at either 90 per cent or full pay. Another system combines a set number of weeks (usually 6) at full or 90 per cent pay with a further number of weeks at half pay.

The treatment of National Insurance benefits are a negotiable element, and in some cases benefits are not deducted from the 90 per cent salary entitlement.

Paternity leave. There is no statutory right to paternity leave. A number of agreements have been concluded and the demand for paternity leave features increasingly in trade union demands. The agreements reached for paternity leave range from 28 days or over to 1 day; the most generous firms are in the publishing business.

11.9 Influence of trade unions on relative wages

It is evident that one of the primary objectives of a trade union is to raise the wages of its members relative to those of other employees. However, it is difficult to measure the extent to which a union is successful in achieving this aim, because the earnings which would have been obtained in the absence of workers being organized cannot be observed. The difference must, therefore, be estimated, and a number of problems needs to be solved in the process.

A common approach is to compare the differential which occurs between unionized and non-unionized workers. The two sets of workers must be as similar as possible: occupations should be the same, human and physical capital inputs should be comparable, and so forth. In addition, it must be possible to ensure that any possible feedback effects have been eliminated. For example, if a union pushes up the relative wage of its members, organizations employing the same type of labour (but which does not belong to the union) may also find it necessary in tight labour markets to increase the wages of their employees in order to keep quit rates down or persuade their employees not to join the union (this latter being referred to as the 'threat effect'). In these cases wages tend to be similar in all organizations (but those employing non-union labour may have greater flexibility in the design and implementation of manpower policies). If these effects are not adequately dealt with, empirical estimates will understate the effects of unions on relative wages. On the other hand, the relative wage effects of unions can be overestimated. If a union secures a high wage from an employer, the latter may subsequently find it possible to hire better quality manpower; the higher wage is then not being paid for the same quality of labour as before, and if the difference cannot adequately be measured, an overestimation is made of the union wage effect.

Difficulties also arise when relative wage effects are estimated by use of regression techniques. Gregg Lewis (1963), for example, surveys a wide range of US studies adopting this approach and attributes the major cause of error to measurement faults in the data and to errors which occurred when adjustments were being made for non-union factors.

As Metcalf (1977) points out, when the union/non-union wage differential is estimated by use of multiple regression techniques, the natural log of earnings is usually taken, so that the proportionate difference is estimated and not the absolute difference (in terms of £x). The proportional or percentage difference in wages is usually held to be the more relevant measure (whereas absolute differences are important in determining rates of return). However, one source of error in obtaining such estimates is that (in the UK) when official statistics provide information on unionization, they do not usually include data on other variables which affect wage differentials, such as human capital characteristics, age, and so forth. If these other variables are omitted, the results will be biased. Errors may also be contained in results which are based on union density, because it is frequently the case that many people who are not union members are nevertheless covered by collective agreements. Coverage data are therefore preferable to membership data, since the latter do not control for spillover effects between union members and non-union-covered workers.

Another problem is that while wages may be partly determined by union membership, it is also possible that union membership depends on wages. Membership and wages are then jointly determined, and this should be allowed for (usually by using simultaneous equation methods to estimate the differential). If this is not done, the union/non-union differential will be overestimated.

When we come to consider the empirical estimates which have been obtained for the union/non-union wage differential, one of the striking features is their variability. This is indicated in *Table 11.2*, where the results of a number of studies are summarized. We should, perhaps, not be too surprised at this general variability of the estimates, for there are a number of possible explanations. For example, we have just considered some of the difficult estimation problems; these may be more successfully dealt with in some cases than in others. Differences occur in the independent variables which are included and taken into account, and they may also be specified in different ways. As mentioned above, union influence is sometimes measured by using a union density variable; sometimes (as in the case of Mulvey and Foster, 1973) it has been possible to use a coverage variable so that all those subject to a collective agreement are included whether they are union members or not. Again some studies allow for the simultaneity problem previously mentioned, while others do not (compare C with M and D with E in *Table 11.2*).

There are also reasons in economic theory for expecting variations in the estimated effect of unions on wage differentials. In Chapter 3 it was pointed out that Marshall's four determinants of the labour elasticity of demand may favour some groups more than others. Unionization and the wage effect may thus be greater where product demand is relatively

Table 11.2 Estimated union/non-union wage differentials

	Investigator	Period	Group	Estimated differential (%)
A	Pencavel	1964	various UK manual workers	0–10
B	Lewis	various between 1920 and 1958	various industries	2–46 depending on period
C	Ashenfelter and Johnson	1960	US manufacturing production workers (simultaneous method)	4
D	Schmidt and Strauss	1967	US full-time workers (simultaneous method)	7
E	Schmidt and Strauss	1967	US full-time workers	10
F	Rosen	1958	US production workers: industries 80% unionization	10
G	Mulvey and Foster	1973	99 varied UK occupations (coverage)	22
H	Sobotka	1956	airline pilots	24–30
I	Mulvey	1973	UK manufacturing males (proportion of employers apply a collective agreement)	25
J	Johnson and Youmans	1966	all US blue-collar male workers	30
K	Rosen	1958	US production workers: industries 80% unionization	35
L	Mulvey and Foster	1973	83 UK manual occupations (coverage)	36
M	Ashenfelter and Johnson	1960	US manufacturing production workers	40

inelastic, labour costs are a small proportion of total costs, the elasticity of factor substitution is low and the supply of substitute factors is relatively inelastic. Variations in the relative weights of these factors will clearly affect the outcome.

In general, these Marshallian determinants are likely to be most favourable for craft and craft-type workers (the result for airline pilots is therefore not surprising). For example, it is likely to be more difficult to substitute capital for skilled labour than for unskilled or semi-skilled workers. However, the elasticity of factor substitution will always be higher in the long run than in the short run. Hence, the union effect will be greater in the short run.

Table 11.3 Variation of union/non-union wage differential over time (Lewis, 1963)

Period	Estimated differential (%)
1920–1924	17
1925–1929	26
1930–1934	46
1935–1939	22
1940–1944	6
1945–1949	2
1950–1954	12
1955–1958	16

Although there are obviously other factors involved, some impression of variations in the union differential over time can be obtained from Lewis's results, as indicated in *Table 11.3*. As Atkinson (1975) points out, the greatest differentials occurred during the depression of the 1930s, when union pressure prevented cuts in the money wages of their members. Conversely, during World War II, when the labour market was tight, the effect of unions was small. Consequently, variations in general economic conditions also influence the union differential.

Questions

1. What was the purpose of the Truck Acts? Discuss.
2. What system of wages payments are you familiar with?
3. What is the 'social wage'? How does it influence wage bargaining? Discuss.
4. How does unemployment influence wage bargaining? Discuss.
5. What management techniques are you familiar with to establish rates of pay?
6. What guidelines were issued to wage bargainers by the TUC in 1979–1980? Discuss.
7. How effective would shorter hours be in combating unemployment in the manufacturing industry? Discuss.
8. Explain why the Marshallian determinants of labour demand elasticity are likely to favour some groups more thn others.

References

Atkinson, A.B. (1975). *The Economics of Inequality*, Oxford University Press
Lewis, H.G. (1963). *Unionism and Relative Wages in the United States*, University of Chicago Press
Metcalf, D. (1977). 'Unions, incomes policy and relative wages in Britain', *British Journal of Industrial Relations*, 15, July

Chapter 12

People, organizations and the government

12.1 Introduction

On a number of occasions in previous chapters we have referred where necessary to the effects of government policy and legislation on the employment relationships between people and organizations. Inevitably, these aspects have assumed much greater importance in some chapters than in others, and the influence of government has been introduced and discussed only to the extent necesary for an understanding of the role of government as an external force affecting the basic relationships considered. While the role of government is not the primary focus of attention here, and would, in fact, require a book of its own for an adequate treatment, it is desirable to obtain a contextual picture of the broad sweep of government policy in so far as our basic subject matter is concerned.

Since every aspect of government policy cannot be considered within the space available, three particular areas have been chosen: manpower, taxation and industrial relations policy. These areas are of obvious importance to the subject matter of preceding chapters and a survey, albeit brief, of developments here will assist in placing previous discussions within a somewhat wider context.

We shall begin by considering the strict economic case for government intervention in a market system. It should be remembered, however, that government intervention is not always made for purely economic reasons, but may result from various political and social considerations. Nevertheless, this approach will help to clarify our thinking and draw attention to some of the underlying requirements for an active government role.

12.2 Market failure and the government

The purpose of a market is to set prices and, through this mechanism, to allocate resources between employing organizations and to allocate goods between people as consumers. Regardless of any value judgement as to what type of economic system one might prefer, the strict economics case for government intervention in a market economy depends on the failure of such a system to perform adequately. Thus, if the conditions outlined in Chapter 1 which are necessary for a perfectly competitive market were present throughout the economy, and if there were no (1) public goods, (2) internal economies of scale, (3) inadequate access to product and factor markets, (4) externalities in production and consumption, then an optimum allocation of resources would occur in the sense that one person could not be made better off without making someone else worse off. Such a situation of Pareto optimality (so called after the man from whose work it was derived) is illustrated in *Figure 12.1*, where two consumers, A and B, have welfares of a_1 and b_1,

Figure 12.1

respectively. Improving the welfare of one consumer without reducing that of the other means that any change must be along a or b (say to y or z) or within the north-east quadrant bounded by them. Starting from x, movements to other points such as m, n or t, would improve the welfare of one consumer only by reducing that of the other. But in a perfectly competitive economy with the four previous conditions met, movements from x to positions such as w, y or z would be impossible (because resources have already been allocated in their most efficient and productive uses and consumers all occupy positions which maximize their welfares[1]).

Markets may fail in respect of any of the four conditions mentioned above and Pareto optimality cannot then be attained. For example, certain goods cannot be sold to people individually but must be consumed collectively. For this reason they are called public goods, examples of which include defence and law enforcement. The problem is that, being consumed collectively, there is no way of discovering the valuation which any one individual puts on such a good, whereas when commodities are sold individually, it is possible for the price paid to be taken as a measure of a person's evaluation of the product. Again, if there are unexhausted internal economies of scale, Pareto optimality is not being achieved because it will then be possible to expand total output by reallocating productive resources. Similarly, if everyone does not have equal access to markets, maximum welfare may not be achieved. For example, some people may be unable to obtain funds to finance education or training, whereas such a reallocation of resources might raise their productivity more than it reduced that of someone else, so that output overall was increased. Lastly, the term 'externalities' refers to the effects which 'spill over' onto others when an action is taken by an economic agent. These spillover effects may be in the form of either benefits which cannot be charged for or costs for which recompense cannot be obtained. For instance, an individual who is educated cannot charge others for the additional benefits which accrue to society at large, any more than people who live near a school can be reimbursed for the cost of increased noise levels at certain times of the day.

Government intervention may clearly be necessary in respect of any of the foregoing causes of market failure. As noted above, if resources are not properly allocated, output may be lower than otherwise, perhaps because people are not being fully developed or because bottlenecks occur within the process of production when certain types of human resources are not available or not provided in sufficient quantity. It is then possible for government action to raise the level of total output as indicated in a simplified fashion in *Figure 12.2*. Here curve *ab* indicates the maximum output combinations of consumer goods and services which are attainable with present resources. Combinations such as *x* require a greater resource input than is currently available, but *z* is generally indicative of those maximum combinations which *can* be attained. If the current situation is similar to that given by point *y*, output can be expanded and the economy shifted to *z* by a reallocation of resources[2]. Government economic measures can therefore be seen as attempts in the short run to shift the economy from points such as *y* to those represented by *z* – i.e. to improve the existing allocation of resources so that output is increased and productivity improved. Over the longer term, government policy is usually also concerned with producing rightward shifts in the production possibility curve so that it goes through points such as *x*, making possible greater combinations of goods and services than can presently be obtained. This is the result of the process of economic growth which has been, and remains, a major objective of government policy, since it determines the extent to which material prosperity is improved over time. When governments intervene in the economy for this purpose, they do so in order to increase the rate of growth above what it would otherwise have been.

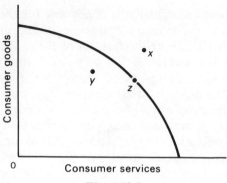

Figure 12.2

If the market system works imperfectly, the possibility exists that government action can bring about improvements in both the short and the long run, although it does not necessarily follow that it will effect improvements and the evaluation of government policy is fraught with difficulties, partly because of the problems associated with disentangling one causal effect from another and the differing time horizons over which consequences must be judged. However, with these considerations in mind, we can now proceed to discuss the previously mentioned areas of government policy.

12.3 Government manpower policy

In the postwar period governments became increasingly aware of the importance of human resource development in the achievement of economic and social objectives. This heightened awareness had several causes in the UK. Not least of these were the high levels of employment achieved by the management of aggregate demand after 1945 and, in the late 1960s and early 1970s, the contraction in the total labour force (as indicated in *Table 1.1*, page 13). Such factors put increased emphasis on labour market bottlenecks and the need to ensure that deficiencies in the market mechanism were made good by government action.

However, direct government involvement in manpower training dates from long before 1945. For example, government training centres (referred to in the literature as GTCs) were established after World War I to retrain disabled ex-servicemen, expanded during World War II to provide skilled labour for the war effort, allowed later to decline but subsequently revived in the 1960s in the form of skill centres (SCs). Postwar government involvement in training should, therefore, be seen in a longer-term historical perspective, although it has expanded considerably in recent decades.

Such expansion of direct government involvement in industrial training was not the recommendation of the Carr Report of 1958. The National Joint Advisory Council sub-committee was set up to consider the implications of a 50 per cent expansion in the number of school-leavers between 1956 and 1962. While advising that the facilities offered by the further education sector should be expanded, it nevertheless recommended that industrial training should remain the responsibility of each industry. However, the Report led to the creation of two new bodies which were intended to assist in the development of industrial training. Thus, the Training Advisory Service was set up to promote new and better methods of Industrial Training Service), while the Industrial Training Council was established to improve the flow of information on industrial training to those who were involved in the function.

From the debate which followed publication of the Carr Report a view gradually emerged which held that not only were there unacceptably great variations in the quality of training, but also that its quantity was in any case too low. In addition, the contribution of human capital creation in the attainment of socioeconomic objectives by government was tending to receive greater emphasis and can be seen as a necessary part of a wider range of policy measures intended to guide the general direction of the economy. But it was felt that too few people were being granted day release for training and that some firms were 'poaching' trained labour from other organizations.

Disquiet with the quality and quantity of training eventually led to the 1964 Industrial Training Act (ITA). This Act gave power to the then Minister of Labour to set up a system of Industrial Training Boards (ITBs) to promote both more and better training. Employers and employees were given equal representation on ITBs, which also included some educational and industrial members. While final control over resources was left with employing organizations, the Minister and ITBs were given responsibility for resources and finance, with the influence on training coming through a system of levies and grants; the levies are imposed on firms to raise finance for training purposes and out of this grants are made to employers for the training which they provide. Hence, the financing and (since ITBs make recommendations on the type which should be given) the quality of training was partly removed from individual employers and employees. An employer can, however, appeal against the imposition of a levy if it is considered that he does not come within the scope of that particular ITB or if the levy is considered to be incorrectly assessed.

The finance raised by an ITB from the levy can be used to provide training facilities, pay the fees of colleges of further education who provide approved courses and reimburse travel and maintenance expenses for those on approved courses. Moreover, ITBs operate in both private and public sectors of the economy, in the latter respect having been established in the gas, water, electricity and transport industries. While government departments are not included in the system, they are intended to adjust their training practices to those recommended by ITBs.

A number of important innovations have been made by ITBs in their development of training schemes. Guidance was given in the formulation of training schemes by the Central Training Council (CTC), which set out a number of principles which should be taken into account and which assist in the improvement of more traditional approaches to training. The Engineering Industry Training Board (EITB), in particular, has introduced radical changes in the approach to training. In many respects the apprenticeship system in that industry had become outdated. Training was often highly informal, unstructured and unnecessarily long. To deal with the problems, the EITB introduced a modular training system of a highly general kind which sought to meet both current requirements and the need for future flexibility. To attain qualified craftsman status, at least two modules must be successfully completed, each module being based on the time required to develop a particular skill. Training in the first year is given entirely off-the-job and in later years block periods off-the-job ae combined with on-the-job experience. Some studies, such as that by Thomas, Moxham and Jones (1969), which investigated the training of textile machine operatives, have indicated that a better balance between formal and informal training can have a beneficial effect on worker productivity and contribute to a reduction in the training period. The OECD (1970) report on 'Manpower Policy in the United Kingdom' saw this kind of ITB innovation as a way of breaking down rigid adherence to age limits in training and obsolete craft demarcations.

A good deal of apprenticeship and other training off-the-job is conducted within colleges of further education (CFEs), which form an important and integral part of the British training and education system. As Morrish (1970), for example, points out, the Mechanics Institutes which foreshadowed CFEs dated from about 1800 and received attention from the government in the latter part of the nineteenth century. More recently CFEs received significant stimulus from the ITA and the CTC recommended a closer relationship between the colleges and training. Their role in training has also been emphasized by the Training Services Agency, which has made use of the facilities and expertise available in CFEs.

The 1964 Act clearly stimulated a great deal of change and expansion in training activity. A further injection was provided in February 1972 by a discussion document called 'Training for the Future' (Department of Employment, 1972), which sought to deal with a number of criticisms which had been made of the government's Vocational Training Scheme (VTS). The VTS had been developing for some time and included provision for the acquisition of clerical and commercial skills in CFEs and firms in addition to the work taking place in government training centres (GTCs), which were subsequently renamed skill centres (SCs). However, after the mid-1960s approximately 90 per cent of VTS work was channelled through GTCs and the system was felt to be deficient in several respects. It was argued that the number of trades available was too small, that waiting periods for some trades were too long (at up to 2 years, with 10 000 on the waiting list), that compared with other countries total training capacity was too small and that co-ordination between the public and private sectors was insufficient.

As a result of the recommendations made in 'Training for the Future' a new stage in the development of British training began. The Training Services Agency (TSA) and the Training Opportunities Scheme (TOPS) were created to replace the VTS, with the Manpower Services Commission (MSC) acting in a co-ordinating role. The quantitative importance of government involvement in training increased markedly. For example, the 15 000 training places on offer in 1971 increased to 90 000 by 1976, while the number of trainees doubled between 1974 and 1976; although largely restricted to secretarial and clerical skills, the numbers of females in GTCs rose from 324 in 1970 to nearly 27 000 by 1975.

From January 1974 the co-ordinating body for British manpower policy has been the MSC. Although accountable to the Secretary of State for Employment, the MSC is a body which is separate from the Government. It has the general objective of ensuring an adequate supply of trained manpower and operates the public training and employment services run previously by the Department of Employment. It is, therefore, concerned not only with training, but also with placing people in employment. Since the MSC conceives of manpower policy as being concerned both with people as factors of production and with those individual needs which centre on employment, its approach encompasses both economic and social considerations (see, for example, MSC, 1976).

While the MSC has direct responsibility for certain employment-related activities (such as the work creation and job creation programmes) it operates largely through the Training Services Agency (TSA), the Employment Services Agency (ESA) and certain other organizations such as the Department of Employment, local authority careers services and the Advisory, Conciliation and Arbitration Service.

The ESA has responsibility for Job Centres, professional and executive recruitment and rehabilitation. In addition, it is also concerned with direct employment services such as occupational guidance, disabled employment, training applications and general employment services for the registration of vacancies and unemployment, etc. The ESA is less concerned with school-leavers (whom it prefers to leave to career officers) than with people already in the labour market. It has a staff of some 15 000 and 1005 local offices in addition to district offices, and decentralization is seen as important in the task of creating a flexible approach which is capable of dealing with changing conditions.

Since April 1974 the TSA has been the arm of the MSC which has responsibility for training. It has three divisions:

(1) Industries Division, which assists industry to meet its training needs.
(2) Directorate of Training, which is concerned with the methods used in teaching and the acquisition of skills, and with planning and policy studies.
(3) Training Opportunities Division, which concentrates on help to the individual in meeting training needs. This is done by use of SCs, which provide a range of courses in construction, automotive and engineering trades, and CFEs, which provide approximately half of TOPS training (with emphasis on clerical and commercial occupations).

In addition to its links with CFEs, the TSA also works through co-operations with the ITBs, which themselves provide coverage of approximately 50 per cent of all employees. It is also active with non-ITB sectors, including a significant part of private industry covering areas such as banking, insurance, finance, fishing and shipping in addition to the public sector.

Clearly, then, and largely as a result of the stimuli received from the ITA and 'Training for the Future', government involvement in manpower training, development and utilization has increased significantly over the last two decades. This expansion has not been without criticism of the activity and approach of the MSC, but, on the other hand, a number of studies have suggested that while improvements of various kinds can be made, this type of involvement has been profitable.[3].

12.4 Taxation policies

A major purpose in levying taxes is to provide revenue with which the State carries out and pays for its various activities. However, both the sums levied and the type of tax have an influence on economic activity and, in some cases, the primary reason for tax being levied (or removed) is its influence on the economy rather than its purely revenue effects. Governments, therefore, can use taxation policy as a means of influencing economic activity in what are regarded as desirable directions. The desired directions need not necessarily be economic (although such implications frequently cannot be ignored) and taxation may serve a social purpose. For example, the taxes on tobacco (especially on cigarettes) and alcohol are partly designed to reduce consumption of these commodities for health reasons.

The subject of taxation, and the wider area of public finance of which it is a component, has ramifications which are too extensive for this section to provide anything approaching a comprehensive treatment even within the limited context envisaged. Therefore, the discussion will be limited to a brief consideration of one or two aspects which will serve to indicate some of the effects that result from taxes of different kinds. In this respect it should perhaps first be noted that, although there may be some offsetting monetary effects, taken on its own the imposition of a tax tends to have a deflationary effect whether levied on incomes or on goods and services. In the former case, an income tax reduces the amount which people have at their disposal for spending or saving. To the extent that spending is directly affected, there is primary reduction in the aggregate demand for goods and services which, since the demand for labour is derived from that for the products which it produces, will lower the demand for people as employees. This may also occur if the initial effect is to reduce savings and therefore also the amount which borrowers can obtain to finance expenditure in excess of their current incomes[4]. Where expenditure taxes are concerned, in the absence of any offsetting falls in other prices, aggregate demand will be reduced, since goods and services subject to the tax will rise in price and, from a given income, consumers will not be able to purchase as many as before. Besides these income effects, there will also be substitution effects as consumers switch from buying goods now subject to the tax to other unaffected products whose prices are now lower in *relative* terms. Thus, the demand by employing organizations for labour will be affected differentially according to the pattern of consumer substitution between goods and services.

An income tax may also have effects on the amount of labour which people are willing to offer to organizations, although even the qualitative direction of change cannot be predicted on an *a priori* basis in some cases.

Indifference curve analysis is usually used to determine the outcome (see, for example, Prest, 1963, or Rees, 1979), on the assumption that a worker has a continuous choice between hours devoted to either work or leisure, with the effect of the tax depending on the relative strength of income and substitution effects. The substitution effect arises because leisure is regarded as a normal good, so that less (more) of it is bought as its relative price increases (decreases). An increase (decrease) in the wage rate increases (decreases) the cost of leisure, since then each hour not spent working involves a greater (lesser) sacrifice in terms of income lost; a worker therefore substitutes work for leisure (leisure for work) when the wage rate increases (decreases), since the price of leisure relative to other goods has risen (fallen). On the other hand, an increase (decrease) in the wage rate increases (decreases) the income of the worker, so that more (less) of all goods can be bought and this produces the income effect. Thus, for a straightforward rise (fall) in the wage rate per hour the substitution effect causes an increase (decrease) in the number of hours worked, while the income effect causes a decrease (increase) in hours worked. The overall net result depends on the relative strengths of each effect.

Now, in the case of a tax on income which takes the form of either a poll tax of £y per head or an income tax which is exactly proportional to income and produces the same yield, the income effects are the same in both cases. However, with a flat rate income tax the price of leisure changes, whereas it does not with an equal yield poll tax, since the same amount is raised whatever the number of hours worked. With the equal yield poll tax, nothing happens to the trade-off between work and leisure and, since the income effect of the tax change reduces the ability to buy leisure, more hours will be worked. With the proportional income tax the outcome depends on whether the substitution effect from the tax change, which will cause the employee to work fewer hours, is more or less than offset by the income effect, which increases hours worked. Since the income effect may be greater or lesser in strength than the substitution effect, no *a priori* conclusion can be reached. If the proportional income tax is replaced by a progressive income tax, so that the tax rates are greater at higher levels of income, the size of the substitution effect is increased, so that fewer hours are supplied; there is, therefore, a greater possibility that the number of hours supplied will fall.

Turning to a different aspect of taxation, an interesting innovation in the British tax structure (severely criticized by *The Economist* in its issues of 7 May and 24 September 1966) came in September 1966 with the levying of Selective Employment Tax (SET), which provided fertile ground for investigators to analyse in terms of the reasons for its introduction and its subsequent effects. Although some commentators have claimed to discern a rising trend in unemployment since 1945, it is possible broadly to distinguish two periods since that date: one in which there was relatively full employment with only 1–2 per cent of the workforce unemployed up to about 1966 and, since then, a rising trend leading to levels of 7 or 8 per cent in 1980 with very heavy unemployment in some of the older industrial regions. Thus, SET came in a period of labour scarcity and a relative weakening of manufacturing industry.

As originally introduced, under SET every employer paid a flat rate on each employee differentiated by age and sex. The tax was broadly imposed in relation to the average earnings of men, women, boys and girls but was refundable to all industries except 'taxable industries', services and construction. In effect, it was a tax on labour employed in service and construction industries (see, for example, Butler and Gidlow, 1966, for details).

In his 1966 inaugural lecture at Cambridge Professor Kaldor put the reason for Britain's relatively low growth rate as being partly due to historic facts which involved premature attainment of economic maturity. In the development of most industrial countries there is a trend over time away from agriculture to manufacturing and services on the outputs of which most of the increases in income are spent. But as real income continues to rise, the service sector tends to expand faster than manufacturing. These changes are accompanied by concomitant changes in the distribution of the labour force as between primary, secondary and tertiary sectors. Thus, by the time of the post-war period Britain had already denuded the agricultural sector of labour; unlike countries such as France and Germany, where there were still substantial proportions employed in agriculture, Britain could not meet expansion in other areas by transferring labour from the primary sector. On the other hand, some people argued that employment in the service industries was too high and inefficient. A major purpose of the introduction of SET, therefore, seemed to be to effect a transfer of labour from service industries (where it was relatively inefficient) to manufacturing industries, which were regarded as important from the point of view of both growth and exports. Growth was associated with manufacturing and manufacturing was highly export-intensive (Musgrave and Musgrave, 1968). At this time value added tax was not in operation and some commentators also pointed out that SET broadened the tax base and was more comprehensive than a conventional tax on services would have been while removing the disparity of treatment in taxation between goods and services, since goods were subject to purchase tax and excise duties, whereas services (except rates and motoring taxes) were tax-free up to 1966.

The basis of the tax was a surcharge on all employees' National Insurance contributions, amounting to £1.25 per male employee, increased in two successive steps to reach £2.40 in the 1969 Budget. These sums were to be refunded completely to employers in transport, agriculture and the bulk of the public sector and repaid, with the addition of a premium, to manufacturing industry. The burden of the tax thus fell exclusively on services and construction.

How far SET was effective in attaining its objectives is difficult to estimate. It was reckoned to increase the cost of labour in service industries by 7 per cent, which would thus result in a substitution of capital for labour and an increase in manpower supply to manufacturing (Musgrave and Musgrave, 1968). However, unemployment began its rise at about the same time and, while SET may have shook labour out of service industries, it does not necessarily follow that these resources were absorbed by manufacturing organizations. As a poll tax (i.e. fixed charge per head) SET bore heavily on the unskilled, older and handicapped worker, but it may have given some help to the export of manufactured goods by what was virtually a subsidy. Also, a report on the effects of SET by Reddaway (1970) showed that abnormally high increases in productivity had occurred in physical distribution trades; although some of these improvements could have been due to other factors operating during the period (e.g. the abolition of resale price maintenance), the report expressed the view that SET had played a major role. In addition, it was argued that SET had affected the structure and organization of retailing partly by reducing the number of counter staff, in some cases by leading to a reduced service (although this effect was probably small), by accelerating the development of self-selection and (to a lesser extent) self-service. In general, SET had been responsible for speeding up changes which would have occurred anyway.

However, enough has probably been said in this section to indicate some of the ways in which government taxation policy can influence the structure of organizations and their operating environment together with the manner in which they may affect the supply of people to employers. For the last section we can turn to survey the economic and political background against which British industrial relations and policy have developed.

12.5 The economic and political background

12.5.1 Pre-war Britain

During the last 50 years vast changes in the relationship between people in organizations and the government have taken place. The 1930s were a period of unprecedented slump and unemployment reached 3 million in Britain by 1932. Wages were cut because the reserve army of labour exerted a very powerful influence on the labour market. It is worthy of note that in the 1930s Britain's terms of trade improved because the price of her exported industrial goods remained steady in spite of the world-wide depression, while the price of her imported foodstuffs and raw materials declined. The effect of this development and its impact on wages and cost of living is shown in *Figure 12.3*. There were no inflationary tendencies and living standards actually improved.

Towards the end of the 1930s the situation began to change. There tended to be an abatement of the economic crisis partly due to

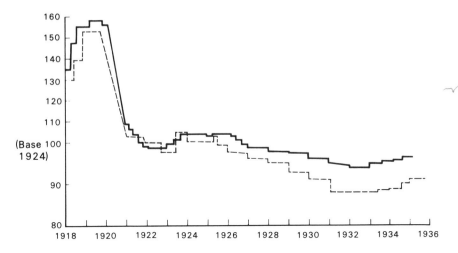

Figure 12.3 Movement of full-time rates of wages and cost of living, 1920–1926.
Ministry of Labour indices; 1924 = 100. ——, money wage rates; - - - -, cost of living

rearmament of both the Axis powers, consisting of Germany, Italy and
Japan, and the opposing powers that were to form the grand coalition
against the Axis. Unemployment in Britain began to decline but
remained at over 1 million well into the war.

With the imminent prospect of war, prices began to rise world wide
and also in Britain. Price rises have formed the background on which
Britain's economic and industrial development has taken place for over
40 years, fluctuating between very modest rises of 1 per cent, 2 per cent
and 3 per cent and 24 per cent in 1975–1976. The reasons causing
inflationary pressures are extremely complex; rises in input costs, shifts
in political power between the West and East and the ex-colonial 'Third
World' and the formation of extremely powerful financial and industrial
transnational firms able to fix prices, the formation of such international
cartels as OPEC and the relative weakness of governments compared
with the economic strength of the transnational firms provide some of
the explanations. The argument that wages have had a decisive influence
on price rises especially in Britain has been popular with governments,
but has been contested by many economists and the trade unions. (See
Table 12.1.)

12.5.2 Post-war Britain

The first 6 post-war years were under a Labour administration, with a
trade union movement that had grown considerably during the war
years. This period saw massive nationalization measures being adopted

Table 12.1

Year	Consumer prices (A)	Take-home pay (B)
1960	100.0	100.0
1961	102.9	102.5
1962	106.9	104.4
1963	108.9	105.4
1964	112.6	106.4
1965	117.7	108.8
1966	122.1	110.8
1967	125.3	115.1
1968	130.8	118.0
1969	131.9	123.4
1970	145.4	135.0

Taken from data in the 1971 *Blue Book of National Income and Expenditure*.

A is an index of consumer prices from Table 16 in the 1971 *Blue Book*. B is an index of the take-home pay per unit. (From a letter by Lt. Col. F. W. Torby, published in the *Financial Times* on 1 September 1972.)

in Britain against a background of growing balance of payments difficulties, especially in relation to the United States. In 1949 sterling was devalued from $4.03 to $2.80. The devaluation caused massive increases in the cost of imported materials and had a considerable influence on prices at home.

The Trade Union Congress had in the meantime agreed to assist the Government's export performance, especially in the dollar markets. The policy of wage restraint was not agreed to without considerable opposition within the trade union movement.

With the change of government in 1951 new nationalization measures ended and in 1953 the steel industry was denationalized and so was road transport. During this period many of the wartime economic restrictions were either removed or eased, but increasing external pressure continued to affect the balance of payments unfavourably. An important financial result was the gradual raising of the Bank Rate, which stood at 2 per cent during the period of the post-war Labour Government. It was raised to 2½ per cent by the Conservative Government and has shown a steady upward trend with some slight fluctuations, reaching a peak of 17 per cent in 1980 (by then referred to as Minimum Lending Rate or MLR).

While these increases were part of government monetary policy designed to combat inflationary pressures, it at the same time reinforced inflationary pressures by being partly responsible for price increases where industry and commerce were dependent on borrowing. It also tended to limit investment, which inhibited modernization of industry, making the latter less competitive and constantly endangering the current account of the balance of payments.

Other events which affected the economy were the several local wars, the most serious being the Korean, Suez and Vietnam war, as well as the 'cold war', which raised expenditure on armaments in all the industrial countries and so increased the prices of all strategic raw materials. Further, the post-war period is characterized by the virtual liquidation of old colonial empires (with the exception of a few enclaves and islands, among which Hong Kong is the most important). In the case of the oil-producing ex-colonies, exercising this freedom to raise oil prices has had a profound effect, especially since 1973, on prices throughout the world.

The formation of the European Common Market in 1959 had a profound effect on the British economy through the spectacular growth of Britain's European competitors. After much heart-searching and negotiation Britain joined the Community in 1972. It has to be said that with increasing economic difficulties EEC membership has steadily declined in popularity and has, in fact, never been accepted by the trade union movement as a whole.

12.5.3 The policy of full employment

During the war years the dreadful legacy of unemployment, the ill health, the operation of means tests, the Unemployment Assistance Board, the hunger marches were often discussed both in the forces and among the civilian population when bearing the assaults of Hitler's Germany. There was a resolve that never again should there be a return to the 'hungry thirties'. This resolve led to Sir William Beveridge's famous Report on the Social Services for a post-war Britain. The plan presented in 1942 was a morale booster in difficult times and people believed it would be carried out. The most important part of the Beveridge Report is entitled 'Full Employment in a Free Society', and it recommended that post-war governments should pursue full employment as a political and economic aim. This was accepted by all political parties and was more or less maintained for nearly 20 years.

But by 1966 the commitment to full employment was being weakened. Already in November 1964 with the budget announced in that month a policy of serious deflation was begun – the Bank Rate was raised to 7 per cent and Britain took on a central bank loan of $3000 m and in December 1964 the IMF loaned Britain another $1000 m. The April Budget of 1965 called for £164 m extra taxation and introduced corporation tax and tightened exchange controls; in May 1965 Britain took on

another $1400 m from IMF. No IMF loans are made without conditions
or 'strings' and the result was a perceptible rise in unemployment.

Frank Cousins's letter of resignation spells this out. It included the
phrase 'our international monetary transactions have been based on
assurances of our intention to restrict internal demand'. In June 1967 we
had the Arab–Israeli war and an Arab embargo on oil to the UK; oil
prices began to rise. In November sterling was devalued to $2.40 and by
January 1968 large cuts in public expenditure were announced. Policies
of deflation have been planned by both governments since then with
obvious results in terms of unemployment. By the second half of 1980
unemployment was heading for 2 million and in many industrial areas of
the north conditions were beginning to be reminiscent of the 1930s.

12.5.4 Incomes policy

The events of 1965–1966 were linked to a new version of an incomes
policy which was set out in a White Paper. This policy was supported by
a small majority by a TUC special conference of trade union executives.
A prices and incomes board was established to set price and wage
increases. The TUC supported this policy. The Prices and Incomes Act
1966 introduced a wage freeze for 6 months, to be followed by a period of
severe restraint. (See Appendix 12.2 for a brief outline of post-war
income policies.)

Eventually the policy of wage restraint broke down and the government blamed the trade unions for Britain's economic difficulties. The
Donovan Commission proposed limitations on trade union power and
the Labour Government published its White Paper 'In Place of Strife',
which proposed legislation to curb trade union powers.

In June 1970 the Labour Government was replaced by a Conservative
administration which put the Industrial Relations Act 1971 on the
statute book and at the same time pursued an incomes policy; among its
measures was the policy of 'threshold payments' under which automatic
wage increases were awarded after a given level of inflation had been
reached. The Industrial Relations Act and especially the unions' opposition to the Heath Government's industrial policies brought a Labour
Government to power in February 1974.

In 1973 during the last phase of the Heath Government, the TUC and
the Labour Party came to an agreement that if Labour was returned to
power it would pursue a 'wage restraint' policy in agreement with the
TUC, provided that it pledged itself to maintain the 'social wage',
provide for a minimum wage and keep earnings in line with prices. In
exchange for advocating wage restraint the TUC would expect a future
Labour Government to put a series of measures on the statute book

which included a repeal of the Industrial Relations Act and legislation on health and safety at work, 'rights at work' legislation and legislation on discrimination both on race and on sex. The Labour Government returned in 1974 carried out its legislative promises. Whether the legislation met the terms of the Social Contract in every detail is a moot point. The crumbling of the Labour majority in Parliament, the opposition in the house of Lords and the Lib–Lab pact made legislation difficult to enact.

On wages and economic performance generally the feeling in the trade union movement grew to the point where, in 1977, the TUC demanded an end to the Social Contract, a return to 'free collective bargaining' and an 'alternative economic strategy'.

The Labour Government continued to pursue its policy of wage restraint and laid down a policy of 5 per cent wage increases in 1978 in a situation where prices were rising still very much in excess of 5 per cent, although the rate of inflation had dropped to just below 10 per cent (see Appendix 12.1). The attempt by the Government to keep wage increases within 5 per cent sparked off a great deal of industrial unrest in the winter of 1978/79, which was labelled the 'winter of discontent'. The election that took place in May 1979 resulted in a Conservative election victory and a comfortable majority in Parliament for the Government.

Questions

1. How, and as a result of what main stimuli, has government involvement in manpower training developed since 1945?
2. Describe the main features of MSC activity.
3. Explain, with examples, why governments may find it desirable to intervene in the economy in respect of education and training.
4. Suppose that an employing organization receives from its ITB in the form of a grant an amount exactly equal to the levy it has paid. Explain why the end result might be preferable to having no ITB system.
5. Show the relative effects of our arguments in question 2 on a typical age–earnings profile which begins with the commencement of training and ends at retirement.
6. Analyse the possible effects of SET in terms of *Figure 12.2*.
7. There were relatively few industrial disputes in the 1930s. Discuss.
8. The policy of full employment was pursued by post-World War II governments. What are the implications for employing organizations?

Notes

[1] The conditions are fully discussed in any intermediate text, such as Koutsoyiannis (1975), Leftwich (1976) or Lancaster (1969).

[2] Position y might also be the result of insufficient aggregate demand, in which case z is attained by reducing the level of unemployment.

[3] See, for example, Adnett (1977), Lasko (1978), Ziderman (1975) and Ziderman and Walder (1975).

[4] Note that we are not considering the use to which the government puts its revenue thus obtained (which, if spent, will have an offsetting effect to the deflationary consequences of the tax) or the monetary implications which result from either changes in the government's borrowing requirements or the supply of funds for lending.

References

Adnett, N.J. (1977). 'Manpower training in the United Kingdom: some aspects of the government's role', *International Journal of Social Economics*, **4**, 2

Butler, E.B.and Gidlow, A. (1966). 'The Selective Employment Tax', *Moorgate and Wall Street Journal*, Autumn

Department of Employment (1972). *Training for the Future: A Plan for Discussion*, HMSO, London

Hughes, J.J. (1978). 'Training for what?', *Industrial Relations Review*, **9**, No. 3

Koutsoyiannis, A. (1975). *Modern Microeconomics*, Macmillan, London

Lancaster, K. (1969). *Introduction to Modern Microeconomics*, Rand McNally

Lasko, R. (1978). 'The work experience programme', *Department of Employment Gazette*, March

Leftwich, R.H. (1976). *The Price System and Resource Allocation*, 6th edn, Dryden Press

Manpower Services Commission (1976). *Towards a Comprehensive Manpower Policy*, MSC, London

Morrish, I. (1970). *Education Since 1800*, Allen and Unwin, London

Musgrave, R.A. and Musgrave, P.B. (1968). 'Fiscal policy', – Chapter 1 in Caves, R.E., *Britain's Economic Prospects*, Allen and Unwin, London

Prest, A.R. (1963). *Public Finance in Theory and Practice*, Weidenfeld and Nicolson, London

Reddaway, W.B. (1970). *Effects of the Selective Employment Tax: First Report. The Distributive Trades*, HMSO, London

Rees, A, (1979). *The Economics of Work and Pay*, Harper and Row, New York

Thomas, B., Moxham, J. and Jones, J.A.C. (1969). 'A cost benefit analysis of industrial training', *British Journal of Industrial Relations*, **VII**, No. 2

Ziderman, A. (1975). 'Costs and benefits of manpower training programmes in Great Britain', *British Journal of Industrial Relations*, **XIII**, No. 2

Ziderman, A. and Walder, A. (1975). 'Trade unions and the acceptability of GTC trainees: some survey results', *British Journal of Industrial Relations*, March

Appendix 12.1: Facts and figures 1960–1980

Year	Inflation (%)	Wage increases (%)	Unemployment (%)
1960	1.6	4.1	1.5
1961	3.4	3.4	1.3
1962	2.6	4.4	1.8
1963	2.1	4.3	2.2
1964	3.3	3.8	1.6
1965	4.8	4.6	1.3
1966	3.9	3.3	1.4
1967	2.5	3.6	2.3
1968	4.7	7.8	2.4
1969	5.4	7.8	2.4
1970	6.4	12.1	2.6
1971	9.4	11.3	3.4
1972	7.1	11.0	3.7
1973	9.2	12.2	2.6
1974	16.1	17.8	2.6
1975	24.2	26.5	3.9
1976	16.5	15.6	5.3
1977	15.8	10.3	5.8
1978	8.2	14.0	5.7
1979	17.2	19.6	5.3
(April) 80	21.8	22.0 approx.	5.3

Sources used:

Allen, G. *Structure of British Industry*, Longman, London, 1967.
Aubrey Jones. *The New Inflation*, Deutsch, London, 1973.
Economist, 11 February 1978.
Pelling, H. *A History of British Trade Unionism*, Penguin, Harmondsworth, 1972.
Proudfoot, M. *British Politics 1951–70*, Greenwood, London, 1974.

Appendix 12.2: Post-war incomes policies

Norm for wage increases	Methods of enforcement	Special features
1948–1950: Cripps + Wage restraint – no set norm	Voluntary through TUC	
1956–1961: Plateau – no set norm	Voluntary – monitored through council on Prices, Productivity and Incomes	Public sector price controls
1961–1962: Pay pause followed by 2–2½% norms based on productivity growth	National Incomes Commission could review agreements referred to it by both parties	
1965–1966: Guidelines 3–3½%	Prices and Incomes Board (PIB)	Exceptions for productivity, etc.
1966–1967: Freeze followed by severe restraint	Statutory – PIB	
1967–1970: Return to 1965 criteria – norms 3–3½%	Statutory – PIB	
1972: Six-month freeze	Statutory	Price curb would be enforced where profits were excessive
1973 (April): Increases £1 + 4% p.w.	Statutory	£250 p.a. limit
1973 (October): £2.25 p.w. or 7% (whichever greater)	Statutory (broken by miners' strike)	£350 p.a. limit – threshold payments linked to prices
1975: £6 p.w. limit	Voluntary	No increases over £8500 p.a.
1976: 5% limit within a range of £2.50–£4 p.w.	Voluntary	
1977: 10% on earnings	Voluntary	Sanctions on firms which pay more
1978: 5–10% on earnings	Voluntary	Rejected

Index

ACAS, *see* Advisory Conciliation and
  Arbitration Service
Advertising
  discrimination in, 182, 190
  of job vacancies, 73, 85
Advisory Conciliation and Arbitration
  Service
  activities, 14
  advice, 225, 226
  arbitration, 226
  conciliation, 226
  functioning of, 225
  importance, 13
  role of, in collective bargaining, 225
Agitators, conflict caused by, 162, 163
Allocation of manpower, *see* Manpower
Applications for job vacancies
  application forms, 85
  letters, 85
  sifting and short list, 86
Authority
  charismatic, 127, 128
  definition, 127
  rational-legal, 128
  traditional, 128

Bargain, *see* Collective bargaining
Birth, standardized rates of, in UK, 39
Bureaucratic theory of organization
  effect of, on individual behaviour, 117
  theoretical model of, 116, 117
  weakness of managerial approach, 117

Capital, *see* Human capital
Carr Report, 253
Change
  as feature of social life, 150
  gemeinschaft and *gesellschaft*, 151
  planning of, 156–158

Change (*cont.*)
  regulation–radical change dimension,
    156
  social, Marx's analysis of, 152, 153
  theories of, 150–154
Cipolla, Carlo M. (population and
    technology), 35, 36
Closed shop, 199, 200
Cobb–Douglas production function, 75
Code of Practice, for promotion of good
    industrial relations, 200
Coercion
  definition, 124
  power as form of, 124
  secondary picketing, 124
Collective bargaining
  ACAS, *see* Advisory Conciliation and
    Arbitration Service
  bargain
    definition, 217
    individual and collective
      distinguished, 217
    organizations with which made, 218
  bargaining structure, persons included
    in, 218
  as central feature of industrial
    relations, 226, 227
  constraints on, 235, 236
  employers' organizations, role of, 226
  health and safety agreements, 222
  law of contract and, 220, 221
  legislative provisions, effect of,
    221–224
  local and national, 237
  management techniques to establish
    wage rates, 236, 237
  outcome of, 233 ff.
  place of, in law, 221
  procedure agreement, 224, 225
  in public and private industry,
    outcome of, 237–244

Collective bargaining (*cont.*)
  redundancies, handling of, procedure
    for, 222
  on shop floor level, 237
  trade union objectives, 227–229
  Truck Acts, 233, 234
  steps followed in, 222–224
  time of work, 222
  unionization by industrial sector and
    establishment size, 238
  wages payment systems, 234, 235
  working population, number of, 218
Commission for Racial Equality
  establishment and powers, 190
  work of, 190
Communication(s)
  barriers to, 144–148
    channels of communications, as, 147
    individual ideas, 144
    language, 147, 148
    size, 146
    status, 145, 146
  cognitive dissonance, 144
  definitions, comparison of, 141
  'grapevine' information, 145, 146
  homogeneity or heterogeneity, 146
  ideas, of, transmission and feedback,
    142, 143
  information and, 142
  jargon, 148
  nature of, 141, 142
  one-way and two-way, 142, 143
  physical factors affecting, 146
  poor, conflict arising through, 161
  process, 142
  records, 148
  stereotypes, use of, 144
  time spent in, 148
  verbal, 149
  words, use of, 148
  written, 148, 149
Competition
  effect of, on market activity, 79
  monopolistic, 80
Confederation of British Industry
  formation and membership, 133
  as pressure group, 133
  representation on other bodies, 132
Conflict
  arenas of, 165–167
  management of, scheme for, 165, 166
  old and new views, 160

Conflict (*cont.*)
  origins of
    class divisions, 161
    conflicting interests, 161
    control, lack of, 162
    personality factors, 160, 161
    poor communications, 161
    work environments, alienating
      nature of, 161
  theories of
    agitator, 162
    communications, 163
    economic, 164
    integration, 163, 164
    societal, 164–165
    socio-technical, 164
    technological determinism, 164
Contingency theory of organization,
  117–119
  development, 118
  main elements, 118, 119
  shortcomings, 119
Contract of employment, 208, 209
Costs
  fixed, 73, 75, 76
    analysis of, 73, 74
    employment costs, 73
    turnover costs, 73
  training, 70–72
Custom, regulatory effect of, 92

Death, standardized rates of, in UK, 40
Demography
  Demographic Transition Model, 36 ff.
  meaning, 36
Discrimination, *see* Race discrimination;
  Sex discrimination

Economic League, aims of, 139
Economy, population and, relationship
  between, 33 ff.
Education
  age participation rate and qualified
    leaver rate, 44–46
  colleges of further education, 254
  comprehensive schools, growth of, 42,
    43
  employment and, relationship
    between, 47–52
  further education statistics, 44

Education (*cont.*)
General Household Survey, 44, 46
higher, estimates for, 46
importance of, 24, 33
nursery and primary schools, 42
productivity and earnings related to,
47–52
as screening device, 48, 49, 86, 87
secondary, reorganization of, 43, 44
training and manpower development,
68–72 (*see also* Training)
tripartite system, 43
Elasticity
in demand for labour, 66–68
Marshall's views on, 67, 68
in price, 27, 28
Emigrants, definition, 39
Employer
health and safety, duties regarding,
201–207
training by, *see* Training
Employers' organizations, 11, 13
Confederation of British Industry, 11,
133
Conservative Party, links with, 138
as pressure groups, 133
role of, in collective bargaining, 226
structure of, 232
Employment
contract of, 208, 209, 220
discrimination in, *see* Race
discrimination; Sex
discrimination
education and, relationship between,
47–52
elasticity of demand for labour, 66–68
employees, role analysis, 112, 113
externally provided manpower,
utilization of, 59–63
factors governing, Adam Smith's
views on, 23
full, policy of, 263, 264
health and safety, *see* Legislation
itemized pay statements, right to, 209,
210
Job Centres, 256
labour demand data, 61
labour market, *see* Market
marginal physical product, 60, 61
market, *see* Market
organizations and, 59 ff.
pricing and allocation model, 3–6

Employment (*cont.*)
protection, *see* Legislation
status of employees, 112, 113
supply and demand schedules, 15 ff.
termination of
notice, 211
unfair dismissal, 212, 213
written statement of reasons for, 212
terms and conditions of, written
statement of, rights to, 209
time off work, 210, 211
training, *see* Training
of women, *see* Women
working population, number of, 218
Employment Services Agency, 255, 256
Engineering Employers' Federation, 133
affiliated establishments, 133
as pressure group, 133
role of, in collective bargaining, 226
structure of, 232
Engineering Industry Training Board,
254
Environment
protection of, employer's duty, 203
workplaces, alienating nature of, 161,
162
Equal Opportunities Commission
establishment, 182, 186
membership and duties, 186
women's working hours, report on,
187, 188

Feedback, as part of communication,
142, 143
verbal communication, 149
Fraser's system of recruitment grading,
84
Functionalism, 153

Group(s)
analysis of behaviour in, 108, 109
definition, 108
leadership study, 110
norms, 109, 110
pressure, *see* Pressure groups
structure, contextual factors, 111, 112
work in, study of, 108
Guilds, 11

Health, *see* Legislation
Hiring, *see* Manpower

Human capital
  age–earning profiles, 52
  attributes comprised in, 19, 20
  as basis of organizational design, 115, 116
  earnings and working life-cycle, 50, 51
  education as, 47, 48
  investments in, rate of return on, 52–56
  personnel selection, 87 (*see also* Manpower)
  productivity raised by, 49
  supply of, 19, 20
  major points in study of, 115, 116
  scientific management compared, 116

Immigrants
  definition, 39
  effect of, on population, 39, 42
Immunities, trade union, 195–198
  curtailment of, 198
Inducement
  as means of influence, 124
  as type of power, *see* Power
Industrial organization(s)
  analysis of, 105
  inputs and outputs, 105
  open system, 104, 105
Industrial revolution, effect of, 11, 174, 175
Industrial Training Boards, 46, 253, 254
Industrial Training Council, 253
Influence
  behaviour as outcome of, 123
  implicit, 123
  meaning, 123
  means of
    inducement, 124
    persuasion, 123
    trained control, 123
Interest group, 130 (*see also* Pressure groups)
International Labour Office, formula for equal pay, 177
Interplanning
  groups, working in, 108–110
  motivation, 107, 108
Interview for job vacancy, 87
  criteria of assessment, 89
  group selection, 87, 88
  methods of conducting, 88

Interview for job vacancy (*cont.*)
  planning beforehand, 88
  purpose of, 88
  references, 89
  selection board, 87
  selection test, reinforcement by, 89

Jargon, 148
Job Centres, 256
Job evaluation, 236, 237
Joint Industrial Councils, 220

Labour market, *see* Market
Language, as barrier to communication, 147, 148
Legislation
  Code of Practice to promote good industrial relations, 200
  development of, 194, 195
  employment protection
    collection of pay, 210
    contract of employment, 208, 209
    itemized pay statements, 209, 210
    lay-offs, guaranteed pay during, 210
    notice, 211
    redundancy, 213, 214
    suspension on medical grounds, payment during, 210
    termination of employment, 211–213
    time off work, 210, 211
    unfair dismissal, 212
    written statement, rights to, 209
  health and safety
    agreements as to, 222
    articles and substances used at work, 203
    employers and employees, general duties, 201, 202
    environment, protection of, 203
    former Acts remaining in force, 207
    Health and Safety Commission, 206
    Health and Safety Executive, 206
    law on, enforcement of, 205, 206
    outsiders, duty towards, 202, 203
    powers and penalties, 205, 206
    regulations, 206
    research, obligation for, 203, 204
    Robens Report, 201
    safety representatives, functions of, 204, 205

Legislation (*cont.*)
  health and safety (*cont.*)
    supervision of, organization of, 207
    trade union representation, 204
  increase in, during post-war period,
      194
  TULRA 1974
    closed shop, 199, 200
    no compulsion to work, 198, 199
    peaceful picketing, 199
    trade unions and immunities,
      195–198
  Wages Councils, 214, 215
Lobby, 130 (*see also* Pressure group)

Malthus, Thomas R.
  'diminishing returns', law of, 35
  'iron law' theory of wages, 7
  Principle of Population, 34
Management, scientific, *see* Scientific
    management
Manager
  meaning, 129
  political aspects of behaviour affecting,
      129
  power, study of, 130
Manpower
  allocation within organizations
    allocative structure
      criteria for entry, 93
      degree of openness, 92, 93
      ports of entry, 93
      rules for determining priorities,
          93, 94
      scope, 93
    benefits and disadvantages of
        internal labour markets, 94, 95
    causes of internal labour markets
      custom, 92
      on-the-job training, 91, 92
      skill specificity, 91
    internal allocation policies, 90, 91
  demand for, fixed labour costs and,
      72–74
  development, training and, 68–72 (*see
    also* Training)
  government policy, 252–256
  hiring
    allocation and planning, 82 ff.
    costs, correlation of, with level of
        skill required, 86

Manpower (*cont.*)
  labour market, recourse to, 82
  planning, 95–100
    difficulties and inaccuracies, 99
    main aspects, 96
    policies, co-ordination of, 97
    summary of process, 97
  recruitment
    advertising, 85
    applications, 85, 86
    educational screening, 86, 87
    Fraser's system, 84
    group selection, 87, 88
    identification of vacancy, 83
    internal and external resource
        markets, 90–95
    interviews, *see* Interview for job
        vacancy
    job description, 83
    maximum efficiency, importance of,
        89
    objectives and hiring level, 83
    personnel specification, 83, 84
    'ports of entry', 84, 89, 90, 93
    promotion, 90
    references, 89
    Rodger's plan, 84
    selection, 85–90
    short list, 86
  role analysis, 112, 113
  seniority, 94
Manpower Services Commission, 46, 47,
    255
Marginalism
  application of marginalist method, 29
  changes in value of variables, 28–32
  marginal revenue product, 62, 63
Marginal physical product, of labour, 60,
    61
Market(s)
  advertising for skilled and unskilled
      labour, 73
  characteristics of, 6, 7
    imperfections, 14, 15
    organizational influences, 9–13
    personalized factors, 6, 7
    social factors, 7–9
  competitive, effects of, 64–66
  consumer welfare, 250
  failure of, conditions for, 250
  fragmentation, view of, 15
  government intervention, 249–251

Market(s) (*cont.*)
  internal labour, 90
    allocative structure, 92–94
    benefits and disadvantages, 94, 95
    causes of, 91, 92
  main function of, 4
  monopoly and monopsony elements,
    14
  oligopolistic, situation arising in,
    64–66
  operation of, 4, 5
  Pareto optimality, 250, 251
  perfectly competitive, assumptions to
    be made, 4
  price reductions, effect of, 64
  pricing and allocation model, 3–6
  public goods, 250, 251
  purpose of, 249
  restrictions on movement, 14, 15
  structures, 78–81
  supply and demand, factors
    underlying, 15–22
  theoretical models
    monopolistic competition, 80
    oligopoly, 80, 81
    perfect competition, 79
  trade union membership, 12
Marshall, Alfred (elasticity of labour
  demand, determinants of), 67, 68
Marx, Karl
  labour, value of, 235, 236
  theories of, 152, 153
Maternity
  antenatal care, time for, 185
  notices required, 185
  pay, 184
  right to return to work, 184, 185
  unfair dismissal, provisions against,
    182 ff.
Monopoly
  effect of, 80
  labour demand and monopolistic
    competition, 64
  meaning, 80
Motivation
  definition, 107
  forces affecting individual's behaviour,
    108
  Maslow's hierarchy of needs, 107

National Economic Development
  Organization Council
  bodies represented on, 138
  meetings of, 138, 139

Oligopoly
  effect of, 80, 81
  meaning, 80
Opportunity cost, 127
Organizations, 1, 2
  analysis of, 105, 106
    assumptions, 102, 103
    perspectives in social science, 103,
      104
    social action approach, 106, 107
    social science, meaning and purpose
      of, 102
    social system as basis of, 104–106
  approaches to design of, 103–107
  change in, 149, 154–158
  collective bargaining and, *see*
    Collective bargaining
  communication within, *see*
    Communication(s)
  controls exercised by, 2
  design of, approaches to,
    bureaucracy, 116, 117
    contingency theory, 117–119
    human relations school, 115, 116
    scientific management, 114, 115
    social action approach, 106, 107
    social system, 104–106
  development, 158, 159
  economic and political background
    post-war Britain, 261–263
    pre-war Britain, 260, 261
  employment and, 59 ff.
  externally provided manpower,
    utilization of, 59–63
  government policy, 249 ff.
  individuals in, 102 ff.
  industrial, open systems model, 104
  influences exerted by, 9–11
  interplanning, *see* Interplanning
  legal relationships of, with people, 194
    ff.
  manpower allocation within
    allocative structure, 92–94
    benefits and disadvantages of
      internal labour market, 94, 95
    causes of internal labour markets,
      91, 92
    internal allocation policies, 90, 91
  manpower and planning, 82 ff.
  motivation of employees, 107, 108
  power and control, 113, 114
  as social entities, 2
  structures, 10, 110, 111
  technology, relationship of, 111

Organizations (*cont.*)
   variations, 111
   trade unions, *see* Trade union
   value conflicts created by, 2, 3
Overtime, by women, 186

Pareto optimality, 250, 251
Payment
   collection, 210
   guaranteed, during suspension on
      medical grounds, 210
   itemized statements, right to, 209, 210
   during lay-offs, 210
   particulars as to, in terms of
      employment, 209
Personnel specification, use of, in
   manpower recruitment, 83
Persuasion as means of influence, 123
Picketing, 199
   secondary action, 124, 128, 197, 198
Piecework, payments for, 234
Political behaviour
   definitions, 123
   nature and importance of, 122
Population
   birth rate, fluctuations in, 38
   death rate, reduction in, 38
   demography, use of, 36 ff.
   economy and, relationship between 33
      ff.
   emigration and immigration, 39
   ethnic minorities, growth of, 39, 42
   food and, differing rates of increase,
      34, 35
   live births, fall in, 38
   migration, effect of, 39, 42
   sex and age structure (UK), 41
   size of, economic factors affecting, 34
Power
   coercion as form of, 124, 125
   compliance, avoidance of, 125
   definitions, 124
   dependency and compliance, 125
   descriptions of, 126
   relationships and responses, 125
   types of, 126, 127
   use of, 127
Pressure groups, 130–132
   international, 137
   political behaviour of, 122
   political parties distinguished, 122,
      131
   power organized by, 124–127 (*see also*
      Power)

Pressure groups (*cont.*)
   protective and promotional, 131, 132
   study of, 122
   types of, 132
      employers' organizations, 133
      professional associations, 132
      trade unions, 133–139
      understanding of, 128–132
Professional associations
   objectives, 132
   as pressure groups, 132
Psychology, individual and social, in
   study of organizations, 103

Race discrimination
   Act of 1976, main provisions, 188–191
   advertising, 190
   Commission for Racial Equality, 190
   definition, 188, 189
   equal opportunities and race relations,
      188
   genuine occupational qualifications
      excepted, 189
   incitement to racial hatred, 191
   legal procedures and remedies, 190
   positive action, 189
Recruitment of employees, *see*
   Manpower
Redundancy, 213
   calculation, 214
   compensation for, general provisions,
      213, 214
   procedure for handling, 222
References, 89
   objectivity, 89
   short-listed candidates, 89
Research, obligation for, 203, 204
Robens Report, 201
Rodger's recruitment grading plan, 84
Role analysis, 112, 113

Safety, *see* Legislation
Scientific management
   approach, faults of, 115
   human relations approach compared
      with, 116
   labour supply analysis, 115
   organizational design, as approach to,
      114
   tasks involved in, 114, 115
   Taylor's principles of, 114
   screening device, education as, 48, 49
Selection board, use in recruitment, 87
Seniority as determinant of job rights, 94

Sex discrimination, 179
  advertising, 182
  against applicants and employees, 180,
    181
  applies equally to men and women,
    180
  damages, 182
  definition, 179
  in employment field, 180
  enforcement of provisions as to, 182
  Equal Opportunities Commission,
    182, 186, 187
  positive, in favour of women, 186
  private households excepted, 181
  sex as genuine occupational
    qualification, 181
  small firms, 181
  unlawful acts, 182
Shop-stewards, 135–137
Smith, Adam
  factors governing employment, 23
  population and growth, views on, 33,
    34
  scientific management, views on, 115
  Wealth of Nations, 33
Social sciences
  division of labour among, 104
  meaning, 102
  organizational life, study of
    purpose of, 102
    social system, 104–106
  perspectives in
    individual psychology, 103
    social psychology, 103
    sociology, 103, 104
Sociology, *see* Social sciences
Status
  effect of, on communication patterns,
    145, 146
  formal and informal, 145
  hierarchies, 146
Strike, as industrial conflict, 165
Supply and demand schedules, 15 ff.
  'added worker hypothesis', 18
  'cobweb' cycles, 20
  demand for labour services, 21, 22
  'discouraged worker hypothesis', 18
  elasticity in demand, 27, 28, 66–68
  labour services, supply of, 15–17
  leisure and family, 17, 18
  marginalism, 28–32
  multiple regression analysis, tests by,
    18

Supply and demand schedules (*cont.*)
  net advantage and equilibrium, 16
  participation rates for women, 18, 19
  supply, measurement of, 16

Taxation
  income tax, 257, 258
  policies, 256–260
  Selective Employment Tax, 258–260
  social purposes of, 257
Trade dispute, definition, 196
Trade union(s)
  agreements binding in honour only,
    221
  branches, 135
  contributions, 135, 136
  definition, 195, 196
  density in 1974 (UK), 219, 220
  gentleman's agreements, 221
  health and safety representation, 204,
    205
  history, 13, 133, 134, 194, 195
  immunities, provision of, 195–198
  legislation, 13, 195
  manager as member of, 2, 3
  meaning, 11
  membership, 13, 134
  objectives in collective bargaining,
    227–229
  police and armed forces, position of,
    218
  political levy, 138
  political party influences, 137
  power, use of, 124
  as pressure groups, 134
  protected activities, 196–198
  relative wages, influence on, 244–247
  'secondary action' by, 197, 198
  shop-stewards, 135–137
  Trades Councils, 137, 138
  TUC
    EOC report, views on, 187, 188
    establishment, 11, 135
    General Council, 137
    key decisions, 1979, 239–244
    Labour Party connection, 131
    regional, 138
    representation on other bodies, 131
    structure of, 135, 231
  union/non-union wage differentials,
    246
  unionization by industrial sector and
    establishment size, 238

Trade union(s)
wage increases, unemployment caused by, 66
white collar membership, 11
Training, 82
analysis of, 68–71
apprentices, 99
benefits of, 69, 70
Carr Report, 253
Central Training Council, 254
colleges of further education, 254
costs, 70–72
correlation with level of skill required, 86
Directorate of Training, 256
Engineering Industry Training Board, 254
financial payments to employers, 70
flexibility and adaptability, 68, 69
formal and informal, 69
general and special, 69
government involvement in, 252, 256
importance of, 24
Industrial Training Boards, 253, 254
Industrial Training Council, 253
manpower development of, 68–72
methods, 69
on- and off-job, 69, 91, 92
retention of services after, 70, 71
skill specificity, 91
trained control as means of influence, 123
Training Advisory Service, 253
Training Opportunities Scheme, 47, 255
Training Services Agency, 254, 255
divisions of, 256
Vocational Training Scheme, 255
Truck Acts, 23

Unemployment
resulting from technological change, 51
trade union membership and, 12
wage increases causing, 66
Unfair dismissal
pregnant women protected from 183
(see also Maternity)
re-employment after, no compulsion on employer, 199
Union, see Trade union(s)

Variable proportions, law of, 59, 60

Wages
age–earnings profiles, 50, 51
'cobweb cycles', 20
coin of realm, payment in, 233, 234
differentials between occupations, 22–24
earnings of full-time males, 51, 57
education and earnings, correlation between, 48
equation to marginal revenue products, 86
equilibrium wage below acceptable level, 8
factors correlating with, 48
hours worked and hourly wage rates, relationship between, 17
incomes policy, 264, 265
'iron law' theory of, 7
job evaluation, 236, 237
management techniques to establish rates, 236, 237
minimum wage legislation, 7–9
movement of, 1920–1926, 261
payment systems
bonus payments, 235
measured day work, 234
piecework, 234
time rate, 234
pressures engendered by, 7
price and wage rises, 1960–1970, 262
profits and losses, effect of, 21, 22
relative, influence of trade unions on, 244–247
social wage, 235
Truck Acts, effect of, 233, 234
'wage fund' theory, 33
work and time study, 236
working life-cycle in relationship to, 50, 51
Wages Councils
appointment, 215
legislation, 214, 215
powers and functions, 215
Wages Regulation Orders, 220
Women
average hourly gross earnings, decline in, 179
concentration of, in certain industries, 176
earnings as proportion of men's earnings, 178
employment protection
antenatal care, time for, 184

Women (*cont.*)
   maternity provisions, 182–184
   right to return to work, 184, 185
  equal pay
    Act of 1970
     comparison with men's work, 178
     conditions and grounds for pay
      equality, 177, 178
     legislation following, effect of,
      178
    ILO formula for, 177
  Factories Act protection, 186
  female employment, development of,
   174–176
  franchise, obtaining of, 176
  hours to be worked by, 186
  legal position of, in employment, 176,
   177
  maternity provisions, 182–184

Women (*cont.*)
  nightwork, 186
  overtime, 186
  periods of employment, 186
Work and time study, 236
Workforce
  advertising for, 73
  education, effects of, 42 ff.
  expansion of, growth and reduction of,
   60
  externally provided manpower,
   utilization of, 59–63
  quality of, effect of education on, 42 ff.
  role analysis, 112, 113
  structure of, 33 ff.
Writing
  communication in, 148
  records and documents, 148, 149